Welfare Capitalism—and After

Also by Bert Cochran

Labor and Communism

Welfare Capitalism —and After

BERT COCHRAN

SCHOCKEN BOOKS · New York

First published by Schocken Books 1984
10 9 8 7 6 5 4 3 2 1   84 85 86 87
Copyright © 1984 by Bert Cochran

Library of Congress Cataloging in Publication Data
Cochran, Bert, 1916–
   Welfare capitalism—and after.
   Includes index.
   1. Economic history—1971–   2. Welfare state.
3. Capitalism. I. Title.
HC59.C6   1984   330.15′5   83–42719

Designed by Ed Kaplin
Manufactured in the United States of America
ISBN 0–8052–3868–9

Contents

2210640

Foreword

This book attempts to trace underlying historical trends toward state-managed economies to their culmination, and to do so from the vantage point of the capitalist metropolitan centers. The inquiry is therefore directed primarily to the industrialized democratic countries. Although we know that nations have grown more interconnected than they ever were before, and that the great multinational corporations are binding economies through their own intricate networks, there is essential validity in looking at the process from the watchtowers of Washington and her allies.

After World War II America took over the reins of advanced capitalism to impose a world tutelage more thoroughgoing than Britain's in her heyday. Even thirty-five years later, with American hegemony on the wane, the capitalist powers, added together, retain dominance. The result has been a unique, ambivalent international standoff. On the one hand the enlargement of the Soviet world, Soviet industrialism, and Soviet attainment of rough or near military parity with the United States constrict the capitalist domain. Capitalist perspectives are further clouded by the arrival of the ex-colonial nations on the world arena. Their rising assertiveness and their maneuvering between the two superpowers weaken the world complex, making it more vulnerable to disorder. On the other hand divisions and inadequacies, deprivations and absurdities within the Communist sectors, as well as general chaos in the Third World, have reinforced the power, particularly the economic primacy, of the centers of capitalist industrialism. In the words of a prominent African scholar: "Even the largest of the Communist countries are sensing a growing dependence on the world market, which is in turn dominated by capitalism and its methods."

It has to be kept in mind as well that the ideological banners of anticapitalism have been badly tarnished. In the early years of the Russian Revolution, when the country's economy was creaking and her peoples going hungry, the Soviet idea radiated prodigious force in both Europe and Asia. The revolution lacked worldly goods but was rich in moral promise. Now the Soviet Union, a developed industrial state, has lost creativity, idealism, and appeal. Stalin's successors can send vehicles into space, match nuclear-tipped missiles with America's, grant loans and ship military wares to friends abroad, but they lag far behind their capitalist rivals in technological mastery. They are apostles of an authoritarian regime which contrasts invidiously with the parliamentary democracies. China's ferocious Cultural Revolution, and its abrupt reversal after the prophet's death turning yesterday's demigods into today's villains, undermined communism's appeal. As for the more bourgeoisified national insurgencies of our time, they shed their inspirational aureoles even more rapidly by reason of their violent excesses, supressions, and governmental sterility.

On the plane of decision-making, the less-developed countries (LDCs), Communist and quasi-capitalist, because of their poverty and backwardness are necessarily objects, not subjects, of the world economic order. This is not gainsaid because a cartel of oil-producing countries has been riding high, its 1973 embargo and subsequent price escalations effectively blackmailing the industrialized world. The hand-wringing that ensued in the latter quarters brought home, to be sure, altered power relations. A few decades earlier the Western powers would have responded to such pretensions by dispatching gunboats to the Persian Gulf and landing troops at the pipelines. Now, in a world of impassioned nationalisms, recourse to arms is calculated to be counterproductive (thus far). Nonetheless the spectacular enrichment of scions of Arab royal houses, of their business associates, and of ex-colonial parvenus elsewhere, as well as their big investments in Western real estate and banking, represent transfers of wealth, sizable though they are, but not a shift in the location of economic centrality.*

*This was during the Organization of Petroleum Exporting Countries' (OPEC) fat years when there was supposed to be an oil shortage. Now in the lean years when there is an oil glut the cartel is teetering, maneuvering desperately to keep some control over the market by drastically cutting prices. Western bankers, who are good at keeping figures, estimate that the drop in prices will cost the cartel members some $25 billion. The high-rollers become the high casualties during an economic downturn.

So while a number of these nations will continue to have their say on the world stage, and as time goes on an increasingly influential say, and while the Soviet Union remains and will continue to be a formidable rival, it is still correct to portray the conclave of advanced capitalist countries as the centerpiece of world economic initiative and influence.

When I first started gathering data for this book I wanted to focus on what to me was the evident disintegration of the Welfare State, and what that could portend for the social concords forged in the industrialized countries. For that reason I wanted to test my hypothesis that bedeviled Britain might be prefiguring in some way the shape of other, stronger market economies. More extensive investigations have validated the supposition to my satisfaction. I am aware that England is atypical in important respects; nonetheless many insolvencies undermining her economy have since made their appearance in more successful industrial nations. England, in my portrayal, represents an extreme, but not a unique, manifestation of a systemic predicament.

If it is true that the distempers which the industrialized countries have been experiencing are not of an ephemeral character, that they are premonitory warnings of systemic troubles to come, then the problems facing advanced capitalist societies go beyond the exhaustion of Keynesianism. These overdeveloped societies are confronted with the need for critical decisions since familiar Welfare State remedies are increasingly irrelevant, and monetarist and fiscal neoconservative therapies are part of the problem, not of the solution. I will argue that in a historic sense that is the case, that in the matter of some decades major modifications of existing social and institutional orderings will become both indispensable and inevitable.

Since none of the parliamentary industrialized societies are pregnant with political revolution, since existing revolutionary sects command virtually no popular following, and since there is nothing on the horizon to indicate that that will change in the decades ahead, what classes, subclasses, orders, or associations will supply the wherewithal to put through reforms of this magnitude and character? The answer is necessarily geometric. Nevertheless the history of the changeovers that took place in Germany, Italy, and Japan in the 1860s, demonstrating how societies were able to clear the Augean stables by administrative and military sweeps (designated by historians "revolutions from above") has relevance for the industrial powers in their current predicaments.

When Western society moved from feudalism to capitalism there was need for a comprehensive modernization: in law and civil rights; in the powers, conduct, institutions, and administrative modalities of government; in the redistribution of power within social classes. There had to be a changed cultural-value climate if new economic configurations were to flourish. To one or another extent the historical requirement was met and these countries moved to a new historical stage.

This is not to recreate the unilinear cosmologies of a Comte or Spencer (or possibly of a Marx as suggested in the historical sections of the *Manifesto* and of *Capital*). Neither is it meant to imply that history moves along predetermined lines guided by a suprahuman agency. However, the Western European countries, and Japan under her own peculiar imperatives, were caught up in the developing commercial and industrial stream and they had to adapt their national institutions and customs to navigate satisfactorily in it. In our time, in a vaguely analogous movement, we see such adaptation at work as precapitalist countries move to superimpose market-economy ordinances on their feudal or tribal societies.

It was the Western European experience out of which national and capitalist revolutions originated. And despite all the nation-building in the Third World in our time, the European nation-state remains the prototype which others seek to emulate. Early capitalism, convinced of its progressive mission, exuding an optimistic worldview, gave birth to a self-confident elite that won legitimacy for itself from relatively educated populations. Great wealth was accumulated in manufacturing and commerce, and great cities arose flaunting the physical and intellectual attributes of metropolitan civilization. When with that came national politics and a public press, persuasion took its place alongside force, the civilian power alongside the military, as instrumentalities of rule. When institutions could be popularly based, they showed resiliency in adapting to changing circumstances.

The one violent popular outburst that drew a line of blood between past and present—what Marx thought was the model for gaining capitalist hegemony—proved to be the single exception. There was not another successful social overturn of the French Jacobin kind. Only a unique combination of subclasses in simultaneous insurgency succeeded in carrying it through. After the classic eighteenth-century bourgeois revolution in France, another half century elapsed before similar revolutions were attempted in the German and Italian states, and the states of the Austro-Hungarian Empire. The special combination that made for victory before could not be recreated, and by the summer of 1849 the insurgents had been turned back everywhere. That did not finish off middle-class aspiration. What could not be won by Jacobin frontal assault was won by opportunist, adaptive, deceptive strategy. Within two decades a capitalist spirit permeated all these societies, providing the energies that gave them sustenance, shape, and order. Businessmen and their intellectual henchmen carved out substantial domains for themselves in the economic and social spheres, and eventually in government as well. The revamped states discarded past semifeudal arrangements and emerged as authentic capitalist formations. Engels, Marx's coadjutor, wrote in retrospect that "The gravediggers of the Revolution of 1848 had become the executors of its will."

The changeovers in Germany under Bismarck and the Prussian monarchy, and in Italy under Cavour and the House of Savoy, illumine the operations of sociological change called for by historical needs when the uncommon set of factors required for a popular revolution are not present. If major social classes checkmate each other so that customary government comes to a dead end; or if an emerging elite, in carving out its own superintendency, is determined at the same time to prevent the lower orders from pressing their own claims, and therefore arrives at a workable compromise arrangement with the old establishment; or when the old regime has lost its legitimacy and force while the new group coming up is too inchoate and feeble to assert its dominance—the way can be cleared for a reforming Bonapartist regime to take hold of the reins of state and to impose altered social arrangements by bureaucratic and military means. When a section from the upper echelons feels compelled to act and the middle and lower echelons are unable to take the initiative, transformation can be pushed through from the top down by an ad hoc council originating in traditional elites.

The element of mass fervor, popular intoxication, organized mass activities and movements may occur, as was the case in the Italian *Risorgimento* with its Garibaldian irregulars and their conquest of Sicily and Naples. But it was Cavour and his aristocratic and business associates who set policy in the proceedings and determined the course, just as it was Bismarck and his allies several years later who achieved German unification with their own methods. In short, history is the great opportunist: if one avenue to achieving its purpose is shut off it will find another avenue; if both avenues are closed it will tunnel out a third.

It goes without saying that the world of the twenty-first century will not be a replica of the Western world of 1860. If we examine the half dozen largest capitalist states—the United States, Germany, Japan, France, England, and Italy—we see at a glance that they vary profoundly in language, cultural history, religion, niceties of legal categories, political modalities, etc. If several or even two of them put through structural reforms, they will do so disparately in accordance with their antecedent heritages and folkways. For the matter at hand, however, it is their structural similarities that are of interest. They are all developed capitalist states with parliamentary systems of government. They have business and property relations based on roughly related legal principles. Some are stronger and richer than others, but they are suffering from the same order of disabilities and insufficiencies, beset by related predicaments. Equally significant, their classes, their social and political personnel, mesh within an intricate constitutional mechanism so that change is envisioned by all major social groups as incremental in character.

Parliamentarism and its attendant electoral processes have an enormous hold on people's thinking. Parliamentarism is so pervasive that leading Communist parties in the West had to abandon their Leninist rhetoric and cut their links with Moscow at the first opportunity available, if, as their leaders perceived it, they were to make any progress in their national environments. They felt compelled to pledge allegiance to the very ideas Communist parties were created to discredit. Parliamentarism has performed yeoman service for welfarism, promoted loyalty to ongoing institutions, given countries like Britain and the United States a continuity through the shocks and pitfalls of economic disorders and wars. That is its strong side. Its weak side is that it fosters demagoguery and cynicism among political professionals, furnishes nesting places for power brokers for the well-placed, breeds a politics of complacency and inertia. It suffices, and is often estimable in more or less normal times. If the socioeconomic crisis of our era widens into a political crisis as well, however, parliamentarism will set the stage for the emergence of a new breed of politicians who, proclaiming the state the embodiment of the national purpose, will have the nerve to push through measures clearing the blocked pathways that the postwar regimes proved unable to take.

Robert L. Heilbroner, the economist, has made cogent observations about this crisis of our epoch in a number of his writings. "At critical junctures," he said, "crisis seems to usher in changes that alter the institutional underpinnings of the system"; and he was of the opinion that the present historic crisis can be understood in terms of the institutional shifts that are called for and will probably be brought about. It is not required that one agree with Heilbroner's particular catalogue of miseries serving to disqualify those processes that have sufficed in the past but will not suffice in the crisis ahead. Variations and alterations can and should be introduced into the catalogue, as I will elaborate later in the text, but the totality of contradictions points to the inescapable need to monitor, supervise, and direct the economic process. This is a program for comprehensive national planning, the purpose of which is not just to reopen clogged production circuits but to protect a society from dissolution—to protect, as it were, the very possibility of orderly survival and advance.

I use the terms "state" and "government" more or less interchangeably, for I hold with Laski that for all practical purposes they are the same. I am aware of the large literature and the many concepts on the subject; I know that some Hegelians thought of the state as an immanent intelligence directing social change and that Kantian jurists located it within the legal order, the state embodying a property of law itself, etc. In my usage either term is a convenient shorthand for the full panoply of public sovereignty, in this country comprising all parts of the federal government including regulatory commissions, ad hoc agencies deputized for specific and special duties, the Federal Reserve System, as well as the many state and local authorities to which the exercise of some segments of the state's sovereignty is delegated. So far as I am concerned, therefore, interactions between society and the state, attributes of sovereignty in the people as well as in the state, and similar and related matters, belong in the realm of analysis, not in the definition of the term.

Although I have avoided theoretical discussions, my leading

assumptions in the matter are evident. I do not consider the state
an agency of a ruling class. Neither do I support a pluralist notion that the state is up for grabs: that any and all groups and
individuals can rip off pieces of it for their own ends, whatever
these may be, if they display sufficient acumen and energy. Governments, especially democratic governments in modern history,
are called upon to play a large mediating role between classes,
reconciling conflicting interests and through an intricate mesh-
ing of gears satisfying myriad specialized solicitations. Anyone
studying the history and practices of welfarism cannot fail to be
impressed with the ability of the modern state to impose reform
rearrangements—often against the wishes of powerful elites—
and to grant concessions to underprivileged groups, thereby de-
fusing dangerously overcharged social connections. Similarly,
one is impressed with the ability of upper-class circles to absorb
into elitist ranks representatives of oppositions or of hitherto
despised minorities, thereby enlarging the participatory citizenry
with a stake in the maintenance of social stability. For all that,
political legitimacy is usually forged on the basis of defending
and maintaining the established legal and social foundations of
the society, and with that the property rights of economic elites.
It should also be kept in mind that upwardly mobile politicians
on the make have an affinity for the well-connected and the rich.
These are the boundaries within which change can take place.

Without going further afield on this issue it seems to me
sufficient for the purposes of this book to understand that in
transition periods the state is able to lift itself above contending
classes or factions to put through structural renovations to save
society from being torn apart by intractable contestants or from
succumbing to inevitable disintegration. It is true that in the case
of the builders of modern Germany and Italy the lawgivers allied
themselves with archaic monarchies and sought to build protective ramparts for their perpetuation—but that is not the only way
a modernizing transformation from above can take place. It depends on the respective strengths of the forces in play, as I will
discuss in the final chapter. A transforming regime of this nature,
once it has carried out its program and consolidated its system of
controls, will probably become a stern upholder of the new status quo, a defender of the privileges of those new elites presiding
over and administering the institutions of governance. If that
occurs, it will be up to a new generation of theorists to sort out

the materials, and a new generation of practitioners to fix the remedies. Sufficient unto the day is the evil thereof.

I must ask the reader's indulgence in going over certain historical materials that may not seem to bear immediately on the main argument. The socioeconomic crisis that I am discussing is not a passing indisposition. It is a crisis whose cause is not in any one maladjustment, disability, social friction, or mistaken policy. It is rather in the entire ensemble of contradictions, legacies, constricting possibilities, growing disruptions, that at a certain level of pressure will force the issue for change. Although individual subjects are put (and have to be examined) in their separate compartments, it is the interactions that are important, the dynamics that take precedence, the convergence and interlinking of a number of debilitating factors of separate origins that bring into focus a central social trend.

Acknowledgments I am indebted to the director of Columbia University's Research Institute on International Change for enabling me to make full use of its facilities; to him and my other associates there for their helpful criticisms of my work in progress; to the staff for assistance of many kinds; to the reference librarians at the Columbia University Libraries, particularly the Lehman, Business, Butler, and Law Libraries, which I used most extensively; to the personnel of the New York Public Library, the John Watson Library of the Conference Board, the Tamiment Library of New York University, the Library of Congress, and the National Archives in Washington, D.C.—for their professional guidance.

B. C.

Welfare Capitalism—and After

1. Crackup of Britain's Welfare State—I

1

The term "Welfare State" was introduced into the language when the Beveridge Report on social insurance was presented to the British government in 1942. The promise of social security underwritten by government generated a tidal wave of mass enthusiasm, and Sir William Beveridge (active in these matters since the early years of the century) suddenly found himself a celebrity in both England and this country. It was an old idea developing incrementally whose time had come. Welfare measures of some sort had been introduced throughout the Western world in the 1930s, and Franklin Roosevelt's New Deal was rightly considered the prototype of the modern Welfare State. When the Labourites took over in England after the war, they moved farther and faster along the same road.

As policy, welfarism was by then a hundred years old. Its origins went back to class struggles in nineteenth-century Europe. Ameliorative legislation had been adopted from time to time to cushion the shocks of economic distress, what Joseph Chamberlain, the Birmingham industrialist and government leader, called "ransom legislation." Concessions were granted to quiet unruly lower classes, or to forestall their becoming unruly, or to split the more moderate from the more radical. In the case of the Ten Hour Bill adopted in England in 1847, which Marx thought was the first victory for British socialism, it came as a by-product of the conflict between two segments of property owners, an achievement, according to Karl Polanyi, of "enlightened reactionaries." Once socialism and laborism grew as political forces in Europe, the pace and substance of welfarism expanded, culminating in the era before 1914 in Bismarck's social insurance program and Lloyd George's National Insurance Act of 1911. Consequently what was new about Roosevelt's New Deal, and even more distinct about the Labour government's 1945–1950 series of reforms, beyond the immensely greater coverage and comprehensiveness of benefits and guarantees, was the shift from calculated beneficence, philanthropic largesse, or noblesse oblige, to a philosophy of the state's obligation to ensure minimum levels of comfort to its entire citizenry.

When the British electorate ousted Churchill in 1945 and the Labourites swept into the House of Commons with a majority of 146, social meliorists the world over turned to that country in anticipation of the coming exploits of middle-of-the-road democratic socialism. The first postwar generation of French technocratic planners coming on the scene under Jean Monnét likewise thought Britain would supply them with basic techniques and organizational principles. In the interwar years, let us recall, the Soviet Union had been for many the mecca of planning, full employment, the future society. Even Sidney and Beatrice Webb, the Fabian oracles of "the inevitability of gradualism," fell in with the popular enthusiasms in the depression-ridden 1930s. Now Stalin's Russia had lost its allure, and expectations were high that moderate socialism could show the way.

The Labourites started with an advantage. They took over from the wartime coalition government a mechanism of interlocking directorates and commissions, parts of which, suitably modified but without the need for controversial innovations, could serve as the machinery for planning and structural reorganizations. This was no mere collection of ossified bureaus handing out mimeographed sheets of regulations and procedures: it exercised powers over the economy. To this was added a psychological advantage. The British people had been conditioned in the war to a regimen of controls and disciplines. This had made government interventions and some kinds of planning respectable for many, and not without precedent for others. As a matter of fact the going mood among civilians and returning soldiers was that government had the obligation of securing people's rights to a decent job and decent living conditions, that it was a positive duty of government to ensure that the war sacrifices had not been in vain, that England would never go back to the era of the desperate past.

The Labour Party, which had proclaimed itself socialist in 1918, reiterated both the goal and the particulars in the election manifesto of 1945. A number of industries would be nationalized; those remaining in private hands were to be subject to "constructive supervision" to prevent monopolistic abuses and to guarantee full employment. There was to be government planning, a program to reequip factories and schools, a set of priorities to achieve maximum production, reestablish the export trade, and ensure "fair play" to consumers. In addition the banners proclaimed price-controlled housing, free secondary education, free medical care, social insurance, progressive taxation. In short, a significant step was to be taken toward socialism, the ultimate goal; in the meantime they would create a more civilized, humanitarian society, "free from the horrors of unemployment and insecurity."

On the face of it the first postwar Labour government made good on a substantial part of its promises. From 1946 to 1948 it nationalized the Bank of England, the coal industry, and transportation, entailing the national railway system plus 1600 miles of canals and internal waterways, as well as sections of civil aviation, and the remaining parts of the London transport system. Later, long-distance road haulage, control of electricity generation and transmission, and that of gas, were placed under the Ministry of Fuel and Power. Other takeovers included building materials, land, housing, wholesaling, telecommunications, and cables. At the end of its term the steel industry was nationalized after a fierce struggle with the owners. (Steel was still a money-maker in those days. On this transference the Tories balked and pledged to return the properties when they took office.) All told, at the conclusion of Labour's tenure in 1951 a little over 20 percent of industry was in government hands, encompassing an employment roll of about two million, not including the usual municipal and national government and civil service employees. Living styles of the working population were revolutionized by the program of subsidized, low-rent housing, the planning and direction of which was turned over to the municipalities; some 1,100,000 dwellings were built in the initial five years. Midway in its term the government brought into operation the National Insurance, National Health

Service, and National Assistance Acts (incorporating the substance of the original Beveridge recommendations). Among other considerable achievements these put an end to the long, dolorous history of Britain's poor laws.

Yet in what became the hallmark of the Welfare State, the government was more successful in providing social services and insurance guarantees than in restructuring the economy on which, ultimately, all taxation and security provisions are dependent. When the observer descends from the mountaintop and examines the different edifices on the ground, what had appeared a well-laid-out city is seen to be an architectural hodgepodge with rickety structures lining major thoroughfares.

Most of the industries taken over by the government belonged to the "derelict" class, suffering from systematic abuses of underinvestment, technological neglect, and inferior management. The nationalizations, rather than working any hardship, were a boon to the owners. The Economist, spokesman and watchdog of the business community, noting the overwhelming support for public ownership of the mines, opined that it was "difficult for anyone to get very excited" about nationalization of civil aviation or cable and wireless communications, issues which it saw "at or near the margin of indifference." Robert Brady pointed out that all the nationalization or seminationalization programs were based on earlier recommendations made by Conservative-dominated factfinding and investigating committees. In the case of the Bank of England it was largely legal legerdemain. Keynes was of the opinion that the Labour program here would make no difference "with the personalities the same, and knowledge no greater." A highly regarded Tory, Quinton Hogg (Lord Hailsham), wrote, "No one is much better or worse off as the result of what can only be described as an elaborate game of make-believe."

There were other reasons why capitalists and conservative politicians did not become unduly exercised over the initial nationalizations. First, to avoid provoking hostilities the government decided to pay more than generous compensation for what in most cases were run-down, unremunerative, ramshackle holdings. Except for the Bank of England and some parts of the gas and electricity concerns they were in need of huge investment inputs for technological renovations. The government takeovers in effect relieved the free enterprisers of costly decisions. Call it state capitalism, state socialism, socialism for the rich, or just state Lady Bountiful—what the Labour government did was bail out owners of properties that had lost their capacities for substantial (or for any) profit-making. These owners, newly emancipated, with liquid capital in their hands, could and did proceed to use their compensation funds to invest in rapid-growth, high-technology enterprises. The nature of the government's burden can be gathered when we consider that by the middle of the 1950s the government had encumbered the four major nationalized industries—coal, transport, electricity, gas—with additional debts for indispensable capital renewal amounting to about eighty cents for every dollar that had been paid out for compensation. Robert Brady noted that the nationalizations had "not altered the general structure of ownership of securities, or of income claims on the community's real resources, except, possibly, somewhat to improve the status of the rentier."

A further reassuring note to industrial managers and security holders was that the nationalized industries were entrusted to public corporations whose personnel, managements, modes of operation, and salary schedules were no different than those in private industry. The individual appointed to head the National Coal Board, Lord Hyndley, was a leader in the largest collier company. Most of the regional, district, and colliery directors and managers were the old personnel or their similars. This was the typical pattern of staffing. The appointments to the Transport Commission, the Electrical Authority, the Gas Council were invariably drawn from the existing managerial hierarchies, and subsequently there was continual movement to and fro in the public and private sectors. Fully half the public corporation directors served at the same time on the boards of private corporations. The 1951 Acton Society Trust study of the composition of nationalized industry boards found that of ninety-five full- and part-time members, fifty-two came from top managerial positions in private industry and sixteen were trade unionists serving in individual capacities; the remainder was an assortment of retired military officers, barristers, and civil servants. "There is thus," read the report, "a considerable measure of factual basis for the employees' complaint that 'the old gang' is still in power." The Rogow and Shore itemization of the officers at the different institutions reads for page after page like a listing of dollar-a-year men in the American War Production Board during the war.

Consequently it is not surprising that workers rapidly lost interest in nationalization. A number of Yorkshire miners interviewed by an American investigator gave vent to their disillusionment: "The mine bosses are the same. . . . The Coal Board in London is made up of big bosses and ex-admirals. . . . Nationalization hasn't changed anything." Asked about trade union leaders on national and divisional boards, they replied, "They change when they go on a board. They become bosses. They forget the workers." As Arnold J. Toynbee summed it up later, "From the standpoint of the employee, it is coming to make less and less practical difference to him what his country's official ideology is and whether he happens to be employed by a government or commercial corporation."

2

There is something bizarre in a labor government, with the ship of state officially headed for socialism, entrusting publicly owned enterprises and general economic direction of affairs to corporation executives and upper-class civil servants whose sympathy for collectivization ran from tepid to ice cold. It is incongruous to permit bureaucracies steeped in upper-class conceit to run these enterprises as adjuncts of private corporations and their private purposes. Even had the Labour government not permitted itself to be saddled with the derelicts and basket cases, sooner or later such a scheme was bound to backfire and to discredit its sponsors. Yet for all its intellectual incoherence, the Labour leaders were predestined to follow this course and no other.

The proposition was in strict accordance with party traditions and outlooks. Both Fabians and ethical reformers adhered to gradualism and supraclass rationality. The object of nationalization was not to plan the economy but to increase efficiency. Managing an industrial enterprise had nothing to do with conflicting class aspirations; it was an exercise of professional expertise. Management was a quasi-science or art transcending politics, operative under one or another set of social objectives. So far as the leading Labour officials of that period were concerned, this was all self-evident common sense: hire the "best brains" available, be ready to pay the going price for that skill, then give the men in charge the responsibility and authority to do the job. How else could you operate?

Labour's left-wingers were never satisfied with this program of public ownership. Some supported workers' control or workers' participation. Some wanted to institute something called "industrial democracy." Appropriate resolutions were adopted from time to time in stormy moments at union and party congresses, over the objections of all top officials. But the resolutions never led anywhere, and when the party took office in 1945, Herbert Morrison, the voluble expositor of no-nonsense, feet-on-the-ground public corporation organization, was put in full charge of the nationalization program.

Was the leftist proposition an actual alternative? It had its first tryout in the course of the Russian Revolution. Factory committees were of enormous help to the Bolsheviks in the months preceding and immediately after the revolution in breaking down the machinery of capitalist and czarist rule. As a weapon of destruction they proved invaluable. But the inherent syndicalist tendencies of these bodies to cater to workers' wishes in a single plant or locality, and the outright irresponsibility of some committees, threatened—if the committees were given free sway—to engulf the regime. Lenin's previous pronouncements on the subject had been ambiguous. Now he and his associates hastened to set up a Supreme Council to direct the entire economy. By the 1920 Communist party congress, both Lenin and Trotsky challenged the older verities of collegial and committee decision-making in favor of one-man management. The stress was on discipline, central authority, and increased production. This was accompanied by stern warnings to the trade unions that they would not be permitted to interfere in works operations. E. H. Carr's laconic conclusion was that "Workers' control was abandoned as an impractical aberration."

The fact that the experiment proved abortive in the Soviet Union under conditions of industrial breakdown and Leninist centralizing predilections is not conclusive evidence that it cannot be workable in other, more favorable circumstances. Do management councils in Yugoslavia come closer to Left Labourite concepts? Whatever one's estimate of the success of these councils in achieving independent influence over decision-making or of reconciling enterprise self-management with national planning, they are part of the complex of Communist rule in Yugoslavia. They would not have seen the light of day without Communist sponsorship; they cannot survive without Communist sustenance. Since Left Labourites are not advocates of workers' control as a tactic of transition to revolution, as are some Marxists, what do they have in mind? It has always been left up in the air. They have exhibited confusion over the years in proposing to combine workers' control with traditional parliamentarism, or in attempting to make a party dedicated to class harmony into an instrument of quasi-class warfare. In a characterization of one of its well-wishers, the Labour left is a permanently neurotic personality unable to come to grips with its contradictory mélange of ideas and attitudes—which cancel each other out.

Nationalized industries were run along traditional capitalist lines because the Labour party was bound by traditional values and concepts in a society where the large majority—despite localized outbursts—gave fealty to the dominant middle-class ethos. For that to change the Labour left would have to hammer out a coherent alternative transcending both revolution and welfarist liberal reform, and sizable majorities would have to adhere to its program, a considerable undertaking. Otherwise, no matter how biting the rhetoric of criticism, the Welfare State cannot move beyond standard quasi-Keynesian paradigms.

On one thing both friend and foe are agreed in evaluating Labour's performance. Its record on planning is a nullity. One of the major planks was unaccountably lost in the welter of events. What went wrong? Nothing went wrong. What Atlee, Morrison, Bevin, Cripps, and Dalton meant by planning, they practiced. Others would not agree that that was planning. Andrew Shonfield, who used to be ready to give his blessing to almost any kind of coordinating arrangements, however feeble, lamented that the British Labourites failed to "set up even the rudimentary machinery for long-term planning of the kind which became commonplace in Western Europe during the subsequent decade and a half." Here was a state owning outright a fifth of the industrial properties and in full control of the Bank of England, with the public sector accounting for over 40 percent of all fixed investment and for as much as 50 percent of all building work.*

---

* These figures are counterbalanced to an extent by the state's indebtedness to private interests. Using the data of the mortgage owed to private capital

Yet with this formidable base for planning, even the publicly owned enterprises were not made to integrate their activities. No directive was ever issued to the coal, electricity, or gas boards to work up a unified national fuel policy. The officials heading the ministries to which the boards were formally responsible would think of intervening only in the event of growing deficits, financial scandals, or publicized "old boy" nepotism. In the face of persistent criticism, a permanent Select Committee on the Nationalized Industries was eventually set up, and relevant ministers at times answered questions in Parliament. But the resistance was heavy even to this formal obeisance to public control, and it never went beyond observing formalities.

The coal crisis of 1947 which led to a breakdown in transport and shipping, and temporarily brought great stretches of industry to a standstill, discredited the cabinet's performance and made a public joke of its planning pretensions. Called upon to make good on campaign pledges, the government took refuge in organizational legerdemain. A Central Economic Planning Staff under the respected Sir Edwin Plowden was set up with great fanfare, and below it stood a complicated number of freshly minted committees and boards. It is immaterial that the powers of these impressive-sounding bodies were severely limited and that planning policy, such as it was, came from the cabinet. Planning can be conducted by means of a variety of administrative arrangements, even cumbersome ones, provided the concepts are sound and the will is there.

Neither one was in evidence. The *Economic Survey* that the government issued early in the year made it obvious that the Labour officialdom's notion of planning differed in no particular from the notion of a hard-shell Tory banker. What the Labour ministers had in mind was (1) an information and statistics bureau; and (2) a system of rewards to "indicate" and to "persuade" the principals in the best uses of available resources while leaving decision-making in their hands. Rogow's reading of the document led him to conclude that with such a concept of planning, controls could be kept to the minimum, long-term planning could be dispensed with, and the government would be freed from the burden of any detailed economic regulation.

owners in his calculation, one economist, J. E. Meade, unabashedly estimated that the state's net ownership of property was a negative quantity—minus 14 percent.

Backbenchers organized into the "Keep Left" group in 1947 opined that the distinction was not between democratic and totalitarian planning, as the government paper averred; it was between "real" and "bogus" planning, and that the government was an adherent of the latter kind.

Left to their own inclinations, the Labourites would have relied primarily on a Keynesian budgetary policy to manage aggregate demand, and when impelled, to check consumption in order to free resources for investment—and for the rest, to keep hands off. But it was not to be. An officialdom dedicated to live-and-let-live moderation had been pushed to the head of a country that was hemorrhaging and in perpetual crisis, a Britain that had lost her empire, a quarter to a third of her national wealth, two-thirds of her export trade, and left with a contorted skeletal structure and a tripled national debt. A postwar regime dreaming of orderly, modest reforms thus had to intevene repeatedly in almost every important aspect of the economy: in growth because of its balance-of-payments deficits, in factory building because of shortages of labor and materials, in wages because of inflationary pressures and the uncompetitiveness of much of industry's exports. If the government had no long-range, integrated plan, it had to improvise dozens of quicky plans to plug recurrent leaks, patch up malfunctionings, repair breaks, and align public debt management with control over money supply, credit, and interest rates.

Even in its role of fireman, emergency repairman, and rescuer of derelict free enterprisers, the government's performance was second-rate because of its excessive deference to businessmen and like-minded civil servants. For example, investment controls applied to factory buildings, but not to the plant, machinery, stocks, and vehicles that the factories would use, house, and produce. Exchange controls were in effect, but capital managed to squeeze through the weaker controls of other sterling area countries (one estimate was that illegal export of capital, mainly by undervaluing exports and overpayment for imports, was £2 billion between 1946 and 1949). Much of this was not genuine investment for new projects, but "hot money" whose owners, seeking higher returns, were engaging in currency speculation or shifting their holdings from less to more reliable currencies. Another type of capital export was the wholesale migration of companies overseas to evade taxes (e.g., almost all the copper-mining companies transferred control to either Northern or Southern Rhodesia; Anglo-Egyptian Oilfields departed for Cairo; Sisal Estates found a haven in Kenya). When it was too late, at the end of its term in 1951 the government belatedly passed the Finance Act which made illegal, without Treasury consent, the overseas transfer of a company's seat of management if there was an avoidance of liability for income or profits taxes.

For most, for whom neither migration nor capital export was practical, resistance took the form of a guerrilla war between corporation fiscal managers and Inland Revenue. As in the nationalization of steel, industry mounted a campaign of lamentations and prophesies of disasters unimaginable, a campaign promoted with utter abandon by nearly the entire press. The English were made more conscious of their tax burdens than in any previous period of the country's history, including the war. This vast outpouring, buttressed by scholarly writings, reports, and surveys, made such a strong impression on the public mind (and not only in England) that for years thereafter it was a commonly accepted axiom that Britain was the most highly taxed nation in the world, accompanied by the equally erroneous notion that there had been a decided transfer of income from the rich to the poor.

3

Leftists were unsparing in their criticism of the first Labour government. They summed up the case for the prosecution this way: Although the government put through important welfare reforms, there was no shift of power toward the Labour side. Far from weakening capitalism, Labour's economic reforms, controls, public investments, subsidizations, and socialization of capitalist losses and costs for the infrastructure, in point of fact strengthened the system, extended growth of cartels and oligopolies, and reinforced the economic and social position of ruling elites. In short, rather than taking initial steps toward a socialist commonwealth, the Labour government hammered out a more advanced welfare capitalism. Instead of public enterprise setting the tone and ethos for private industry, private industry set the tone and ethos for the public corporations. (This was made plain when the Tories came back in 1951. Apart from denationalizing steel and road haulage, they were content to administer the system that the

Labour government had bequeathed. And in the next turn of the electoral wheel in 1970, they were content to administer steel nationalization, which had ceased being a profit-maker.) Richard Crossman elaborated in the *New Fabian Essays* the thesis that the Labour government gave birth to "welfare capitalism," not socialism, that the postwar Labour government "marked the end of a century of social reform and not, as its socialist supporters had hoped, the beginning of a new epoch."

Crossman's and related propositions are incontestable. But it is necessary to make two further observations if the British Welfare State is to be placed in its proper historic setting.

The first is this: The demand that the postwar British Labour government should have taken significant steps to socialism is probably fanciful. The constituency was not there to support such a government from the massed onslaughts of conservative figures and institutions. The Labour officials can more realistically be faulted for not taking initial steps to structurally revamp the British economy in order to stanch the bloodletting and to reverse the continual decline. Because of their failure, they were inevitably caught up in the incompatibilities of a depleted, wasting capitalism. As will be shown, with every succeeding Labour government the Welfare State had to be renewed on a meaner, more constricted basis.

Second, there was a certain historical inevitability about the Welfare State's economic incongruity and timidity, and to its disintegration when the percentage of growth plunged downward. In a certain sense the electorate decreed that the Attlee government stay within the limitations of Keynesian welfarism. No one can claim that the Labour party officials were an unknown quantity to the British public. No one in his right mind would have expected socialist decrees from them. Clement Attlee, everybody's choice to head the government, and symbolic of the party's directorate, exuded prissy suburbanite values and attitudes in almost textbook form. Throughout the six years of crisis government over which he presided, he never exhibited strong feelings or views about anything, never defended his colleagues when they were singled out for Tory attack, never summoned his ministers for a basic discussion in an unfolding crisis; he was a reincarnation of Lord Liverpool in labor dress. The only time anyone saw Attlee exercised was when he heard of George VI's death. When he spoke of that, tears came to his eyes and his voice broke. His lifelong reverence for the monarchy, added to gratitude to the king who had knighted him, was the single combination that broke down his exaggerated reserve.

It would be simple-minded to inquire into his general principles, system of thought, or theory of government. He was middle-class Everyman writ large, exuding a composite of utilitarianism, empiricism, traditionalism, and social uplift, all set at the level of platitude. For all his mediocrity and colorlessness, his sharp, cryptic manner in the inner councils and his supreme confidence that British common sense would see any issue through kept the administration in play, whatever course it was on. His thought, however conventional, was free of petty purposes, and he was careful to shun clique associations and maneuvers. That Bevin, Morrison, Dalton, or Cripps, all stronger minds, would have done better in the post is unlikely; that they would not have done nearly as well is almost a certainty. In any case the other luminaries were graduates of the same ideological and policy school.

It was to leaders of this stamp to whom the workers and liberal-minded middle classes gave their support year in and year out (excepting the 35 percent of workers who supported the Tories). When the moderate leaders of the party could no longer count on the big bloc votes of the major conservatively led unions at the annual party conferences in the 1950s, they turned them into a powerless talking shop and shifted authority to the parliamentary party. The Members of Parliament (MPs), formally responsible to an undifferentiated electorate, were even less venturesome in advocating social innovations or giving heed to leftist critics. There had been leftist factions in the Labour party from its earliest days, but whatever their success in injecting inspirational socialist rhetoric in the party's programs and declarations, they never formulated governing policy and there never was the vaguest possibility of their transforming an essentially social-democratic electoral organization into an association of socialist firebrands. Aside from brief outbursts of insurgency in specific localities during times of unusual stress, and a handful of districts that traditionally elected oppositionists, the great majority of the labor electorate gave its confidence to the reliable establishment officialdom.

When Ramsey MacDonald turned his back on the Independent Labour party which had put him into party leadership, the

ILP could not get anyone to sponsor its most modest proposals although 129 Labour MPs were its members in 1923–1924, including five cabinet ministers and the party leader. At the conclusion of a long struggle the ILP insisted in 1930 that its representatives obey party discipline, but only a handful of the 140 MPs stayed with the group. The rest resigned and supported MacDonald in his Tory course and alliance on to the greatest debacle in Labour party history. By the 1950s the leftists usually commanded the loyalties of the majority of the activists, but the party machine could always count on the mass of the labor electorate. Public opinion, shaped in good part by conservative newspapers and age-old instrumentalities of government, weighed in against "extremists." The result was that the occasional leftist victories on resolutions changed neither the character nor the direction of the party, and there was the consistent defection of leftist leaders once they were brought into ministerial or other government posts. Militants who found the party atmosphere of timorous respectability too oppressive for them and broke away to found opposition circles, invariably found themselves consigned to outer darkness. The voting public did not favor mavericks or hotspurs. Marxists predicted that once the empire was gone, the popular mood would veer sharply. The prediction, like others, went awry. When the voters periodically tired of the slow-footed Labour party, they did not seek out Labourite left-wingers or independent radicals; they voted the Tories back into office.

Aneurin Bevan, the one major party leader of his generation who had a touch of the revolutionary about him, probably the ablest, certainly the most brilliant figure in the leadership, could never gain the top post to which his natural abilities would in the course of time have carried him. The most accomplished parliamentary debater of his time, a commanding orator, he was condemned time and again to fight for his very political existence. He was expelled from the party in 1939 along with Cripps and others for advocating a popular front electoral pact with Liberals and Communists in defiance of a National Committee edict. He was saved from oblivion only because of the loyalty of the miners of his home district, Ebbw Vale. In 1955 he was close to being expelled again for speaking against German rearmament, again in defiance of party headquarters, but the uproar was too great for the administrators to be able to go through with it. In

1956 and 1957 he made his uneasy peace with the new Gaitskell right-wing leadership and, like Harold Wilson who had made the same political journey a few years earlier, joined the front bench of the Labour party. He broke with his friends of twenty years when he pleaded with the stunned delegates at the 1957 party conference in Brighton not to send him naked to the negotiating conclave if he became the party's foreign secretary (he was opposed to Britain's unilateral nuclear disarmament). In his own unique career, punctuated by repeated clashes with the dominant right wing, he demonstrated that the Labour party could not be made over into what it did not want to be, could not be revamped in violation of what tradition and a largely conservative public had made it.

4

Propelled by contradictory pressures and motives, the first Labour government constructed not an authentic mixed economy but a rudimentary state capitalism with welfarist features. It was sufficiently vigorous to stage a national recovery that was to improve the lot of the average Englishman. What with full employment, more than one breadwinner in many families, subsidized housing, and free medical care, the majority enjoyed better living standards and fuller lives than before. The minimal reconstruction and reforms accomplished, the inchoate state capitalist regime lacked the outlook, the will, and the tactile organs to correct deep-rooted social and economic inadequacies. For Britain the war struggle had been more devastating than for her overseas ally. She had emerged after her Pyrrhic victory more a battered has-been than a still-formidable wounded lion, without the resources, psychic and material, to resume her old place in the international power lineup.

In this brief review of the main reasons for Britain's historic decline it is necessary to distinguish between those due to specific British circumstances and those in which the British crisis displays features common to all advanced capitalist powers. The distinction cannot always be drawn with assurance; the one cannot always be disentangled from the other. This difficulty notwithstanding, the distinction has to be kept in mind because if England were falling behind her industrial neighbors for reasons unique to herself, it would tell us little about systemic difficulties of late capitalism. If, however, there are common ailments, then the very severity of Britain's syndrome can be of aid in identifying inner malfunctionings.

The next key to keep in hand so as not to get lost in a welter of government enactments and statistics is that both Labourites and Conservatives, despite conflicting ideologies, intervened massively in the economic area; in the case of the Conservatives, in the face of their contrary beliefs and public assertions when out of office. The extension of the state was like something decreed by the gods in a Greek drama that humans could not annul. But repeated government interventions (and consequently, expanding state capitalism) lacked larger coherence because the individual interventions were spasmodic responses to immediate needs. As basic policy they were bound by established capitalist rules, relations, and assumptions. This not only set the outer reaches of what decisions could and could not be made, but it propelled governments into trying to solve burning problems by conventional therapies. At the same time it effectively closed the door to remedies considered outside the bounds of respectability. The result was palliation, less-than-effective tinkering, at times just paralysis, stasis.

Let us start with one of the verities of English economic history. Since the Industrial Revolution Britain has been dependent on foreign trade. By the 1850s a fifth of its national income was derived from sales abroad. In line with this evolution, the capital market of the City of London was heavily oriented toward foreign investment, and the government was often more solicitous in protecting overseas than home investors. Throughout the halcyon days, from 1815 to 1913, when Britain boasted (with some degree of accuracy, at least until the last quarter of the century) of being the workshop of the world, her accumulated balance-of-payments credits were never on goods but came from services, invisible exports, interest, and dividends on overseas investments. At least since 1914 her rate of growth was unusually low and the trend in balance of payments was adverse. So when she emerged enfeebled from the Second World War, she was facing not a new problem of debility but an old trouble now inordinately aggravated.

When her wartime partner abruptly cut off Lend-Lease, Keynes, at the head of a delegation, had to rush to Washington, hat in hand, to ask for succor. Instead of the $5-billion interest-free grant-in-aid or loan to which the British felt they were enti-tled in view of their sacrifices in the common cause, they re-ceived a $3.75-billion loan at 2 percent interest to which were attached provisions for the dismantling of the imperial prefer-ence system and for the free convertibility of the pound sterling. William Clayton, a millionaire cotton broker from Texas, then in charge of economic affairs at the State Department, boasted in a letter to Bernard Baruch, "We loaded the British loan negotia-tions with all the conditions the traffic would bear." On the other side Robert Boothby, a Tory leader, complained that "Com-parable terms have never hitherto been imposed on a country that had not been defeated in war."

Dean Acheson later remarked that it was a disastrous deci-sion made without understanding its consequences. It was these loan provisions that led to Britain's convertibility crisis the fol-lowing year. When the Labour government was foolhardy enough to try to put them into effect, in a matter of a few weeks her gold reserves almost ran out, and much of the loan was squandered in trying to bolster the pound against multinational dealers. From then on, balance-of-payments crises shook En-gland regularly every few years. In 1949 the British deficit rose to £157 million, almost as high as during the convertibility crisis, and its dollar deficit was twice the Marshall Plan aid it was receiving.

The Labour government, under pressure from abroad, cut back social services and devalued the pound by almost 30 per-cent. But devaluation and manipulations in the terms of trade were short-lived palliatives. Competitor countries would retali-ate, and all sides to the transaction were eventually back to where they had been before—with mutual relations the worse for wear. Britain was entrapped in a vicious circle in which her balance-of-payments deficits let to pressures on her currency and inflationary spasms. These would necessitate "cooling off" the economy, with consequent declines in investment, lower growth rates, and unemployment. The deflation in turn would produce at the next stage still greater balance-of-payments deficits, push-ing the economy deeper into the mire from which Britain was seeking to extricate herself. Recourse to foreign loans did no more than tide the government over in the short run while pro-gressively narrowing her freedom of movement and policy options. In short, the deficits were accounting expressions of a deep-seated disorder which could be palliated, not cured, by monetary or administrative adjustments. This was thought of as the British disease at first. Within a few years it had attained international status.

The Attlee and succeeding regimes' extraordinary efforts to revitalize British industry were not all for nought. In the fifteen years after 1948 England's exports were rising annually far faster than in the period 1913–1948. The values of British exports in 1964 in constant prices were three times higher than in 1938; by volume, twice higher. In the 1950–1960 decade her annual rate of growth of total output was over half again that of 1913–1950, the rate of output per head was 70 percent greater, and the rate of output per man-hour almost a fifth greater. But these gains notwithstanding, the United Kingdom was on most major counts at the bottom of the list of the eleven Western European industrial countries, and her share of world exports was rapidly declining. In 1948 her manufactured goods were over 29 percent of the aggregate export of the top eleven industrial nations. This fell to 20 percent by 1954, to less than 14 percent by 1964, to 9 percent by 1977. Her inability to stem the downward slide was signaled by the disproportionate rise of imports of manufactured goods, only 8 percent in 1956, double that by 1970, half again larger in 1978. To summarize the position: From 1870 to 1913 in her years of imperial privilege, Britain's growth rate averaged 2.2 percent per year. In the quarter century from 1950 to 1975 she expanded 2.8 percent per year. But her expansion was so far below that of her neighbors—Germany at 5.7 percent, France at 5.1 percent, not to mention Japan's 9 percent—that she fell and continued to fall behind in the parade.

What happened was that once the Western European states recovered from the war, they went into a historic boom lasting two decades. Their aggregate Gross National Product was more than two-and-a-half times greater in 1963 than it had been on the eve of the war. They were growing from two to three times faster than their island rival. The two defeated industrial behemoths, Germany and Japan, surged back to the field (helped mightily by the United States during the cold war). By the end of the 1950s Germany, like a phoenix risen from the ashes, reappeared as the strongest industrial power in Western Europe. In 1962 she accounted for a fifth of world exports (her 1937 level) and her national product almost doubled between 1950 and 1960 compared to Britain's increase of 40 percent, and the gap continued to widen. By 1976 Germany's percentage of Europe's Gross Domestic Product was over twice England's (Organization for Economic Cooperation and Development data). The major countries' percentages read: Germany, 25.2; France, 19.4; England, 12.1; Italy, 9.5. The question endlessly discussed in the 1960s can be posed again: Why did the victor fare so much worse than the vanquished?

England bore the burdens of having pioneered the Industrial Revolution. In the years of her great ascendancy she had acquired fixed capital assets that had become progressively less profitable, fixed spheres of geopolitical interest that became archaic or inoperative, a military establishment she could no longer afford, and rigid habits of behavior increasingly at odds with the requirements of changed conditions.

If we proceed to break into Britain's circle of woes at the point of the insufficient competitiveness of many of her industrial products because of higher prices, faulty design, poor deliveries, or all three, we notice the related factors (whatever the direction of causality) of lower capital investment and lower rates of productivity improvement than obtained for her neighbors. In all Western European countries fom 1948 to 1962 annual productivity growth increased enormously compared to the pre–World War I period of 1870–1913. England's rate almost doubled, but it was far below those of Germany and France, and was inevitably reflected in the slower growth rate of national product. Say that the year 1950 equals 100; in 1960 productivity per man-hour in the United Kingdom was 129 and national output 140; in Germany, 173 and 260; in France, 178 and 188. The figures in Table 1 verify that England's fresh investments and the productivity of her inputs were decidedly inferior to those of her neighbors.

As the early starter, and shielded for many years thereafter from the harsh winds of rival upstarts by near-monopolist sanctuaries and traditional trading privileges, England was still running many factories with obsolescent equipment. Most of it would have been junked years ago had it not been commercially viable for accounting and tax reasons. The older industries bought and installed their machinery when the markets for their products were larger than they were in the postwar world; they

TABLE 1   Annual Percentage Rate of Growth of Output and Relationship
Between Investment and Output in Real Terms, 1949–1962

	Gross domestic product	Gross domestic fixed capital formation (as % of GDP)	Incremental capital/output ratio (ICOR)
United Kingdom	2.5	16.1	6.7
Germany	6.8	24.3	3.3
Italy	6.0	22.0	3.7
France	4.8	20.6	4.6

were consequently overequipped, and suffered from chronic underemployment of capacity and disproportionate overhead costs.
In the cotton industry, for example, output had been declining
since the early 1930s, and after a short postwar spurt continued
to decline through the 1950s and 1960s. Its unused capacity was
one time rated as high as 50 percent.

The situation in coal, shipbuilding, railways, and the older
sections of engineering differed from cotton only in degree. Conditions were matched on the continent for some older industries,
but unfortunately for England these obsolescent types made up a
large part of the British economic structure. Underemployment
of capacity, high incremental capital/output ratios (ICORs), overmanning, and underinvestment were a complex of structural
faults which would require drastic treatment to remedy. It explained in part both her relative underinvestment and her relative low productivity.

Another aspect of British economics extending her structural
lopsidedness was her reappearance at the end of the 1950s as a
major capital exporter. Like an aging diva drawn irresistibly to
the scene of her earlier triumphs, Britain by 1959 moved again
into developing markets to demonstrate her prowess as an investor. It was estimated that since the war approximately £5 billion
had been added to overseas investment, for a total of £8 billion .
The annual outflow was equal to between a quarter and a third of
net investments in fixed capital at home in the same period.
Later, in 1976, American estimates were that British direct investments abroad ran about $40 billion in book value, possibly a
third of ours. (In a later chapter, some of the baneful effects of

the multinational corporations—MNCs—on the stronger American economy will be looked into.) Whatever the pros and cons here, in the weakened English economy the MNCs aggravated the sicknesses and exaggerated the existing structural ungainliness. Payments to foreigners on foreign investments at home were going up more rapidly than income from Britain's investments overseas. Expansion abroad of British subsidiaries by British multinationals cut sharply into direct exports. Britain's top fifty companies were providing less than a quarter of exports but owned a third of plant assets at home. They also accounted for more than a third of the turnover in the home market. Overseas investments were thus placing an excessive strain on the balance of payments of an already debilitated economy.

5

In considering why Europe's Strong Man turned into Europe's Sick Man, sooner or later people tire of sociology and want to know who is responsible. Since the decline has taken on the character of a Galsworthyan melodrama and since England is both a class-conscious and status-ridden society, either labor or management as the villain of the piece inevitably looms large in the several bills of indictment.

This may appear to be one of those in-house propositions of interest in determining why England has fallen behind in the race but of little relevance to why late capitalism is in trouble. The contrary is the case. (True, some specifics of British labor and management behavior have primary importance for British studies; where they are presented here it is because they constitute necessary background material.) One of the foundation pieces of postwar liberal perspectives was the conviction that Keynesian "fine-tuning" and welfarist innovations had either eliminated or significantly attenuated age-long class antagonisms and for all practical purposes had solved what used to be called the "social question." Consequently the new capitalism could keep the throttle wide open for a continuous journey of expansion and social betterment in full confidence that there would be no interference from any important groups left out of the festivities. However, once Keynesian "fine-tuning" had exhausted itself, welfarism was not advancing but contracting, and unemployment was again running into the millions, then labor–management conflicts and struggles between governments and recalcitrant labor formations are germane for evaluating class relations elsewhere.

To followers of Britain's conservative press the labor establishment—self-righteous officials, militant hotheads, inflexible shop stewards—is responsible for much or most of the country's industrial backwardness. By its never-ceasing strikes, official and unofficial, its resistance to change, restrictive practices, overmanning in plants and offices—in short, workers' unwillingness to work as hard as their counterparts on the continent—labor is dooming the country to decadence and impoverishment. The public indictment only rarely rises to the hysterical shriek of a Peregrine Worsthorne, an editor of the Sunday Telegraph, that British workers are now the "top dogs," that unions can get away with any outrage because of the "contemporary obsession with social justice," and that somebody has to continue the battle for "bourgeois values" no matter what the odds. But the conviction among the many who vote Tory that a good share of the economic difficulties originate here, and that it is time for labor to get its comeuppance, is both widespread and fervently held. How does this check with reality?

England has the largest trade union movement in Europe, over 11 million members (as of 1976) compared to Germany's less than 7½ million, with Germany having the somewhat larger civilian workforce. England's unions also have the deepest penetration, close to 50 percent, matched only by Sweden in its smaller environment, approached by Italy at 39 percent, and with France bringing up the rear at 20 percent. Despite the Trade Union Congress's adherence to the Labour party, the British unions have a Gompers-like suspicion of state interference and prefer to win concessions by their own bargaining with employers. In this respect they are closer to American business unionists than to the more government-enmeshed Frenchmen or Italians. British unions are less centralized, bureaucratized, or state-dominated than German or Swedish unions, and time and again the fervor of the ranks breaks through to set the boundaries within which officials must move. Like the pell-mell organization of British industry, the trade union structure is archaic, a product of labor's chequered past. There are too many unions, too many overlapping jurisdictions; and many unions are too small for effective functioning. But strikes originate in the main in workers' grievances, not because of antiquated organization.

There was a militant thrust after 1945, but only a pale reflection of the offensive after 1918. Nonetheless it led to the re-creation of an independent shop steward organization in certain key industries. In subsequent years it was here that the largest number of wildcat strikes occurred, and the pattern of wage drift (winning of raises higher than those specified in the formal wage agreements) was set. Most of the stoppages resembled guerrilla actions: they were short and involved relatively small numbers, but were strategically well planned and usually effective. To what extent did shop steward floor power, or strikes in general, contribute to the inefficiency of British industry?

The entire proposition has been sensationalized, unconscionably blown out of all proportion to its importance by an unfriendly press. No knowledgeable student of English labor–industrial relations, or work production routine, thinks strikes are a front-rank issue. The statistics do not bear out alarmist assertions, although international comparisons of days lost through strikes have limited analytical value. One would have to know why a particular year was chosen, how that year compared with the years that went before and those that came after, the number of plants and industries affected, the political circumstance of the moment, the amount of violence employed if any, etc. With these reservations in mind, the figures for two selected years are offered in Table 2.

The year 1966 was a reasonably normal one in industrial matters for England and France, even though there was an important seamen's strike in England. Germany was uniquely pacific in the entire era until the late 1970s. Days lost in strikes in England were considerably lower than in France, very much lower than in Italy or the United States, and far higher than in Germany. But 1970 came in the midst of the wage explosion in England, and in the trough of the high strike years in France that occurred in 1967 and 1971. Days lost in England this time were higher than in France, far higher than in Germany, but far below those in Italy and the United States. In other words, it is safe to say that England's strike record was middling, midway between the extreme lows of Germany and a few of the smaller countries on one side, and the highs of Italy and the United States (and Canada) on the other side. It is also necessary to keep in mind

TABLE 2   Days Lost in Disputes per 1000 Workers in the
Civilian Labor Force

Country	1966	1970
United Kingdom	94	443
France	138	87
Italy	778	1117
Germany	negligible	negligible
United States	348	845

that days lost in strikes do not invariably mean lost production. More often than not, production is made up by overtime work, temporary additions to the workforce, or lesser subsequent lay-offs. Orders lost to home competitors do not lessen total production. A strike has to be prolonged and partially crippling to seriously affect the annual product and growth percentages, and there were not many of that kind. Whatever their consequences in individual cases, strikes cannot bear the burden for Britain's decline (although Germany's seamless labor record and all it betokened gave her industrialists an initial advantage).

Where we hit paydirt is the English workers' lower productivity levels (for which managerial ineptitude shares honors with unionists' restrictive practices). Studies over the past quarter century have pointed out that more workers and staff were employed for given operations than were employed in comparable work situations in other advanced countries. The Central Policy Review Staff, a "think tank" set up by the Conservatives during Heath's incumbency, in 1975 reported this type of uncompetitiveness and assigned the biggest reason to overmanning. The National Institute of Economic and Social Research found that Britain trailed her five main continental neighbors—Germany, France, Holland, Belgium-Luxembourg, and Italy—in all six major industrial subsectors with only two exceptions: the English were more efficient than the Italians in textiles and building materials.

A recent study issued by the Geneva-based European Management Forum on competitiveness of industry in seventeen European countries, based on extensive data, tries to arrive at comprehensive judgments by taking into account relevant evaluation and classification factors. Germany and Switzerland place at the top; Britain is in the group that follows, "quite far behind" (which includes Belgium, Luxembourg, and Denmark). Italy is in a far-back third group along with Spain and Ireland. The comment on Germany and Switzerland is worth reproducing:

> These two countries, although having the highest wage costs in Europe and steady currency appreciation, have managed to maintain their competitive position because of their product quality, ability to deliver on time, their after-sales service, and because, with relatively equitable distribution of prosperity, their socio-political consensus and stability are high. This shows that low labor costs do not by themselves render an industry competitive on the international market. Italy, for example, which benefits from relatively low labor costs, is ranked at the bottom on these factors due to runaway inflation, low work motivation and inadequate investment.

Labor productivity, like other social variables, is a function of an interrelated complex comprising investments, work organization, shop traditions, management, and labor relations. It goes to the very roots of a society's makeup. It is impossible to effectively change one of these elements while leaving the others undisturbed. To the extent that low productivity originates in overmanning (and this is due to union resistance to automation) it is because workers fear, with good reason, that they will be relegated to the ranks of the permanently unemployed. Had the Welfare State organized the economy to provide alternative jobs the issue could have been resolved in rapid order. Rising unemployment in conjunction with strong unions made for a compound little suited to speeding up production rhythms.

With similar types of evidence in hand, it is fairly clear as well that British managers in great numbers are as backward as their sternest critics have claimed all along. Barna, in an important study, slightly dated by now but still an authoritative work in the field, examined thirty-one firms in food processing and forty-three firms in electrical engineering. He found great disparities in growth rates, profitability, retained profits, and use or lack of planning; and brought out in the sections that concern us here the inadequacy of supervisory staffs and the innate conservatism and hauteur of numbers of upper-class managers: "The attitudes of many firms can still validly be described in the words of Harold Laski, written a generation ago: 'he must buy not the thing he desires but the thing you have to sell.' " Barna also talks of the aristocratic, contemptuous management "which resents the increased role of women as customers, and which equally resents technological innovation in production and in distribution." Hidebound conceit led to tardiness in introducing new products (which could have been done readily with the existing technology): "The new products were introduced not only from the United States but also, in at least two cases (spin dryers and infra-red heaters), from Germany which at the time had a lower standard of living."

Barna called attention to an article by the architectural correspondent of *The Times* who objected to the "predilection, so widespread among the great industrialists, for buildings reminiscent of past centuries, because those who insist on such architecture deny themselves the freedom and advantage that modern methods of planning and modern building techniques offer them." In the circumstances it is not surprising that many British firms attempt to overcome their defects by offering jobs to men trained in the practices of foreign firms, and that among new firms a large proportion is controlled by foreign companies, or those founded by immigrants and members of minority groups like Jews and Quakers.

Another analyst, Robin Marris, a former Cambridge economist, now head of the economics department at the University of Maryland, similarly pinpointed deficient, ill-educated management as the main culprit for Britain's failure, and called attention to the unwillingness of the better educated to become businessmen. "During 25 years of teaching at Cambridge, none of my students went into industry," he said.*

What is involved is not a simple shortcoming or obtuseness

---

*That these conclusions of some years ago remain fully relevant is underscored in recent reports. The Brookings Institution's 1980 study, *Britain's Economic Performance*, repeats theme by theme the old familiar litany. Richard Caves, one of the two editors of the study, offers the sage advice in conclusion that the English should reconcile themselves to low living standards.

The success of Japanese-owned television and electronics plants in England in contrast to the failure of British manufacturers in the same field is similarly ascribed by British securities firms' economists to the foreigners' superior management and engineering skills and greater devotion to their duties.

Finally, after all the huffing and puffing of over three decades about retraining, at the end of the 1970s West Germany was graduating annually more than twice the number of engineers turned out by British schools and three times the number of more rigorously prepared and examined two-year apprentices.

of this or that individual or set of individuals. If that were the essence of the matter it could be remedied by more intensive training courses and more selective recruiting methods of newcomers. What is involved is that the top echelons of industry are made up of members of a class with ingrained habits of thought, conditioned reflexes inculcated over several centuries in the upper bourgeoisie by means of a network of educational, social, and recreational institutions legitimizing an established ideology of values and attitudes. Because the British bourgeoisie did not supplant but fused with the older aristocracy, and like parvenus eagerly adopted the latter's atavistic mores and mannerisms, a normative pattern emerged that wove together themes of traditionalism, hierarchy, rank, amateurism, and nepotism. "Muddling through" was imprinted as both an iconolatry and a mystique of upper-class superiority. It is the entire complex of the past, material and social, economic and intellectual, that has held British society in thrall. The living are in the grip of the dead. Three decades of threshing about have not succeeded in throwing off the incubus.

2. Crackup of Britain's Welfare State—II

It would have been no body blow to Western civilization had nothing more transpired than that Germany and France supplanted England as the more affluent of Europe's industrial nations. Western culture would survive. The way it happened, and some of the reasons why it happened, however, bear adversely on the perspectives of postwar liberalism and the Welfare State.

In the 1950s continental industries, especially in Germany, had a price advantage over the British because they paid lower wages. The partition of Germany and the expulsion of millions of people from the eastern territories, intended to finish Germany as a great power and to lower her people's living standards, had unexpected effects. As Charles P. Kindleberger explained:

> It was initially widely believed in Germany and among the Western Occupying Powers that the loss of these eastern lands—Germany's breadbasket in which Junker farms had produced the wheat and rye eaten by the workers of the Rhineland and Ruhr—would deal a sharp blow to the German level of living. The influx of expellees and refugees was dreaded for the same reason. . . . The loss of the eastern lands in fact aided West Germany by permitting it to buy its grain in world markets at prices below those charged by the Junker farms of the east. Bismarck's famous 1881 tariff on wheat and iron, and subsequent increases in the duty on grain, had made bread expensive for the German working class. . . . Similarly, the refugees from East Germany turned out to be a blessing in disguise. . . . In static analysis, more labor with given land and capital lowers in-

come per capita. But with a high level of demand, and high investment, more labor may help to hold down wages, hold up profits,
savings, investment, and growth. . . . The influx from the East provided the best possible source of incremental labor to the West—
relatively skilled, readily absorbed culturally, and eager to work
hard to restore its standard of living. The economic miracle in the
1950s and early 1960s until the Berlin Wall of 1961 cut off the flow
owed much to this movement which was originally thought of as a
disaster.

This is half the story. The other half, equally important, is
that wages could be held down throughout the decade because of
a highly motivated, collaborationist trade union organization
committed to supporting the authorities and employers in the
reconstruction effort. Without the unions' championship it could
not have been done. The share going to wages even in the early
1960s was far lower in the two continental countries than in
England, as shown in Table 3. Beckerman demonstrated that by
1960, when GNP per head was slightly higher in Germany than
in Britain, Germany's per-capita consumption was markedly
lower.

Employers of the two continental powers thus enjoyed the
advantage of a differential wage for a crucial decade and a half.
But the advantage was a transient one. England's lower productivity and slower growth were taking their toll; by the second
half of the 1960s Germany and France were moving past Britain
in annual income per capita, and by the 1970s living standards
in Britain were closer to those of Italy than to those of Germany
or France. By 1975 incomes in the latter two were 40 percent
higher than in Britain. English living standards went down first
relatively, then absolutely.

The figures in Table 4 add up to the fact that England was in
the grip of crisis. If in the early postwar years the crisis could be
ascribed to inevitable instabilities and maladjustments in the
wake of a most destructive war, by 1960 no prescience was
needed to discern that the country was caught in a cycle of
constriction the forces for which would not right themselves by
generating their own correctives. The way successive governments proceeded to tackle the problems—governments, let us
note, led by seasoned political practitioners—strongly suggests
that the course will not and cannot be righted by conventional

TABLE 3   Distribution of Income Between Payrolls and Ownership (as percentage of national income)

Country	Year	All wages & salaries	Ownership	Balancing item
United Kingdom	1946–49	73.0	27.0	
	1960–63	73.6	26.4	
Germany	1953	58.7	41.3	
	1963	64.8	35.2	
France	1953	56.5	37.5	6.0
	1962	60.6	33.7	5.7

precepts. It will take a jolting experience and new types of less tradition-bound figures who are ready to work their way clear of both the shibboleths and confinements of middle-class orthodoxies, liberal or conservative.

I will center my attention on the several linked major problems facing British governments: how to break free of the forced "stop-and-go" cycles, how to overcome the related stagflation, and how to gain the right to direct the nation's economic course by government planning. Since governments of other countries, when up against analogous troubles, adopted remedies somewhat similar to Britain's, and since their enactments were grounded on corresponding intellectual presuppositions, the British experience has a generalized importance. In order to avoid repetitiously filling in necessary background material, the propositions will be dealt with as part of the historical flows rather than under individual headings.

At the heart of the model Welfare State's socioeconomic policy was an absurdity. The state was in conflict with itself. On the one hand its managers went to extraordinary lengths to raise tax moneys to underwrite welfare benefactions, all toward the end of mitigating class conflicts, eliminating social tensions, and eliciting social cooperation. On the other hand the Welfare State became an engine to foster class animosities and provoke class warfare. In the process attempts were made to turn the unions, labor institutions built up over years to guard employees' wage and shop interests, into mechanisms to uphold statist corporate programs.

In spite of its far-reaching effects and considerable costs,

TABLE 4   A Comparison of the Major Capitalist Powers in the Early 1970s

Country	Private consumption per capita (in U.S.$, 1974)	Average annual volume growth, 1969–1974 (at constant 1970 prices)	Gross domestic product per capita (in U.S.$, 1974)
Germany	3312	3.6	6195
France	3119	5.3	5061
Italy	1782	3.9	2706
Britain	2142	2.7	3371
Sweden	3647	3.2	6878
United States	4148	2.7	6660

welfarism is a flimsy sports-model body superimposed on a solid capitalist chassis and motor. How was the crisis of inadequate growth rates and other symptoms of the malaise to be resolved? It was axiomatic that an attempt to meet the crisis by reordering economic imperatives in favor of national direction and collectivist arrangements was bad economics, bad politics, and bad policy, and could only lead to disaster. It was thus inevitable that an opposing strategy would be pursued. A government engaged in managing, or at least manipulating, aggregate demand, for whatever purpose, must try to put a damper on wages. Rising wages get translated almost at once, particularly when industry is heavily oligopolized, into higher prices. These in turn adversely affect economic categories from exports to investments. Moreover in capitalist economies it is easier, for both political and economic reasons, to restrain wage increases than to police prices, profits, or investment policies. Wages and prices are often linked in official pronouncements; as a matter of practical statecraft, investments originating in profits have to be encouraged. Consequently the emphasis inevitably tilts toward controlling wages.

The first Labour government was pushed into the fray by circumstances not of its own making. Just as it was averse to planning, it was uninterested in monitoring wage movement. After the fuel, convertibility, and balance-of-payments crises hit in 1947, the officials had no alternative. However, it was still welfarism's honeymoon period, and it could all be done amicably. Sir Stafford Cripps, the ex-leftist chancellor, introduced a White Paper at the beginning of 1948 which yoked wage increases to productivity increases. The statement was hazy on profits and rents, and there was no mention of price controls. The trade union officialdom was cooperative. It was the first Labour government since the MacDonald rout and everyone in the labor movement was anxious to make a success of it.

The pseudo-voluntary wage restraint was remarkably effective for two and a half years. Using a base rate of 100 for wage rates and retail prices as of mid-1947, wages and prices stood at 104 in January 1948. When the policy fell apart in December 1950 wages stood at 110 and retail prices at 114. Real wages had gone down. Following the devaluation of the pound, members in union after union were in revolt. As soon as prices shot further upward with rearmament for the Korean War, wage restraint was swept aside and the continued exhortations of Trade Union Congress officers were pointedly ignored.

When the Tories returned to office, they did not tamper with the social services and nationalizations (except steel and haulage, which were turned back to private ownership). But the spirit was that of the Bourbons returning to Paris after Waterloo. Among the ministers, permanent civil servants, and Tory ideologues there developed, in the words of Shonfield, "an aggressive cult of antiplanning." In the files of the Treasury there still rests the project introduced in the early 1950s under the title "Operation Robot," intended to abolish with one stroke all restrictions on the shipment of sterling abroad and to permit free entrepreneurs, under the unimpeded sway of world market forces, to make decisions without interference or regulation. Since not all Tories had been mesmerized to the point of obliviousness to reality by airy clubroom exchanges (it took thirty years to work themselves to that pitch), the scheme was rejected by the cabinet, but not before it had been vigorously pressed by a number of influential ministers and civil servants. Even with the rejection, the underlying assumptions behind the proposals were not discarded. From the vantage point of the academics of *Political and Economic Planning*,

> There was neither such a strong and persistent determination to intervene to make competition work and thus increase efficiency as in Germany, nor a policy for stimulating growth by target planning

or structural reform, as in France; nor even a serious sustained effort to increase productivity by attacking obstacles to growth, as had been the aspiration in the early postwar period in Britain.

For much of the decade the Conservatives' "You never had it so good" sloganeering came across because they were able to ride the crest of a cyclical upturn. Lady Luck was marching at their side. The prime minister, Harold Macmillan, scion of the publishing house of the same name, had been brought in to rescue the party after the Suez debacle. A throwback to the Edwardian era, he was fond of repeating on suitable occasions Gladstone's dictum that "no man should ever lose a night's sleep over any *public* disaster." The man-in-the-street appreciated the aristocratic insouciance because for the moment the public was in the throes of consumerism, sampling with delight the flood of goods available after rationing was abolished in 1954. Hence, the man-in-the-street could take in stride recurring balance-of-payments deficits, speculation against the pound, hurried loans from international bankers, or government cutbacks of budgetary outlays, since his living standard was still the highest in Europe and he was living better than his forebears when the sun never set on the Empire. With the end of the decade came the end of the euphoria. The economic decline caught up with him and the Conservative joyride was over.

In early 1961 the Organization for European Economic Cooperation (OEEC, forerunner of the OECD) published an eagerly awaited report that in England (and elsewhere) excessive wage increases were an independent and important source of inflation, that they were due to trade union initiatives, that the cure was a strict incomes policy. There was another run on sterling in July, followed by another round of deflation directly instigated by the Bank of England. Thereupon the government bit the bullet and Selwyn Lloyd, the chancellor, announced in Parliament the promulgation of a Pay Pause. This consisted of a straight wage freeze for nine months in the public sector, and the formal request that it be extended to all private industry as well. When the Pay Pause expired in April 1962 it was supplanted by a wage norm of 2–2½ percent as the upper limit for raises. There were no proposals for limiting price increases. Earlier there had been a reduction of business taxes.

Concomitantly the government experienced a sudden, not entirely explained, conversion to planning. Since the Conservatives had already been in office for a decade, and Lloyd, the organizer of the enterprise, had been one of the antiplanning coterie in the 1950s and his record at the Treasury was that of a fiscal martinet, less generous spirits suspected that the conversion was meant to entice labor officials to support the government's incomes policy. Be that as it may, a National Economic Development Council (NEDC) was duly set up and a staff was put to work under the chairmanship of Sir Robert Shone, former leader of the Iron and Steel Board.

The planning offered by the Tories in the less than three years that the NEDC carried on under their administration was called "indicative planning," the name of a technique perfected and trumpeted in France. How much the French variety contributed to French growth will be considered in Chapter 3. There is little doubt, however, that the British variety of the species was a notably anemic one. The NEDC's major activity was to conduct a study of the implications of a 4 percent yearly growth from 1961 to 1966. The target was tested for its feasibility and an inquiry was put out to seventeen industries covering about half of industrial production. None of the industries, public or private, was committed in any way. The publication of the report was itself supposed to constitute a weapon because it would induce managers to think in terms of a growth rate that would otherwise have appeared unduly optimistic. The one and only instance offered, justifiably or otherwise, where this theory of moral suasion was alleged to have had an effect was in electrical supplies. "The Plan," as it was called, targeted an annual investment increase in manufacturing of 3.3 percent; it was actually 0.2 percent. Most of the other targets were similarly awry, or irrelevant. By the end of 1964 "Tory planning" had no admirers and few apologists. The Conservatives under Macmillan did little more than add another page to the Attlee government's ledger of planning as a public relations ploy.

As for progress in easing the pains wracking the body of a sick Britain, there was none on growth, productivity, exports, or price stabilization. What the prudent Conservatives did was to leave their Labour successors a deficit on current account of £400 million, at that point the largest peacetime deficit in the century, and a balance-of-payments deficit of twice that amount.

They had also exacerbated class resentments. A Gallup Poll in December 1961 found that 56 percent of the respondents thought a class struggle was in progress. The promulgation of the Pay Pause marked the exact point where Labour pushed ahead of its rival in the opinion polls.

2

The head of the new Labour government was Harold Wilson. An ex-left-winger associated briefly with Bevan, he had built up a reputation for adroitness, nimbleness, and an ability to move quickly with the tides without losing his balance or air of detachment. These talents, when added to his proficiency as a House debater, made him a formidable political personality. He was an economist in his own right, had trained as a young man under Beveridge, and had been president of the Board of Trade in the old Labour government. Wilson brought along with him as his economic adviser Thomas Balogh, the somewhat leftist economist with a reputation for astuteness in precisely those economic matters that had been plaguing postwar England; Peter Shore, who had collaborated with Arnold Rogow in penning the authoritative critique of the Attlee government and was a general factotum and last minister of the specially created planning department; and a number of others, some more prominent, some less prominent, of like attitudes.

Moreover the new government came in on a program that was nothing if not bold, self-confident to the point of brashness, promising improvements in generous measure. Wilson refurbished the old Fabian ideology of efficiency reeking of settlement house social uplift with the strident accents of post-Keynesian technocrats confident that their day for social engineering had arrived. There would be full employment, a faster rate of industrial expansion, a sensible distribution of industry throughout the country, an end to the present chaos in transport and traffic, a break on rising prices, and a solution to balance-of-payments problems. And these beneficences were to be gained "by a deliberate and massive effort to modernize the economy, to change its structure and to develop with all possible speed the advanced technology and the new science-based industries with which our future lies. In short, they will only be achieved by Socialist planning."

If at any time in past election campaigns Labour spokesmen

had underplayed planning, Wilson more than made up for the neglect. In the 1964 campaign there were plans galore: the big National Plan for economic growth; then plans for the regions, for transport, for tax reform, for structural refashioning. There was no plan for additional nationalizations; nationalizations as conducted under autonomous public corporations were in bad repute. In compensation the platform featured additional welfare planks: a capital gains tax, democratization of education, bigger national insurance benefits, repeal of the Rent Act. As the message was belted out in the party manifesto, "the country needs fresh and virile leadership. Labour is ready. Poised to swing its plans into instant operation. Impatient to apply the New Thinking that will end chaos and sterility. . . ."

The boasting having been so extreme, the more humiliating was the total failure of the second postwar Labour government. Like Laocoön and his sons, Wilson and his ministers found themselves coiled and throttled by the same serpents that had beset the previous governments. No sooner was the Labour cabinet installed in office than it had to scurry around for international bank loans to meet the bills, and from that moment to its defeat six years later it moved from crisis to crisis. Labour ministers found themselves adopting the very policies they had castigated the Tories for pursuing only a few years before. When they were voted out of office, planning had become a music-hall joke, unemployment had risen to over 600,000 (a new high at that time), and Wilson's attempt to impose a punitive Labor Relations Act almost brought the party to a split in a Ramsay MacDonald–like crisis of confidence. The nature of the British malaise and the frustration in trying to find a solution within existing economic and social dispensations are now familiar to us. It will suffice to follow through on what happened to planning, why the government was determined to hold down wages, and why most of the promised welfare reforms had to be abandoned.

There was extensive reshuffling of bureaus and commissions, and a new Department of Economic Affairs was brought into being. But it was the same type of planning that the Tories attempted in Macmillan's last years. The same questionnaires were sent out to select groups of managements to indicate the percentage of growth that should be aimed at. A year after Labour's return to office the National Plan was unveiled: 25 percent growth to be sought between 1964 and 1970, or 3.8 percent annually. As an example of how the Plan figures had been worked out, each industry had been asked to what extent it expected to increase exports on the assumption of a 3.8 percent production increase. The questionnaire was accompanied by a note stating that exports would have to double the existing rate if the growth target was to be achieved. The managers said, in effect, fine. They had made no commitments, and were not asked for any. Despite its impressive 475-page format published in the form of a White Paper, and with many pages devoted to informative discussions of the nature of some of the problems, the Plan in fact had nothing to contribute to the solutions. For good reasons it was greeted with skepticism by all leading financial writers, many of them advocates of indicative planning. What made the Plan a pure exercise in public relations was that it was undermined from the start by the rest of the government.

The large deficit set going the rumor on the international money-markets grapevine that the pound was to be devalued. Wilson held back since he had determined to call a special election to gather in a more workable majority than the bare majority that had sent Labour to Whitehall the year before. He knew that the inevitable deflation and distress that would follow devaluation would scarcely endear him to the public. In any event he had recourse to crisis management; he slapped a 15 percent surcharge on imported goods, raised the bank rate, arranged $3 billion in credit with the central banks, and applied for an additional $1-billion loan from the International Monetary Fund. Thus by July 1965, two months before the Plan was unveiled, an expansionary policy had already been foreclosed.

A year later the government faced another moment of truth. In May and June there was a six-and-a-half-week seamen's strike and a new heavy run on the pound. This time Wilson (returned to office in March with a comfortable majority) put through deflation with a vengeance. Public expenditures were slashed, the purchase tax and bank rate were raised, unemployment shot up, wages and prices were frozen. George Brown, in charge of the Plan, followed with a plaintive confession: "How does this affect the National Plan? I will be absolutely frank with the House; it means that the rate of growth we attempted to set, and on the basis of which we predicted all other things for 1970, is no longer available." Thereupon Samuel Brittan, the financial writer, composed this mock epitaph:

On July 20, 1966 the demise of the National Plan was announced. It had of course been suspected dead for a long time past. The doctors had diagnosed congenital defects as soon as the infant was born; and its chances of survival were never rated highly before its birth in September 1965.

Wilson's expert juggling only delayed until spring a further balance-of-payments deficit bringing on a new sterling crisis. In November Wilson threw in the towel. The pound was devalued from an exchange rate of $2.80 to $2.40, to be followed by a deflationary budget with all welfare spending cut back drastically. Thus in a final stroke what had been left of Wilson's social service program was eliminated.

In his apologia for failure to carry out his promises, Wilson later wrote:

> The Governor of the Bank of England became a frequent visitor. . . . It was his duty to indicate the issues on which, in the City's view, it was necessary to win confidence if a disastrous haemorrhage were to be averted. . . . That is why we had to listen night after night to demands that there should be immediate cuts in Government expenditure, and particularly in those parts of Government expenditure which related to the social services. It was not long before we were being asked, almost at pistol point, to cut back on expenditure, even to the point of stopping the road building program, or schools which were only half constructed. . . . Was it his view, I asked him, that we should cut them off half-finished roads, left as an eyesore on the countryside, schools left without a roof, in order to satisfy foreign financial fetishism? The question was difficult for him, but he answered, "Yes." . . . I said that we had now reached the situation where a newly elected Government with a mandate from the people were being told, not so much by the Governor of the Bank of England but by international speculators, that the policies on which we had fought the election could not be implemented. . . . The Governor confirmed that this was, in fact, the case.

Unfortunately for Wilson's case, this was not a new unforeseen development that upset the Labour party's well-laid plans. He was aware of these contingencies before the election. "You can get into pawn," he explained earlier, "but don't then talk about an independent foreign policy or an independent defense policy. . . . If you borrow from some of the world's bankers you will quickly find you lose another kind of independence because of the deflationary policies and cuts on social services that will be imposed on a government that has got itself into that position."

There are hints here and there in his memoirs that the international speculators were in a conspiracy against the Labour government for class reasons. While the British press was always more tolerant of a government's difficulties if that government was Conservative, there is little evidence that there was any concerted international bankers' movement to embarrass the Labour government or to bring it down. The International Monetary Fund (IMF) directors, like medieval ecclesiastics, invariably offered to all those unfortunate enough to be in need of their loans the same simple remedies to drive away evil spirits: cuts in public spending (especially for luxury items like social services), currency stabilizaton, free trade in moneys and goods. As for speculators, the major operators of transnational currency movements in the postwar world are the multinational corporations. For the purposes of this specific account, their money managers are not concerned with ideologies but with currency values. Their working rule is to enhance profits and finance their own transactions. They move into markets with superior interest rates and move away from any currency that may be devalued. The ability of treasurers of these corporate leviathans to shift from one currency to another within a matter of days or hours places weakened economies at their mercy; it forces governments to set policies in deference to their anticipated movements.

A government intending to put through basic structural changes in defiance of orthodox dispensations, and in order to make the economy a servant of equalitarian aspirations, has to insulate itself from the pressures of the money powers, not only abroad but at home. The more thorough the intended transformation, the more positive must be the nation's ability to withstand the retaliatory blows of the old establishments. The population has to understand that this means not just a majority vote in Parliament but a protracted economic battle requiring endurance and resolve, a battle in which costs will have to be borne and sacrifices will have to be made. What the leaders of the British Labour party lacked was not education in economics or adroitness in parliamentary politics, but the will to embark on such a perilous journey; confirmed liberals in practice by training and associations, such a radical course was outside the purview of the possible for them.

3

We left the wages situation at the point when an electoral majority was turning to Labour in the early 1960s as the Macmillan government was forcing through wage freezes and wage controls. That there was going to be trouble for the Labour government on this front as well was evident from the start. The candidates had been arguing before the election that the unions would cooperate much better with a Labour government to control wages and make sacrifices for the obvious reason that a Labour government was dedicated to social justice, etc. When the Labour party took over in October 1964 it tried to make good on its gratuitous boasts.

Although British earnings had been lagging behind those of the continent, output was improving far more slowly so that unit costs remained comparatively high. Also, as usual an economic crisis was at hand. The pressures were very great to reimpose wage curbs as a major tactic for making British wares competitive and holding down price inflation. Trade union officials' disposition to cooperate in the game was reinforced once the government made provisions in the budget to raise pensions, abolish health service charges, and introduce a capital gains tax. Employers were not elated by the announcement of a capital gains tax, but its effects were a long way off while wage controls were immediate. (Price controls were theoretical, not practical; excess profits and dividends were supposedly to be corrected by future unspecified fiscal provisions—a low-grade danger.)

It was in this atmosphere that the new voluntary incomes policy was launched. The corporative nature of the undertaking was brought out in the way the White Papers were written up. The rule in legislation is that employer and trade union organizations are barred from seeing a draft of a bill before its publication. In this instance representatives of both private parties took part in the drafting. The ceremony at Lancaster House where George Brown, head of the Economic Affairs department, heralded the end of class conflict was a television spectacular. The news was splashed across the newpapers, and 50,000 copies of the tripartite Statement of Intent were dispatched around the country to be pinned up on factory walls and in trade union offices. If ballyhoo could do it, the Labour government was on its way.

A National Board for Prices and Incomes, headed by an eleemosynary-minded industrialist, was set up to ensure that the norm of annual increases limited to 3–3½ percent would be lived up to. Before April 1965 there were wage commitments and settlements in the pipeline affecting ten million employees not governed by the norm, and in mid-April the retail price index was up four points in the six months since the election, the largest half-year rise since 1952. Things were not moving according to schedule; by the end of August a worried ministry asked union and employer heads to support legislation for statutory wage and price controls. It was reported at the time that the government was counting on additional loans, and the United States was prepared to mount an immediate rescue operation for sterling provided there was a British commitment to introduce incomes legislation by the end of the year.

The General Council hesitated, remonstrated, and at the twelfth hour, with many sighs, agreed to compulsory controls, following which the proposal was adopted at the 1965 Trade Union Congress (TUC) and at the Labour Party Conference. The government White Paper of November outlined how the scheme would work. For prices it was much the same procedure as before: the board would keep track of a small number of key consumer items; for wages, the regulations incorporated a union wage-vetting procedure under which the TUC would initially examine wage claims before their referral to the prices and incomes board. The TUC thus institutionalized the role it had played informally in 1948–1950. The Confederation of British Industry, in contrast, refused to supervise either the wage or price decisions of its members. It argued that it was a voluntary organization and could not presume to exercise discipline over those who were its members by voluntary decision.

When the Labour party was returned at the end of March with a solid majority, the machinery for incomes legislation began to turn. The prices and incomes board was reconstituted on a statutory basis. Then came the stinger. The bill also required that the government be advised of all wage claims and settlements; there was to be a thirty-day standstill, or where referred to the board, one of four months. And there were penal provisions: anyone striking to compel employers to settle was subjected to fines of up to £500. In July 1966 came the massive deflation, and the elaborate multistage incomes policy was turned into an outright wage freeze for six months followed by a further six months of "severe restraint." Nor were the agreements that had already been made, covering some six million workers, permitted to stand. The government required employers to break their contracts and defer payment for six months. The General Council officials, having involved themselves so deeply, plunged in further by endorsing the freeze. While relations with the government ministers were no longer as ebullient as they had been with Attlee's ministers in those more hopeful days, union officials still accepted the government's reasoning on how to deal with the crisis. Several months later when the government put the penal clause into effect they went along again. Their motive this time was self-protection. They knew that union endorsement of the wage freeze would break down if some of the ranks could win increases through direct bargaining and that they themselves would be discredited because of their passive acceptance of the freeze. It was far safer for them to let the government keep the ranks in line and to have the freeze applied across the board.

Rising prices during the year of wage freeze and "severe restraint" resulted in a decline in real earnings, so the mood was explosive at the September 1967 Trade Union Congress. Resolutions for the repeal of the incomes law passed without even a card vote. George Woodcock, the TUC secretary, on behalf of the entire General Council heatedly opposed another, stronger resolution offered by several unions which "deplored" government policies of deflation and unemployment, rejected government interference in collective bargaining, and called for an extension of public ownership as vital for planning. Woodcock protested that such a stand was putting into question the TUC's policy of accommodation. Frank Cousins went after Woodcock for wanting "the bureaucrats who sit on the platform" to determine by themselves what the TUC should be doing—and the resolution passed.

The Labour government and the labor ranks were no longer moving, even rhetorically, on the same rails. The fruitlessness of the government's economic decisions was pushing it toward increased controls over the unions, while the unions wanted to disentangle themselves from corporative arrangements. After the devaluation in November the government felt constrained to keep wages from rising in response to the inevitable inflation. It therefore brushed aside union officials' proposals to substitute a new incomes policy to be administered by them, and made clear that even more stringent measures were to be introduced, a policy soon codified in a White Paper, *In Place of Strife*. The announcement that new legislation would be pressed called into question the relationship of the unions to the party, inaugurating a period of acute tension between the two. The number of trade unionists paying the political levy was declining, and one union, the sheet metal workers, voted to disaffiliate from the Labour party. When the parliamentary Labour party discussed the proposed legislation, the MPs were shaken by the declaration of Emanuel Shinwell, the party's elder statesman, who had a reputation as an extreme disciplinarian, that he would not vote for the bill: "I am more concerned about saving the party than saving the government," he explained.

The reaction of most of the General Council was hostile in the extreme. The Labour government, it was felt, was aping the Conservatives in misleading the public that strikes were the main issue confronting the country, and putting a taint of criminality on legitimate union activities. The punitive proposals were flatly rejected. The council members had been told in no uncertain terms by constituent union officers not to equivocate or waffle. By the end of February virtually every major union executive had declared his opposition to restrictions on the right to strike. At the same time a challenge was mounted in the industrial arena at Ford. Auto workers went out in a wildcat strike on February 21 against an agreement reached between the unions and the company. The Engineering and Foundry Workers and the Transport and General Workers Unions both made the strike official a week later. A temporary injunction secured by the company was ignored by the officials, and a plea for a permanent injunction was turned down by the High Court. Ford finally settled with the unions in mid-March. In the wake of the victory, and the successful defiance of the government, committees of union officers and stewards were set up in major centers by a Liaison Committee for the Defense of Trade Unions.

The unions' aggressive stand cracked the solidarity of the parliamentary Labour party, and in March, despite major pressure from the government, fifty-three Labour MPs voted against the government's motion and forty more abstained. Wilson was faced with a full-blown revolt. Concomitantly the National Executive Committee of the party took the unprecedented step of breaking with the government on both incomes and antistrike legislation. The NEC feared that the course Wilson was on would snap the indispensable link between unions and party. When Wilson, convinced that his government's credibility was at stake, called up an antistrike bill linked with incomes policy, the crisis came to a head. An unprecedented special congress was called for June. In the eight-week interim, union locals were passing resolutions demanding replacement of cabinet members, suspension of financial support, disaffiliation from the party, the calling of a protest strike. Similarly the mood in the parliamentary Labour party grew stormy: sixty-three MPs pledged openly to vote against the bill and thirteen more were committed to abstain. The General Council, for its part, adopted a forthright declaration of noncooperation to put before the coming congress. Their hands thus forced, Wilson and his associates, despite their magisterial airs, had no alternative but to back down. They had received notice that neither the parliamentary party nor the cabinet could be counted on to support their legislation.

What remains to be explained is why such an experienced crew of politicians and administrators, headed by such a wily prime minister, were so fanatic in attempting to virtually freeze wages, and when confronted with resistance, to tame the unions with antistrike and other punitive enactments. Government figures, wily or nonwily, are forced into an either/or law of alternatives. If they do not adopt one course, willy-nilly they have to work for the alternative one. Wilson had diagnosed England's economic ailments as technocratic, and amenable to technocratic remedies. He had opted for the technocratic solution as the sure way to break out of persistent crisis. To the extent that technocratic rejuvenation was the way out, it required near-frozen wages if technocracy was to work at all. Once he and his confrères boxed themselves into this way of thinking, the workers appeared to them as foolishly myopic, their officials demagogic, the unions as instruments obstructing the way to the uplands. Not for the first time has an insurgency sought to devour its own children.

It has to be kept in mind that inchoate state capitalism was an enormous engine for using tax money to relieve private businesses of numerous risk-taking and investment obligations, and of providing crutches for many disabled business clients. There were tax allowances and rebates, investment grants, regional employment premiums, miscellaneous subventions. Under both Labourites and Conservatives truly enormous sums, billions of dollars, were ladled out, with additional subsidies provided in the form of below-cost prices for services from publicly owned industries.

The Labour governments were the initiators of these state-capitalist–induced modernizations. The Attlee government had from the earliest days advanced grants to update obsolescent plants and to improve industrial ambience from apprenticeship training to statistics gathering. Under Wilson this program was extended, integrated, and conceptualized. He created a new Ministry of Technology which built up close relationships with crucial industries—electronics, computers, machine tools, engineering—to which it made investment subventions and donated the results of government-sponsored research. Under this aegis an Industrial Reorganization Corporation was formed with an initial sum of £150 million at its disposal to assist industrial mergers and promote restructuring—all on the theory of making British corporations "capable of fighting European giants on equal terms," as Wilson put it.

The program was a total failure so far as thrusting Britain into a position of equality as regards growth, productivity, unit costs, exports—for reasons alluded to earlier. As with a little-understood ailment that will not respond to the physician's customary potions and pills, these ministrations availed little and the gap between Britain and her rivals continued to widen. But the program did produce unwelcome side effects. It strengthened the independent power of private corporations and their bureaucracies. It set into motion, or at any rate accelerated, the concentration of British industry, reinforcing existing tendencies to oligopoly and cartel allocations. It rigidified price structures and inflationary propensities. It canalized economic decision-making to the corporate elites and their civil service allies. Raymond Vernon wrote that according to a study covering 1955 to 1969, nearly 4 percent of the manufacturing enterprises listed on British stock exchanges were absorbed each year in the merger movement (in Germany the absorption rate ran to 3 percent), and that "the national markets of Europe, taken one at a time, seemed to display an increasingly concentrated structure." Britain's Office of Fair Trading determined that after the takeover boom of the 1960s and

1970s, the largest 100 firms accounted for 40 percent of total net output in manufacturing in 1973 as against 27 percent twenty years earlier.

On the narrower question of wage and price controls, the Wilson disaster does not necessarily demonstrate that a control policy is unsuitable under any and all conditions. To be sure, there are big risks: wage reductions achieved may be only temporary, and controls lead to distortions in labor markets, encourage under-the-table settlements and black-market practices, and saddle governments with self-perpetuating, wasteful bureaucracies. Nevertheless there have been instances, and they can be cited, when such a restraining enactment educated publics in disciplines of reciprocity and eased inflationary pressures. But trying to employ coercion and to apply sanctions against an aroused and strong labor movement without any attempt at restraining prices or demonstrating that wage restrictions were contributing to society's larger objectives was the sure way to impel labor ranks to demolish the roadblocks the first chance they got and to race to make up for lost time.

That is what happened. Toward the end of 1969 there was a wage-and-strike explosion; 6.8 million working days were lost in strikes, over 45 percent more than in 1968. The next year the figure jumped to 11 million. A high proportion of these strikes was unofficial, and in many of them stewards and local officials negotiated wage increases higher than those the national leaderships set forth. The gains were not spectacular, and much of them were eaten up by the inflation, but real income increased for the typical wage earner by 1.3 percent annually over 1969 and 1970 compared with 0.5 percent in the previous four years. For the entire period from April 1965 to June 1970 hourly wage rates went up 6.5 percent, earnings went up 7.3 percent, and retail prices increased 4.7 percent. Whether it would have been very much different without all the huffing and puffing, and bringing on the crisis of 1969, nobody really knows. Derek Robinson, formerly of the National Board for Prices and Incomes, is one who thinks the incomes policy "had little overall effect," that "the immense stresses and strains imposed on the labor market . . . were an excessive price to pay for merely postponing wage increases. . . . Those who believe that the incomes policy had some beneficial effects rely only on impressions and non-quantifiable factors."

Once election time arrived all the actors played their assigned parts in the time-honored ritual. The Labourites closed ranks: the trade union officials rallied round; the government, in its last months, refrained from applying the statutory powers of the incomes law; the party's election manifesto trotted out the familiar panegyrics to planning and economic growth. Unfortunately the ranks were uncooperative. The turnout was the lowest since 1935. Heavy working-class abstentions enabled the Conservatives to come back.

4

The new prime minister was Edward Heath, an uptight, priggish organization man, called by some newpapermen the Clem Attlee of the Conservative party. But unlike Attlee, who was all briskness and imperturbability for getting on with the job, Heath had gained a reputation for unpleasant censoriousness, a hard taskmaster when he was chief whip under both Eden and Macmillan. He was neither very much liked nor did he have much personal support in the party. He was wooden and unimpressive on the platform and on television, and had frequently been mauled by Wilson when the Conservatives were in the opposition. But he hungered for success, was determined to prove himself, was organizationally solid, and came across in the election campaign as the salesman for a tough managerial crowd.

Only a few novel policy modifications which the Tories brought into play need detain us. They displayed in the beginning the same delusions that had their predecessors in thrall in the 1950s. This time the managers, confident that they had more leeway in carrying along a tired and disappointed people with free-enterprise experiments, moved more aggressively to dismantle parts of the economic apparatus of the Welfare State. The Industrial Reorganization Corporation (IRC) was abolished. The Prices and Incomes Board was dissolved. A number of regional planning councils were disbanded. However haltingly, the march was heading back to the free market. But not for long—in very little time, confronted with realities, the Conservatives had to reverse themselves. They had to junk their cherished dogmas.

The struggle with Labour, as one could expect, was re-launched, an unpostponable priority. If Wilson could not succeed because of his dependence on the labor constituency, then the Conservatives, with their middle-class and upper-class constituencies, ought to be able to carry the day. One of the first major moves was to enact an Industrial Relations Act more onerous than the one Wilson had proposed. It was bad figuring. The strike wave which had started in Wilson's last year was still gathering strength when this law went into operation, and Heath was confronted with a more united and resolute opposition than the one that brought Wilson to heel. There were huge demonstrations and several one-day political strikes. There was a free-for-all inside Parliament. The government, after suffering defeats in the mine and rail disputes, had five shop stewards jailed in connection with a dock stoppage. With that, a general strike was imminent. Opposition had already developed to Heath's bull-headedness among employers and press owners. To halt the ominous drift toward class war, the Law Lords quickly met as a final Court of Appeal, reversed the Appeal Court ruling, and the five dockers were released from prison forthwith—to repeat their defiance of the Industrial Relations Court to millions of television viewers. Thereupon the law was shelved. Heath and his coadjutors had completely misjudged the situation.

Since the endemic inflation and deficits had not been washed away by the healing waters of the unfettered market, the defeat forced Heath to reenact an incomes policy. The law called for a temporary freeze to be followed by (Phase II) a sharp limitation on all wage increases until the end of October 1973. When Phase III was unveiled at the beginning of that month, limiting basic increases to 7 percent (equivalent to an average of £2¼ a week) at a time when prices were rapidly advancing again, the union leaders broke off negotiations with the ministers. Once the miners union rejected a settlement within Phase III, the policy was in crisis. On November 17 the union banned overtime work. At the new year the government announced that owing to the lowering of coal reserves, industry would be put on a three-day week—an edict that lasted two months. In early February the miners took a strike ballot and a strike was set for February 10. Two days before the strike was to start Heath, who had already demonstrated that he was disaster-prone, announced a new general election at the end of the month. He fought it out on straight "government versus the miners" grounds, and was rebuffed again as he had been rebuffed earlier. The Labour party contingent returned to Whitehall, but it was a sorry victory. There was no majority; Labour held only four seats more than the Conservatives, and its percentage of the popular vote (37 percent) was the lowest since 1935.

It was mentioned that the Heath government had to change front on interventions and subsidizations. This had been (and remains to this day) a big item in the conservative press, and was an important talking point in the 1970 Tory preelection presentations. Labourites were jeered for wasting public money trying to save yesterday's declining or dying industries which on the morrow would in any case be taken over by the less-developed countries. The Tories pledged that they would put a stop to these handouts. In the free society there was no place for "lame ducks." Everyone was going to have to pull his own weight. That was how free enterprise would bring out the best, and that was why the IRC had been junked: it had bailed out too many sick and sinking enterprises.

Shortly thereafter the Heath government got entangled in the affairs of the bankrupt Rolls-Royce Company to which it offered £42 million in aid. Two months later, when the financial gap had widened to £150 million the government put in a receiver, and later had to salvage parts of the company by nationalization—one of several instances of ideology at war with policy.

Another "lame duck" was the Upper Clyde shipbuilding group which the Labour government had been underwriting and supposedly nationalizing. The yards were old, inefficient, riddled with antiquarian procedures, and shipbuilding was a declining industry. Heath's inheritance included government ownership of 48 percent of the company's shares, but all the input had not reversed the mounting losses. Finally, in 1972 the government reluctantly threw another £35 million into three of the yards and a little later spent still more public money to persuade an American buyer to save the Clydebank yard itself. (Unemployment at this time on Clydebank was over 12 percent of the workforce.) Later, *The Economist* jeered (when Labour was back in office) at this "infant industry protection for dying geriatrics like British shipbuilders. There can be no recession in which it has been less sensible to protect yesterday's industries, because tomorrow these are all going to the South Koreans." The editors concluded: "Britain serves as the awful example of the country which for 30 years has subsidized its stagnation in yesterday's industries, both by its crutches for lame ducks and by 'incentives' like its investment allowances."

The reason the Tories under Heath lacked the courage of their convictions was that in a declining economy, keeping hands off while all manner of uncompetitive plants shut their doors only aggravated already dangerously rising unemployment. Laissez-faire, when tried, was not bringing on lusty expansion and the rise of fresh enterprises in newer industries. It was causing a further contraction of already contracting home and external markets. If numbers of British companies could not make the grade with government subventions, how were they going to do it without them? There is no difficulty in finding new investments, British and foreign, for thriving concerns. The techniques have not been devised, however, for enticing investments into stagnant or decaying enterprises, which in the British case are not the exceptions but the rule. Britain's capitalist forefathers who handed down the City of London's revered precepts did not have to face the problem of a society in slow economic rot.

Between 1960 and 1972, despite the bipartisan St. Vitus dance of over a quarter century, Britain fell from seventh to fifteenth place in GNP per capita among OECD countries, and yet another notch by 1980. Full-blooded inflation hit them all, but Britain got it earlier and worse than any other important industrial country, 203 percent in the 1967–1977 decade (as against 122 percent in France, 172 percent in Italy, 86 percent in the United States, and 58 percent in Germany). Unemployment, another world systemic ailment by now, stood at one and a half million, 6 percent of the workforce in 1977 and 1978, rose to two million by the summer of 1980, and soared above three million in the closing months of 1981. The Cambridge Godley group of economists predicted that along the present course there would be five million unemployed in ten years' time.

When the Tories at last found in Margaret Thatcher their "iron maiden" who would not blanch in the face of miscalculation or disaster, many of them concluded that there was much to be said for rising above one's principles. The New York Times, by no means an unfriendly observer, thus grimly sums up the Thatcher government's record after a bare year in office:

The Conservative economic potions—a shift from income to sales and tight controls on money—had had an unintended effect. Instead of stimulating private investment and enterprise, and reducing Government's intervention in the economy, they worked . . . to double the inflation rate to 22 percent [over two times the rate when Mrs. Thatcher took office]. That in turn . . . raised the Government's minimum lending rate to a record of 17 percent and discouraged private investment. It also overvalued the pound, sucking in imports and pricing Britain's exports out of world markets. Far from reviving, British industry is worse off than even a year ago. Unemployment is approaching two million, the highest since the Depression of the 1930s and more than double the number that helped bring down the last Conservative Government in 1974.

Did the *Times* have advice to offer Mrs. Thatcher on how to cope? Yes: "An opportunistic muddling through is required."

There is another problem with trying to get out of an economic mess by elbowing aside your neighbors. It is a mistaken strategy for a nation to try to solve its difficulties by piling up surpluses in foreign trade. It would be a recrudescence of mercantilism in modern dress. If one perceives the trading activities of nations as a race between rival contenders, there can only be one or two winners. The rest will be losers and hurt in the race. And even the one or two victors will have their victory turn to ashes when the injured ones throw up bulwarks to protect themselves and keep out their rivals. Beggar-thy-neighbor policies were tried in the 1930s and found wanting.

Reading today's business publications of the major industrial countries is a disheartening experience. They all advise their nationals to do the same thing: get out of the old, worn-out, labor-intensive industries; get into the industries of the future from which the big leaders are going to come and the big profits are going to be realized. High technology will constitute the Elysium of tomorrow: computers, digital processors, word-processors, management systems, integrated circuits, high-speed automation equipment, biological synthesizing, food processing. That may be advice that can be successfully implemented by one, or possibly two, countries. But can all of them enter a do-or-die competition of this nature without falling flat on their faces and skewing their economies in the process? Unlike the theory of the open universe, world trade, particularly in such specialized fields, is not capable of infinite expansion. That was one of the reasons why Keynes wanted government control of investments. Only with that could "international trade . . . cease to be what it is, namely, a desperate expedient to maintain employment at home by forcing sales on foreign markets and restricting purchases, which, if successful, will merely shift the problem of unemployment to the neighbor which is worsted in the struggle."

Without meaning to do so, many business editors are filling out prescriptions for an international trade war, not for peaceable trading relations and normal balance-of-payments reconciliations. To proffer such advice to anyone is reckless. To proffer such advice to Britain, with its historical and institutional distortions and archaisms, is to indulge in fatuity wholesale.

That the entire English position could be stricken, that the English people's living standards could plunge downward, all in the matter of a few decades, without unhinging the country's political institutions will be pointed to by future historians as one of the wonders of the world on a par with the Hanging Gardens of Babylon and the Colossus of Rhodes. Still, no peoples and institutions are exempt from the assaults of time and tide. It can therefore be surmised that the British will in due course demonstrate that they do not stand outside history's sway. Unsurprisingly, we can already hear premonitory mutterings on the scene that presage disturbances to come. The propositions I will refer to may not be earth-shaking in and of themselves, but they are symptomatically most significant.

First is the appearance of what has been called the second generation of Cambridge economists—Godley, Neild, Posner (the first generation included Keynes and Joan Robinson). These worldly philosophers reject strategies of tinkering and palliatives; they are scornful of additional tactical expedients to energize the hitherto fruitless quest for classical economic equilibrium. They call for nothing less than a "siege economy." They believe that the country's troubles stem from trying to maintain a status which it is not equipped to hold: importing too heavily at the expense of domestic industry, retaining sterling as a reserve currency at the expense of balance-of-payments deficits. They propose to control and restrict imports so that the home market will take up the slack of unused plant capacity; they want to regulate all foreign trade and transactions to reconcile them with internal projects and needs; etc. They are not political radicals, but they are offering radical solutions. Their program represents a sharp departure for established academics, all the more remarkable for coming out of Cambridge, one of the twin blue-ribbon establishments of British academia. The Godley group will be heard from again since it is the only qualified academic school offering a fundamental program to resolve the British crisis.

The second development is the appearance of a New Left formation in the Labour party identified with Tony Benn. The arrival of still another leftist group in the Labour party, or its proposals for a sweeping reorganization of the economy, would not necessarily rate big writeups in the Sunday supplements. What is of interest here is the inner character of the group and the widespread support that its proposals have generated in party ranks. Of all the leftist caucuses inside the Labour party in the past sixty years, the Benn group is the most Jacobin in tone, the most implacable in temperament. Benn and his associates are more concerned with turning the party into a disciplined order dedicated to radical change than to soft-pedaling their radicalism at election time so as not to antagonize the party's numerous middle-of-the-road adherents.

They forced through a conference resolution to subject freewheeling Members of Parliament to party control. They are proposing to adopt action planks for socialist reorganization and to compel elected representatives to speak up for them. They did not flinch when their militancy led to the departure of a group of moderates on the opposing side, nor did they offer compromises when the right-wingers formed their own party to the detriment of the Labourites' chances for victory in the next election. Whatever the future holds for Benn and his group, or for the Labour party itself for that matter, this entire development prefigures a sterner mood in British politics once leaders can no longer avoid confronting the realities.

That Mrs. Margaret Thatcher—a zealot with a doctrinaire streak—has emerged as the undisputed boss of the Tories is in accordance with the theory of probability since that is the trajectory that the Tories have long been traveling. That she and her henchmen could be expected to accelerate Britain's plunge to disaster, given their ideological obsessions and upper class arrogance was likewise in the nature of things. That after presiding for four years over a destructive and bankrupt regime she could

bring her party to an electoral triumph—that is a true phenomenon the explanation for which might best be sought from the
more mystical exponents of Jungian psychiatry. Before the Gil-
bert-and-Sullivan war over the Falklands, opinion polls recorded
that she was the most unpopular prime minister in four decades,
commanding the grudging acceptance of no more than a quarter
of the voters. After the war, her support continued to soar enabling the Tories to muster 43 percent of the popular vote.

The Economist, in its summary before the election, pointed
out that the Thatcher government of 1979–1983 did worse than
all 23 other OECD countries, that it has a "lousy economic record." One need go no further if that is the judgment of the Tories'
coadjutor and patron saint. Not just Tory promises, but Tory
perspectives have turned to ashes. Instead of cutting down
spending by monetary control, tight money brought on a sharp
rise in interest rates and the flow of pounds to New York where
interest rates were still higher. This evaporated the promise to
reduce taxes. The original 10 percent cut in income taxes was
simply a shift of the tax burden in favor of the rich when the
value-added tax (VAT), a British variety of sales tax, was doubled to 15 percent, to be followed by increased excise taxes on
automobiles, gasoline, and other consumer items. The bottom
line at the end of 1982 was that taxes as a proportion of earnings
had risen by 10 percent as had public spending as a percentage
of national income. The makeshift and spasmodic veering did
not save the Thatcher government from having to borrow £13½
billion in 1980–1981, 6 percent of the gross national product,
one of the highest ratios of borrowing in the world.

If monetarism proved to be a worthless therapy to bring the
slump under control, supply-side economics was no more helpful. Manufacturing output at the end of 1982 plunged to its lowest level in fifteen years, industrial investments fell by over a
fifth, national income was down by 5 percent despite the North
Sea oil bonanza. To complete the dolorous account, exports were
shrinking at an annual rate of 4 percent, and—the sure sign of a
decaying internal market unable to hold its own at home—imports of finished manufacturing goods doubled in volume since
the mid-1970s.

The promise to stop supplying crutches to industrial lame
ducks has gone the way of Heath's assurances a decade earlier—
and for the same reasons. Enormous sums adding up to billions

of pounds have been handed to the British Steel Corporation, British Shipbuilders, British Leyland, Rolls-Royce, and others. One cabinet member made the acid reference to the industry minister, "There's a job waiting for Sir Keith Joseph in Oxford Street. He's been practicing the role of Father Christmas for the past twenty months."

Mrs. Thatcher's one accomplishment was to push down inflation to an annual rate of 5 percent, approximately half the rate when she took office (after the inflation rate had gone wild in her first year). This had nothing to do with monetarism or the Bank of England's high jinks. It was essentially due to the tested Victorian remedy of depression, mass unemployment, mass shutdown of workplaces. The area between Birmingham and Wolverhampton, once the heartland of Britain's industrial might, is now a region of abandoned factories and rotting warehouses with the old canal system of the area reduced to noxious streams of putrescent water. Elsewhere in the North, entire sections of cities look as if they had been picked clean by swarms of locusts. The unemployment rate is heading toward 14 percent of a workforce of 23 million, 3½ million workers without jobs, two and a half times greater than when the "iron lady" entered 10 Downing Street.

In the light of this devastation and disintegration, affecting smaller business owners as well as workers, how account for her remaining the toast of the rich in the privacy of their clubs? Aside from the ersatz lion's roar over the Falklands her regime offers definite pluses for those in the upper and middle classes for whom the Welfare State is an abomination and socialism or even talk of socialism a contrivance of the devil. Although it has been politically impossible for Mrs. Thatcher's ministers to hack away at social services with quite the abandon displayed by Reagan's technicians, they have been doing yeoman work selling off to private investors parts of nationalized industries that are good profit-makers.

Another stroke of luck for the Tories has been the softening up of the unions, something Heath tried but failed to do. The credit does not go to more cunning generalship or greater resolve on the part of the present government, but to changed circumstances. The economic slump is the deepest and longest-lasting since the 1930s, and as is usual in the initial stages of a downturn, it has frightened, not emboldened, workers. British unions (like American unions) are in disorderly retreat. Membership has dropped by about a million. Strikes are at the lowest point in a decade and a half. (In the U.S., too, the number of strikes has fallen to the lowest point since World War II.) Union ranks see little profit in walking picket lines under present conditions. Wage-raise agreements are running below the inflation rate. There are also preliminary reports of productivity gains because of the massive layoffs and closures. As one would expect, all this has improved profit margins. And as one would further expect, the Confederation of British Industry finds that "business confidence" is very high.

However beneficient the market forces, Mrs. Thatcher and her ministers do not intend to shirk their own duties for this restorative work. In line with The Economist's advice that "The only limit on reforming the unions when they are down should be a determination to pass measures that have a chance of sticking," they pushed through preliminary restrictive legislation, and now other punitive measures are due.

The one proposition that all observers noted in the bizarre election of 1983 was its underscoring a sharp polarization taking place in British society. On a different level, and in changed circumstances, Britain is the home again of Disraeli's "two nations," with one nation showing as little comprehension or sympathy for the other as a century ago. The polarization was disastrous for the Labour Party at this juncture. The right-wing split made possible or was mainly responsible for the Tory victory. And the alignments are not yet completed, for the Labour Party still harbors a moderate wing that elected to stay in the party but which does not go along with major party pronouncements. But the polarization will not stop with the Labour Party. It is bound to lead to other consequences, not all limited to the parliamentary plane, and not all of them necessarily favorable for reactionaries and status quo loyalists. Fundamentally, the attempt to turn the clock back (or as close as one can get) to the 1920s of Stanley Baldwin is a chimerical one. The tacticians of the short term are recklessly mortgaging the future of their own class. Before five years are out, the books will show incontrovertibly that Britain cannot afford Mrs. Thatcher.

3. French Planning Revisited

1

The direction of advanced capitalism can be gauged from another angle by taking note of analogous ailments affecting France, considered the model by Western planners in the 1960s. That France assumed such a role will be accounted one of history's anomalies. Here is a nation whose cultural heritage should have made her more inept than England in postwar reorganization and competition. The country, dominated by a bourgeoisie that had forcefully dismembered the *ancien régime* in the classic bourgeois revolution of all time, went socially conservative the day after to the point of mimicking some of the attitudes of the aristocracy it had displaced. These traits were exhibited in chemically pure forms in the military establishment where faded provincial aristocrats, driven from seats of power, found refuge: the cult of élan, imperialist mystique, disdain for commercial pursuits, worship of caste, the revel in ethnic and racist superstitions.

The most durable, potent, and conservatizing institution the bourgeoisie fashioned, and one which constituted the cellular nucleus of its rule for a century and a half, was the French family. It has been aptly said that in the pantheon of organizations it takes its place beside the Catholic church, the Roman army, the American corporation, and the German general staff as a notable creation of the human mind. The need for family primacy, perpetuation, and social predominance entered into the molding of a traditionalist unenterprising economy in a country that had been industrialized but had never had an industrial revolution. The small- and medium-size firm held a strong position well into this century, often servicing conglomerations of regional markets, not a national market. It was part of an intricate matrix of time-honored, untouchable relationships by which unenterprising enterprises were protected and preserved through tariffs against the outside world, and through cartel arrangements that assigned them predominance on their own turfs against more resourceful, lower-cost producers. *Les familles d'esprit* dominating the entire scene was a homogenized product of a fixed social world in which representatives of the upper bourgeoisie and government bureaucracy commingled freely in their homes and resorts, and married off their sons and daughters within the gilded circles. Civil servants with the right connections and attitudes, or themselves members of the upper classes, were regularly coopted into important, lucrative posts in business firms, while talented, ambitious business activists were permitted, when needed, to enter the ranks of their betters.

This sluggish economic order had its major prop in a large peasantry determined not to tolerate any innovations that would disturb its proprietary standing. Swollen in size through the sweeping agrarian redistributions of the great Revolution, according to some rough estimates from four to six and a half million in a population of some twenty-eight million, it made up at the time 85 percent of the total population. Small-scale, hidebound rural proprietors, their conservatism, technological and political, posited by historical circumstance and the slow penetration of industry, were the mainstays of political reaction and immobility. France's agricultural modernization along capitalist lines, either in the American or British manner, was impeded by the needs of successive governments to appease the peasant's passion for his own plot of ground and his attachment to traditional modes of production. As late as 1946 agricultural proprietors, family kin, hired employees, and sharecroppers accounted for 37 percent of the national workforce in western France, and agriculture took in almost 60 percent of the active population.

The ultra-centralized state bureaucracy, an inheritance of the Revolution and going back to the unlimited monarchies, sired a succession of feeble, unstable regimes earning France in modern times the appellation of the stalemated society. By means of various combinations, a coalition of center parties presided over the

Republic's affairs after the Second Empire, its dominance associated with a breed of accommodating politicians adept in blanketing the latent labor–capital conflict with a vacuous, bombastic rhetoric. The 1930s depression tore the center apart and discredited the politics of immobility. No sooner was the Léon Blum Popular Front installed in the summer of 1936 than the country was shaken by a tidal wave of sitdown strikes and plant seizures. It appeared that France was to usher in a Welfare State akin to the American Rooseveltian model. But a stiff-necked, tradition-bound bourgeoisie would not reconcile itself to social-democratic welfarism. After 1936 France resembled two armed camps preparing for civil war. The class standoff was a factor in the subsequent paralysis of the army before the Nazi legions.

How could France, torn by internal dissensions, beset by powerful factions on both ends of the political spectrum intent on tearing down the parliamentary order, resting on an economy that had performed wretchedly throughout the 1930s, emerge after the war the putative paragon of growth, expansion, and indicative planning? Some explain the phenomenon by the cathartic effects of the manifold catastrophe: France's crushing defeat in war, the disgrace of most of the old elites along with the figures of the far right in the ill-starred Vichy regime, capped by the forced departures of her troops and colonialists from Vietnam and Algeria. The result was an internal regrouping of the country's constituent elements. The new generation coming up in the political, educational, and business fields could not accept tradition in the way its fathers had. The discrediting of the old conservative crowd enabled a group of go-getting technocrats to push to the fore. Doors had opened for them to take the initiative. The younger middle-class professionals, or soon-to-become professionals, realized they would have to display extraordinary drive, risk-taking, and proficiency if France, in her disgust with past mentors, was not to entrust her fate to a left which they feared and despised.

The country was swinging leftward after the war. De Gaulle, the popular hero but arch-traditionalist, had to go beyond Blum to keep the captaincy of the ship of state in the post-Liberation turbulent waters. Heading a Popular Front (somewhat Bonapartist) government which included two Communist and four Socialist cabinet ministers, the all-national regime of reconstruction proceeded to clear the ground for the emerging Welfare State.

There were only a few, feeble objections to the nationalizations which took in the northern coal fields, gas, and electricity, the Bank of France and the big four private banks, the insurance companies, and Renault. Radio and telephone communications and rail transport were state-operated before the war. Blum's government had nationalized munitions as well, and had created a mixed holding company, the Société Nationale des Chemins-de-fer Françaises (SNCF), of which the state owned 51 percent of the shares and to which were entrusted aircraft and other industries—and the device was used elsewhere. All told, the state-owned sector was roughly comparable to Britain's, controlling enterprises making up more than 20 percent of total industrial assets. From 1947 to 1953 state investments made up more than half of the total gross capital formation. Even at the end of the 1950s it was over a third of the total (probably over two-fifths when nationalized holdings in competitive sectors, banking, and public financing of housing are included)—all adding up to a third of the entire national product. It was the minimum the government could do to maintain legitimacy. The public clamor for social justice could not be ignored. For the moment the Old Right was making itself scarce. The big capitalists and their associated prewar notables were thoroughly discredited. People's memories of their collaboration with Vichy and the Nazis were still fresh.

2

France faced a reconstruction task no less daunting than Germany's. She had fallen behind before the war. Britain's industrial output in 1937–1938 as a percentage of 1913 was 139, Germany's was 144, France's only 119. On the eve of the war, and on emergence from the war, she was a country of retarded industrialization and agriculture, kept backward by the smallness of industry and farmers' parochialism and an export structure typical of semi-industrialized countries. The population rate had been declining from the turn of the century; this took a great spurt upward in 1946 and thereafter reached its highest level in a century and a half—making France more comparable demographically to her two big neighbors.

Although manpower losses were much lighter than in the First World War, property and equipment destruction was heavy, and the entire economy was misshaped and shopworn. The base from which reconstruction had to start was abysmally low. In May 1945 industrial capacity was about 40 percent of 1938 (itself a depression year). Large-scale inflation had been the rule for a decade; from 1938 to 1945 the money supply had increased between five- and sixfold. By the end of that year the Paris index of retail prices (under theoretical price controls) was five times that of 1938. Since the black market was a major institution through 1948, the figures understate the actual leap in living costs.

Two things have to be kept in mind now for orientation purposes. First, expansion and the plenitude allegedly resulting from planning did not start until 1953, after the conclusion of the Marshall Plan infusions. For eight years the economy was creaking and recovery was painfully inadequate. Second, what was happening in Germany—big profits, heavy investments for new plants and equipment to replace what had been destroyed, and the general rationalization of the economy made possible by low labor costs—was occurring in a major way in France also. Wages had been kept at an abnormally low level both by the Nazi occupying authority and by the Vichy government, and Liberation brought no substantive relief. From 1946 to 1949 wholesale prices rose more than fourfold, wages less than threefold (again, disregarding indispensible buying in the black markets). In the last year of that period it appeared as if the inflation had spent itself and prices began to decline a little; then came the Korean War and a new price outburst. By mid-1951 wholesale prices stood a third to a half higher than in 1949. *Le Monde* calculated at this time that "ten months of the raw material boom cost [France] the same amount as all the aid she received under the Marshall Plan." The following lament of a contemporary was typical of the perceptions of many:

> Housing was wretched, and efforts to solve the problem were deadlocked. The Korean crisis made it seem that the United States and Russia were spoiling for a fight. The French, with the experience of two world wars behind them, believed themselves fated to have their land become again a battleground of forces over which they had no control. . . . By 1950 the feelings of helplessness and despair were strong. People traditionally inclined to accept the worst with a fatalistic shrug and the words "C'est comme ça!" found little to hope for. . . . "Pauvre France!" they said, "On est foutu!" (We're done for!)

According to Simon Kuznets, there was no significant gain in per-capita net national product between 1949 and 1953 as there had been even in the productively poor 1924–1933 period. As late as autumn 1954 a United Nations survey noted that "the French economy continues to suffer from deep-rooted weaknesses, which have cramped economic progress and made France lag behind in comparison with other countries of northern, western, and central Europe." John Sheahan was able to write that "It was still possible in the early 1950s to consider the postwar trend as completely consistent with a picture of long-run incapacity."

The gaps and cracks left in the wake of her slow, lopsided reconstruction resulted in huge deficits averaging one-third to two-thirds of budgets. These were surmounted somehow with American loans and grants by 1952 totaling over $4 billion, of which $2½ billion consisted of Marshall Plan aid grants. This hardly kept her finances in order for the military was a voracious claimant. Like Britain, France did not want to give up the glories and revenues of an extensive empire. Two years after Liberation, 1.8 million men remained in the armed services, and in 1952 she was spending a tenth of her product on defense. Her military outlay exceeded that of West Germany to the same extent that capital formation in West Germany exceeded France's. Then there was the drain of the Indochina war from 1946 on. When the agony was over in 1954, more than $8 billion, most of which had come out of the French budget, had to be written in red ink.

As of the early 1950s, from the vantage point of the worker or low-salaried white-collar employee or small shopkeeper, the glowing promises of the Resistance had vaporized. The share going to industry for profits and reinvestment was far greater than in England, slightly greater than in Germany, a maldistribution of the national income aggravated by a highly regressive tax system. Average income was much lower than in England or the smaller northwest countries, and was being overtaken by Germany. Wage differentiation had been and continued to be inordinately wide. Averell Harriman, who at the time was a factotum of the Marshall Plan organization in Europe, and whose natural inclinations would be to see the businessman's point of view, made the flat declaration, "In France, the worker does not receive a fair share of the national income." The left had squandered its early advantages. The Communists—the left's major contingent in the postwar decade—were losing adherents and well-wishers because of their slavishness to Moscow and their heavy-handed, leaden responses to daily events at home. For all their vociferousness they proved unable to change even slightly the proportionate distribution of wealth.

There was a wide extention of social security provisions, with the entire social security system administered by local, regional, and national boards that included labor representatives. Without a doubt this helped mitigate social tensions. Then, during the 1950s better-situated workers had a foretaste of coming middle-class comforts. Television sets and Vespas made their appearance. The consumer society was elbowing its way forward. The spontaneously erupting strikes in August 1953, involving three million workers at their height, supplied additional incentives for pay raises. By the end of the decade hourly wages of industrial production workers went up by another half (with rising productivity and two devaluations helping to keep France competitive in her exports). Later, in the mid-1970s, her per-capita consumption, 6 percent below Germany's, was almost 50 percent greater than Britain's; her per-capita GNP, similarly 6 percent below Germany's, was some two-thirds larger than the average product of Western Europe as a whole. The wage spread remained unusually large, leading *The Economist* to describe France as "the combination of a modern European economy with the inequalities (in certain respects, not all) of a banana republic."

As disturbing to the technocrats as labor strikes in the 1950s were the Poujadist rural outbursts. But the farmers were soon tamed by concessions and profound inner class differentiations. As with the Populist movement in the United States in the nineteenth century, turbulence gave way to lobbying and pressure politics. Within a few years a regulation businessmen's association dominated by the richer farmers, operating on capitalist lines, succeeded in winning government support for higher prices, protected markets, and various subventions, open and concealed. The protection of native agricultural proprietors has become a common feature of late capitalism in all advanced countries.

Nationalization was another story. The left, and all sorts of sympathizers and peripheral supporters, as in England harbored vast hopes that this was the initial step in the creation of a socialist commonwealth, and as in England these hopes were quickly dashed. French public enterprises proved no more socially oriented than the British, and for the same reason: managers were motivated by marketplace concepts, governed by business criteria, and functioned in the commercial milieu. Andrew Shonfield remarked that "the banks after nationalization were run by the same type of manager, and on exactly the same commercial principles as before. The authorities seemed to go out of their way to demonstrate that there had been no change." Sheahan wrote in a similar vein, "The consensus of the best studies of the question is that the government firms have acted very much as private enterprise might have done in the same markets." Sometimes they appeared more capitalist than the capitalists. Sheahan quoted from a French study on the functioning of nationalized enterprises: "The nationalized firms have known how to develop their productivity, enlarge their field of action, and watch their costs. In an economy where the spirit of conservatism has too often taken the place of the spirit of enterprise in the psychology of the private entrepreneur, the nationalized sector sometimes appears to be the last refuge of those traditionally 'capitalist' virtues: audacity, the taste for large-scale operations, dynamism."

The publicly owned Renault firm struck observers as a classic example of the Berle-Galbraith management-run corporation brooking no interference from outsiders. The company was nationalized by executive decree in 1944; the minister of finance appointed an industrialist as director; when he died in 1955 he was replaced by a similar social type. Pierre Lefaucheux, the new director, made it clear in his speeches and by his conduct that the company was to be run just like a private firm. The major difference was that after paying taxes the company would assign one-third of its profits to the government rather than to private shareholders, one-third was to be retained for investment, and one-third was bonuses. A public review board was set up at the time of nationalization, but both the board and a parliamentary commission generally limited their interventions to composing laudatory boilerplate about Renault for their annual reports. All nationalized firms were also obligated to submit their capital budgets to the finance minister and several government commissions, but managements dominated decisions; very rarely were their proposals challenged. If a company started losing a lot of money and called for government subsidies, it would be a different story.

Because nationalizations in France took class revenge against big property owners as Nazi collaborators, not as large a percentage of derelict and crippled industries was adopted as in England. For this, and for technocratic reasons alluded to, the French nationalizations were more successful than were the British. In the expansionary decades, productivity increased more rapidly in French nationalized coal, electricity, and railroad industries than in the same British nationalized industries (as productivity in French industry in general rose at a faster rate than in British industry). A number of these state-owned companies became leaders in introducing innovations, pioneering technological advancements, displaying unusual ability for profit-making. This has not saved them from cheap jibes and tendentious attempts at denigration.

Government ministers have at times used nationalized industries as pawns in their not-too-successful attempts to control prices. Private corporations have employed their considerable influence to demand and obtain below-cost prices for publicly produced materials and services, then cited losses by such firms as evidence of the innate inefficiency of state enterprise. In other instances state enterprise managers were more concerned with private firms' profits than their own firms' costs. Sheahan observed that "it has not been a common practice for state firms to use their buying leverage in the aggressive style [of American firms]. Rather, they have come under the influence of the most actively interested selling groups, even to the point of siding with their private suppliers against outside alternatives." State enterprise is restricted by the business community's implacable opposition on ideological grounds; state enterprise managers seek to accommodate their industry's behavior so as not to interfere with the private sector's demands and wants, or to damage their own standing in the business world. In the prevailing climate, nationalization necessarily conforms to business and political conventions.

Industrialists and financiers who had to reconcile themselves to extensive postwar nationalizations were resolved when they regained their self-confidence and standing that nationalized companies would operate in accordance with business mores—and that there would be no further nationalizations.

After the alarms and apprehensions of the first months passed, business leaders knew that they could live with these neocapitalist arrangements, and might even draw private benefits from them. But they never called off their campaigns to discredit state ownership, to convince the public that it was an unnatural hermaphrodite. The campaigns had a preventive purpose. Despite the way state enterprises were set up, they necessarily made a professional government-employed elite more prominent in the direction of business affairs. It was feared that if state control were carried beyond a certain percentage of the whole, the entrenched power of the business community would be undermined. As Giscard d'Estaing put it when he was finance minister, "beyond 40 percent, it's socialism."

From the other side the rank and file employed in these nationalized enterprises saw no advantage accruing to themselves. Wages and working conditions were modeled on those in private industry. Workers had no more say in running state-owned plants than private ones. All yearnings for workers' participation in management and decision-making were as ruthlessly smothered as in England. Hence workers and reformers were becoming skeptical that state ownership of industry was the way to a better society. Under nonsocialist governments nationalizations led to results associated with state capitalism, not state socialism. (These disappointments notwithstanding, the coming of a new Socialist regime has spelled a new ambitious program of further nationalization. Despite the flood of conventional scholarly dissertations and heady journalistic prose in the interim years to the effect that "Now we all know better than to think that nationalizations are either necessary or important," governments are unable to direct a national economy, or to even think of doing so, without having a good measure of ownership.)

3

There is no need to draw parallel columns with the English data on strikes, union work rules, shop practices, or management performance, since France's track record was high on growth, productivity, increases of exports, etc., in the two expansionary decades. In that period, she was the glamorous achiever to be emulated, unlike the wastrel across the Channel to be shunned. The innovation responsible for this success was "indicative planning." This is an appellation that does not carry the luster it once did (certainly no one will write ecstatically about it the way Shonfield once did), but French planning is still assigned a modest niche in the pantheon by technocratic-minded academics.

The story rightfully begins in the autumn of 1944. The Provisional Government, under strong leftist pressure, set up a superministry under Pierre Mendès-France to prepare a comprehensive national plan and oversee its operation. This resuscitated the ministry set up under Blum's Popular Front government—and like its predecessor it was successfully and speedily knifed to death by Treasury and other establishment agencies. Against Mendès-France were such indisputable facts that he was a too-self-confident Jew, a crusading Keynesian backed by the left, and also had grandiose ideas about reorganizing the economy. It was an entirely different story when Jean Monnet came forward with his proposed plan shortly afterward. Monnet was a known and accepted quantity, and whatever opinions leading industrialists at first had about the value of planning, they knew him as a technician the business community could be comfortable with. They also figured that the Plan brochure, with the seal of the Republic stamped on its cover, would be a handy instrument to ward off any more excitable demands for further nationalizations.

Monnet was made to order for the job. He was the bourgeois incarnate in appearance and dress, well groomed but unflashy, a carefully barbered, oval-shaped, balding head emerging from a nondescript figure, the neat little mustache an indispensable adjunct to the incisive nose and a political cardinal's eyes. He was mistakenly viewed as a great technician; he was actually a great wheeler-dealer, a political contact man, and had been, in his earlier years, a salesman for his father's wine and brandy business. What he had a talent for was gathering technically proficient men around him, a more tactful, less vain French version of Bernard Baruch, and like him, wealthy in his own right.

It is not my purpose to review in detail or orderly manner the seven or eight plans promulgated over the past three or so decades. There are many such books and articles, a number of which I have drawn upon for my own orientation and analysis. Another detailed account would be unnecessarily repetitive and outside the purpose of this exposition. What I want to bring out is the specific set of principles underlying indicative planning as revealed in thirty years of practice and the relation of planning papers to governing decisions, and finally, to investigate whether we are dealing with an organizing mechanism that has transformed the old capitalism or whether this planning is one of a number of not necessarily integrated techniques, instrumentalities, contrivances, evolutionary increments, which in their totality distinguish late industrial capitalism from its pre-1930 Depression model, a pattern of organization routine systematizing without breaching the older profits-and-market determinants.

The involuted origins of planning, a response to imperatives similar to England's, was not without its element of irony. Left-wing people had a hand in its creation: they were the main architects of the ideological climate; they fashioned the battle cries; they were the only ones in a position in the immediate postwar period of exaltation to rally sizable ranks to the appropriate banners. Leftist votaries had the vague idea that some kind of socialism or semi-socialism would eventuate at the end of the nationalization and planning processes. But the middle-class technicians, backed by power institutions, took over the workings and fitted planning, as they did nationalization, into the machinery of neocapitalism.

Once the old traditions and verities waned because of the moral eclipse of the prewar eminences, the technocratic spirit and the gospel of expansion suitably shorn of their revolutionary excrescences, took hold like a conquering army. The credo did not originate with, nor was it confined to, the brain-trusters assembled by Monnet. Technocracy, in its putatively value-free, politically neutral guise, was taken up in the top circles of industry, finance, and government. In a relatively short time it became part of establishment ideology. The emergence of the technocrats, in both private- and state-owned industry, did not represent a shift of power from old elites to new ones; it represented a substantial reordering of personnel, concepts, and mores within the existing economic and social order, marked by the enlargement of the role and power of the state, and consequently of the state bureaucracy.

The initial crew of Monnet planners were proselytizers in the business community, manipulators inside the government bureaucracy, dedicated apostles of a planning that would not disturb market arrangements and ownership prerogatives. The Planning Commission was not at first, or at any time, a big organization; the full-time payroll was about 130, including typists, secretaries, and chauffeurs; the planners numbered no more than forty. Its small size was due to Monnet's deliberate decision, having Mendès-France's experience in mind, to fit the Plan into the existing structure of the bureaucracy. Some of the planners' major experts were on loan from other departments and subject to departmental discipline. The very files and statistical data came from the Ministry of Finance as did most of the econometricians.

Monnet and his associates saw as their first task the need to quiet property owners' fears that somebody was trying to introduce socialism by stealth, that profits would be interfered with, decisions rammed down their throats, or a bureaucracy built up to monitor their movements. Very quickly it became apparent to even the Henry Fords among them that there was nothing to worry about, indeed that Monnet's kind of planning might have advantages. Old-fashioned businessmen were invited to take part in roundtable discussions with technocratic hustler types like Pierre Massé of Electricité de France (later head of the Planning Commission), or Louis Armand of railroads (SNCF), whose energizing go-getting traits would presumably be absorbed by the less enterprising brethren. Laying out a national input–output chart would bring home to business leaders, it was felt, how their own investment decisions affected the whole, as well as the large advantages to be garnered by forward activities of expansion-oriented managers.

Inside the government the Planning Commission never had significantly greater powers than those granted its British counterpart. None of its program is or was enforceable by law. Nor has it had any authority over state-owned enterprises. From the point of view of the Treasury, the planners' targets and projects were only one proposition to be taken into consideration among many others. Interviews with Commission and Treasury officials established that implementing the Plan was only of marginal importance in making budgetary and policy decisions. If these decisions cut across the Plan's main aims, as they often did, it was nothing to get excited over. The very haziness of the Planning Commission's authority saved it from extinction, in the opinion of students of the question. According to Granick, "The effective functioning of the Planning Commissariat is explained by the fact that none of its big-brother ministries has considered it a threat worth clubbing." Prof. Pierre Bauchet has written similarly: "The Planning Commissioners have followed a policy of conciliation and not of authority and coordination. One is right to think that only this policy has preserved the Plan from being completely destroyed."

How was the Plan prepared, and what effect did it have on economic movements? After the initial projection and paperwork, determining the implications of alternative growth rates and other variables, planning commissioners and Treasury officials got together to fix the draft Plan growth rate, investment commitments, and other basics. Cabinet members sometimes intervened, and when they did, often promulgated their own measures, however these would affect the Plan. The Finance Ministry was at all times the responsible controller. The First (Monnet) Plan, unlike several that followed, was a laundry list of investment targets and priorities designed to funnel resources into a selected group of strategic industries, not an overall analysis reconciling multifarious interdependencies. It ignored, deliberately or otherwise, among other factors, the inflationary effects of diverting scarce resources to its projected investment program; it included no studies of the effects of necessary heavy imports on consumption and price levels. Monnet and his associates, like field generals with single-track minds, set out to rehabilitate and modernize a production plant that had progressively deteriorated during four years of war and twenty years of prewar decadence—and let others at staff headquarters occupy themselves with logistics.

The commission ran into difficulties very quickly because of the raging inflation. By 1948, the second year of the original four-year plan, it was clear that most of the targets would not be reached. Available investment funds had been grossly overestimated, as had returns on investments. Since in 1948, 1949, and 1950 one-third of planned investment was to be financed out of Marshall Plan funds, the Marshall Plan administrators, realizing what was happening, proposed that the timetable be extended to 1952, the terminal date of their own program. The revised version of the Monnet Plan thus called for an investment effort over six rather than four years. This also became the occasion to drastically change around targets and outlays. The revised 1949–1952 edition bore a relation to the original of the scarred, limping veteran to the young soldier setting out for the fray.

More wounding to the planners' *amour-propre* was their treatment at the hands of Antoine Pinay, who came in as premier in the spring of 1952. The self-styled "Mr. Average Consumer," a hitherto obscure member of the extreme right, both a former Vichyite and a former small manufacturer of leather goods, proposed to cure the inflation (and the recession setting in in the middle of the year) by old-fashioned methods. His medicine was a stiff dose of deflationary castor oil. A special bond issue was also floated with great fanfare and officially hailed as a huge success, but that was just public relations flummery. Over half of it represented a simple exchange of older securities for better-paying new bonds; the remainder reflected a shift of savings away from investments. Both Pinay's elixirs undercut the therapy of the Plan, and Pinay had not even bothered to tip his hat to the planners. (Monnet was no longer among them. Moving rapidly, as always, onward and upward, he had left the commission in 1950 for the European Coal and Steel Community.)

This cavalier treatment of the planners was in evidence again when the left-center government of Guy Mollet came in in 1956. The Socialist Ramadier, the finance minister, offered a spending program that included additional welfare concessions to increase consumer demand. The resultant declining ratio of investment to national product undercut the Plan's schema of growth. The Fourth Plan (1962–1965), duly passed by Parliament before its start, in effect was scrapped midway, for the retrenchment insisted on by Valéry Giscard d'Estaing, a *polytechnicien* aristocrat, then Treasury head.

It was this recurring conduct on the part of successive governments of adopting policies to suit their own preferences without thinking of the Plan, and of the planners being insulated, and insulating themselves, from the hurly-burly of the marketplace, that called into question their precise role. In a confidential document, *Les Motifs d'Execution du Plan,* the planners confessed that "the plan remains a marginal organism in the governmental and administrative organization." They went on to point out their limitations in influencing critical decisions since they were cut out of participation in decisive matters. In a word, alignment of going economic policies with the plans ranged from limited to nonexistent.

4

In theory, when the draft plan is agreed upon by the Planning Commission and the Treasury it is ready for submission to Parliament. In practice, Parliament is excluded from decision-making. The commission was created by an executive decree in 1946, and that was the way the First Plan came into existence also. Credits for the plan were voted by Parliament the following year, but not distinguished from the rest of the annual budget. Only with the Fourth Plan (1962–1965) was the blueprint submitted to Parliament ahead of time. The deputies made some minor changes, inserted a sonorous preface, and sent it along. As Shonfield observed, "There was no serious attempt made to exercise control over it." Elsewhere he remarked, "The planners made no secret of their belief in the iron law of oligarchy." and quoted one of the commission's senior members who described planning as "a rather clandestine affair." For a few years in the early 1960s under the Fifth Republic, discussion of the Plan was encouraged in De Gaulle's denatured Parliament. This was considered useful since the general was trying to make French planning an ideological export product. But it was only a passing tactic.

Once the Plan is official, the program is put into effect in the vertical commissions. There were twenty-three such commissions for the Fourth Plan, involving about a thousand persons. With government officials, programmers, working groups, special task forces included, the total was over three thousand. In the Sixth Plan, when for political reasons a big to-do was made of "participation," almost three thousand attended the modernization commissions' sessions. Again in theory (to make the necessary distinction), vertical commission members, named by the government on recommendation of the Planning Commission and serving without pay, include representatives of management, labor, agriculture, consumer groups, government officials, and technicians. Moreover the commissions proceed in the spirit of participatory democracy; decisions are arrived at not by cold-blooded majority votes but by general accord. In practice the whole show is run by government mandarins and business captains. The others have a ceremonial, not a functional role to play.

Shonfield said that French planning can be viewed "as an act of voluntary collusion between senior civil servants and the senior managers of big business. The politicians and representatives of organized labor were both largely passed by." Some have pointed out that businessmen, civil servants, and technicians made up the overwhelming membership, whereas trade unions had only token or minor representation. Others explained labor's underrepresentation on the grounds that unions do not have enough trained personnel for such participation. Bauchard showed that the character of these commissions necessarily makes the trade unionist who does show up an interloper. His presence is barely tolerated in a private club where other members are all blood relations. Although Bauchard's proposition is well taken, and unions are underrepresented, these factual details are irrevelent to the main issue. Unions are underrepresented by their own decision, not by governmental exclusion, and have refused to participate at all in a number of the plans. They do lack technically trained personnel but could, without difficulty, enlist the cooperation of sufficient numbers of competent, leftward-inclined professionals if by doing so their role in government planning would be materially altered. But this is not the cutting edge of the matter. The fact is that the plan machinery is programmed as a government–business affair designed for certain ends. Were union officials to descend in serried numbers on the commissions to upset the decorous proceedings, the real decision-making would simply be shifted to more informal tête-à-têtes (where most understandings actually are worked out).

Although the basic model is drawn by the planners in close consultation with Treasury officials, business representatives are never far from decision-makers. The people on both sides of the table are from the same social milieu, share common assumptions, speak the same language, are attuned to the same received wisdom. The operation takes place in a business climate in which pantouflage (the shift from civil service to a high-paid job in private industry, similar to the advancement of some of our military men from Pentagon procurement divisions to boards of directors of major defense contractors) is the rule, not the exception. Studies detail that a quarter of all finance inspectors get upgraded to executive positions in private companies. François Bloch-Lainé, a long-time senior civil servant and later head of Crédit Lyonnais, wrote that ranking government officials consider planning an exercise in which business and government executives "decide everything among themselves, behind a curtain of opaque 'technicity,' in clandestine meetings where agreements are too easily reached among civil servants who have already pantouflés and civil servants who would like to pantoufler."

The question is academic aside from this consideration because before the draft plan reaches the modernization commissions, it has been the subject of comradely bargaining and agreements between leading members of the three parties to the transaction. Indicative planning "in its purest form," according to Shonfield, "is made to work because the quality of the analysis done by the planners convinces the men wielding economic power, in the private and public sectors alike, that the conclusions offered them provide good advice." It worked out that way at first. The ideas animating government technicians were to put publicly paid-for skills and resources at the service of entrepreneurs to renovate enterprises, raise labor productivity, trim down work forces, reduce costs, improve profits, and strengthen investments, and when necessary help managements achieve these ends by subventions, forced mergers, and cartelizations. How could businessmen fail to be convinced?

Shonfield, in the mid-1960s a harsh critic of British planning and a fervent admirer of French planning, was hard put to explain the difference between the two since concept, methodology, and implementation procedures were largely the same. Such institutional and administrative differences he managed to extract are either of tertiary importance or of questionable validity. He made much of the "established intimacy" and "continuing dialogue" between government and business managers in contrast to the English businessmen's preference for a corporative approach and for state power dispersion. What does this amount to as an explanation of the purported success of one and the admitted failure of the other? British industrialists did wreck Cripps's Development Councils in the late 1940s, but that was because of their traditional suspicion of and hostility to all initiatives coming from Labour. Even then there was more backdoor cooperation than was publicly acknowledged in business modernization endeavors. By the time the Tories formally endorsed planning, corporation lawyers and accountants had quieted businessmen's fears and convinced them that their privileged positions and incomes would not be taken from them, that it was necessary to get accustomed to the changed postwar atmospherics. When Labour was installed again in 1964, relations had already approached, if they had not already reached, the French ideal of intimacy. Campell Adamson, for example, who had been industrial policy coordinator at the government economic department from 1966 to 1969, left that year to become director-general of the Confederation of British Industry.

It is true that the Tories, on returning to Whitehall in 1951, wanted to get back to business-as-usual. But reactionary primitism gripped the French political establishment time and again in these years as well. Pinay, the small hides-and-leather man, substituted a program of deflation and price freezing for the newfangled notions of planning and expansion, one of a number of instances when the Plan became a talisman, not a guidepost. These periodic departures led up to the de facto abandonment of the schema under Giscard who made no secret of his opinion that planning was largely claptrap.

There should be no exaggeration either of the planners' vaunted use of state disciplinary powers to win approval for their projects by granting or withholding financial favors. This could have been of importance up to 1952 when almost two-thirds of investment was financed out of public or publicly controlled funds. Even then the consanguinous relations existing between government and business officials deprived the lending process of all terrors. The power to grant or withhold subsidies, special loans, and related favors is compelling only when planners are dealing with managers of small firms dependent on government largesse. For the big firms, which are the mainstays of the Plan and around whose activities the Plan revolves, it is a simple matter to have their accountants touch up their internally devised and motivated investment programs so as to fit them under one of the titles qualifying for incentives. "The fact of the matter is," we learn in an authoritative study, "that only the biggest companies raise additional capital by public issues . . . and they can always list some of their activities under the Plan's 'approved' categories. It is easy for them to choose from among the numerous operations they undertake each year those which will most interest the Planners and finance the others out of their own resources."

In the end Shonfield falls back on a mystique. He confesses that what credit the planners deserve for France's rapid expansion is less important than the "widespread belief" that they were navigating the ship, that the mythology was a crucial independent factor. Well and good. That is the more acceptable explanation. The planners were important in the scheme of expansion less because of the specific influences of their specific plans, which were often discarded, than because their doctrine of expansion, competition, modernization, and technical prowess suffused the entire establishment: in government, in industry, in academia. When Monnet first got started, the high functionaries by and large were hostile and suspicious; before long they became converts and made the Plan the instrument of their own ideologies and purposes. The explanation for France's overtaking Britain in the pursuit of common objectives has to be sought in the entire ensemble of French economic activities, not centered in the papers and projects of the plan commissariat. Bernard Nossiter, at the time foreign correspondent of the *Washington Post*, made large claims for indicative planning in *The Mythmakers*. "Then I went to France," he wrote in his subsequent book on Britain, "and saw how little indicative planning had to do with anything."

5

Once France came on difficult times, her officialdom let the Planning Commission drop out of sight. It was an irrelevancy to the country's plight. By the Fifth Plan (1966–1970) the commission organization men had honed their econometric techniques to a high pitch of virtuosity. The attempt to encompass resources allocation led to the logic of attempted reconciliation of the major components of the economy, suggesting a variety of binding controls—and the draftsmen found that their econometric model was at odds with a socially riven society, and engineering logic at odds with political logic. After the May 1968 revolt, in which strikes were more widespread than in 1936, the Fifth Plan was in limbo. The government no longer paid any attention to it, the public lost interest in it, and the planners themselves tried to forget about it by focusing their attention of preparations for the next plan. When the Sixth Plan collided with the economic crisis of the early 1970s, it was all over: the pretensions, the illusions, the hubris. From that time on it has been strictly stop-and-go, with more stop than go. When the time came to work on the Seventh Plan, no government directives were forthcoming. The Planning Commission was paralyzed, the personnel unsure whether it would be permitted to continue or was going to be disbanded.

At last in the fall of 1974 the government decided that it would be unpolitic to permit the commission to formally expire. There would be a Seventh Plan after all, but Premier Chirac instructed the incoming commissioner to stick to a small number of general objectives since times were too uncertain to permit long-term, quantifiable goals. The resultant product resembled a staff orientation memorandum combined with a brochure of Chamber of Commerce puffery. French planning now belonged to the genre of the American president's economic reports drawn up annually by his economic advisers.

To recapitulate: With her advanced-training schools churning out a generation of high-powered engineers and managers, it was as a gung-ho technocratic achiever fired by the gospel of modernization and international derring-do that France entered the major leagues. Indicative planning was only a single strand of the intricate program, and generally was only of symbolic and decorative importance in giving elegance to the design. Indicative planning was also an oversold product. Its conceptualizers had become too boastful. They convinced themselves, and sought to convince others, that indicative planning could accomplish things beyond its powers.

If its role was this picayune in French economic affairs where it had its greatest play, the question arises why I refer to planning in the Foreword as an instrumentality for resolving the ongoing crisis of our era. The answer is that I am not talking about the French kind of indicative planning. Indicative planning is not planning at all, in the essence of the matter. Indicative planning is not an attempt to direct an economy in order to stem systemic tides of disintegration, overcome critical deficiencies, straighten out deformities. It is rather an attempt to steer investments into specific high-profit sectors in order to make these industries competitively battleworthy so that the business majors can conquer more markets than their rivals. In short, the terminology may be similar but two entirely different propositions are under discussion, as I will make clear in a later chapter. To plan an economy in any meaningful sense of the word the directorate has to have control over the crucial elements— materials allocation, money supplies, investments, manpower assignments, authority to reconcile and harmonize disparate sectors and parts—that go into realizing the plan. If one does not have the ability to control these elements, one cannot plan. What one can do is to form an alliance with business to stimulate growth and exports while cleaving to the established rules and modalities.

It is telltale, its superior twenty-year performance notwithstanding, that the French economy was riddled with the same
incoherences as Britain's. They ran the gamut from adverse balance of payments, followed by periodic forced devaluations, to
rising price inflation before, during, and after recurring cyclical
recessions. France, growing faster than Britain, absorbed the
shocks more readily until her economy struck the shoals of the
1970s' stagnation; then the rotted underside was exposed, with
unused plant capacity and unemployment edging up to British
levels. Six years before Mrs. Thatcher arrived at the head of her
free-marketeers to deliver once again Conservative Truth gar-
nished with Friedmanite relish, the French team of President
Giscard, and his appointed prime minister, Raymond Barre, led
the way. They were single-minded doctrinaires: it is not experience that counts, it is their dogma which is bound to yield desired results if only carried through with all necessary resolution. Like the British Tories in the 1950s they thickened the air
with pronouncements about the iniquity of state intervention
(dirigisme, in this case), the perniciousness of controls, the need
to unshackle industry so that it can invest and produce. No
sooner was Barre installed in office than he unveiled his three-
year plan to undo the damage of the past decades by giving the
country a stiff dose of old-fashioned purgative. The opening gam-
bit in the by-now-familiar play was deflation, get the pumps
working to "wring inflation" out of the water-logged economy,
stop subsidizing the "lame ducks," let the free market reward the
aces and pronounce sentence on the laggards. This was September 1976. A year and a half later, as soon as the left was defeated,
all industrial price controls were lifted. The notoriously regressive taxation system, contrary to promises made, was left un-
touched. Wage raises were to be held down. Subsidies to public
enterprises were to be cut. Credits to private companies were to
be restricted. Industry managers were told that they had been
granted what they wanted: now they had to make good. They
could no longer count on the government's using public resources to bail them out. Boussac, a large textile concern which
had run up debts of $100 million, a third of which were owed to
the government for taxes and social security payments, was permitted to go into bankruptcy. The big Terrin shipyards in Mar-
seilles and major steel works in Lorraine were given the go-ahead
signal to jettison thousands of workers so as to cut costs.

Manchester liberalism had a great play for three-and-a-half or four months. Then, like Heath in England before him, Barre caved in before the realities. Faced with the collapse not of an individual firm but the entire steel industry, the Giscard free-market champions had to swallow their brave words about letting the "lame ducks" perish. They arrived on the scene of disaster with a rescue plan—an "ironic contradiction," the *Wall Street Journal* called it, to Barre's free-market protestations. The rescue plan was nothing less than the most drastic state intervention since the sweeping postwar nationalizations. It made the government the majority shareholder of the steel industry, taking control over the companies running the Usinor, Scilor, and Chatillon-Neuves-Maison combinations.

Inevitably the losses were to be socialized out of the public treasury. There was to be a moratorium of the industry's huge debts totaling $12 billion. Some 21,000 jobs were to be eliminated, on top of the 16,000 workers displaced from the payrolls eighteen months before. The proposal was to nurse the industry back to health under a government hospitalization plan through mergers, closing of obsolete plants, and cutting out excess manpower. When the formulae were translated into the language of jobs and dismissal notices went out, violent riots and strikes swept through Lorraine and tens of thousands marched on Paris demanding their jobs back. To quiet the unrest, a compensation program was enacted providing early-retirement pensions and alternative compensations. The cost to the public treasury was estimated at $1.6 billion in addition to the $2.3 billion already spent by the summer of 1979 in writing off the steel industry's bad debts. Another thing: A million unemployed used to be considered politically untenable in France. The Giscard–Barre team broke through the barrier with unemployment moving toward the two-million mark, almost 9 percent of the workforce, by the time they were voted out of office. As has been occurring in recent slumps, rising unemployment did not lead to a drop in prices. So much for the Gallic version of prudent conservatism.

That the Giscard–Barre regimen was offered after the Heath experience, and that the Thatcher regimen could be offered after the Giscard–Barre experience, underscores for us the kind of problem-solving we can expect from Anglo-French politicians closest to business interests. Callousness yoked to doctrinaire obtuseness discredits the very traditions that Conservatives are so frantically trying to uphold.

4. American Goliath

My purpose in juxtaposing England and France was to highlight similarities in economic deficiencies and to underline the common drift to state expansion in response to comparable stimuli. In this respect all countries of the trilateral consortium—Western Europe, Britain, North America, Japan—belong to the same order since they have a common set of structural characteristics. That does not mean that private-property–based and market-oriented countries—preponderantly industrialized, urbanized, parliamentary, oligopolized, consumer-ridden—are carbon copies of each other. The contrary is true. Their institutional arrangements, their cultural modalities, their mores, their political formations range, as do their languages, along a spectrum of progressive differentiation. Like exposed geological formations these provide clear evidence of the impacts of their variegated histories.

Thus Italy is a very lax tax collector; England is a reasonably efficient one. Sweden has little nationalization but close state superintendency; England has considerable nationalization but weaker state control. Japan, whose changeover from feudalism to capitalism was administratively fabricated and occurred only a century ago, displays traits of feudatory consanguinity in the close-knit association of business and government officialdoms. In Germany the changeover took place at about the same time and was also directed by a landowning, militarized (Junker) elite, but the industrial and banking interests are jealous of their independence, opposing government interference (rhetorically, at any rate) no less uncompromisingly than their American counterparts. Just as the capitalist system of production showed an ability to take root under monarchies and republics alike, and was consolidated through populist upheavals from below and elitist manipulations from above, so the state capitalist trends of our day find realization under free enterprise as under social-democratic regimes.

These trends in Western Europe and Japan would be inconclusive were the United States an exception to this rule. For though this country is not the capitalist leader it was forty years ago, she is still the powerhouse and protector of world capitalism. Consequently if it is seen that the United States is drifting in the same direction in the face of an official ideology that deplores too much government, then a transnational tendency to statism is buttressed.

Our official ideology can be described as one sustained paean to the limitless blessings of free enterprise. The familiar counterposition of creative, efficient private businessmen, propelled by solidly realistic profit motives, to the bumbling, wasteful, ineffectual, often visionary government bureaucracy is a litany that has entered into the ritual of national affirmation, a genuflection to the recognized deities required to establish one's bona fides. This is the ideology of a very rich, very powerful, capitalist class that for well-known historical reasons is characterized by an excessive self-confidence.

The twelve Roosevelt years, both through the Depression and World War II, did irreparable damage to the businessman's thesis of a nightwatchman government. But the businessman's power and wealth kept the ideology alive and persuasive; indeed as the United States emerged from the war as the colossus astride the continents, towering over both enemies and allies, the business class was able to refurbish a prestige that had been tarnished in the bitter depression years. It claimed and was generally given the credit for building the "arsenal of democracy" which ensured the victory.

It is worth reviewing some of the highlights of recent economic history, since America, during its hegemony, was the determinant in the reconstruction and the chosen paths of development of the other capitalist nations.

Churchill was not exaggerating when he declaimed, "The United States stands at the highest point of majesty and power ever attained by any community since the fall of the Roman Empire." Its colossal production plant, underemployed and decaying in the 1930s, was unleashed in mobilizing for the Second

World War. There followed a dazzling display of the inherent capabilities of advanced technology and organization when given free rein to perform. With the avalanche of goods issuing from her factories and facilities, the United States was able to act as supplementary supplier to both Britain and Soviet Russia, while outfitting her own enormous military hosts for a two-front war in both Europe and Asia.

In 1945 American GNP was 60 percent higher than it had been in 1939, and shot up another 40 percent in the next decade. At the same time her historic high standard of living compared to that of Western Europe had risen by another half during the war. In 1946, with the shift back to civilian conditions, per-capita income stood over a third higher than in 1929. Tables 5, 6, and 7 tell the story.

These are the figures of an industrial goliath destined to scale new heights of greatness. Contrary to prevalent fears that there would be a serious downturn after the war similar to the one of a quarter century before, the United States—bursting with corporate liquid assets and personal savings—led the way to an era of spectacular growth. In 1944, when victory over Germany was in sight, the United States had already grasped the scepter of leadership that England had held to 1913. By common consent the United States became the world's banker and architect of the new brave world-to-be. At Bretton Woods the agreements and institutions were set up for the new international order. Gold and the dollar became the two reserve currencies: the dollar, for all practical purposes the international currency, with sterling a poor auxiliary second.

By grants, loans, and a variety of money, goods, and techno-logical transfers, the United States was the major force to help the stricken industrial powers repair the war damage and go on to an era of historic expansion. Even if there were no Soviet Union in existence, and no cold war, Washington would have been constrained to play the benefactor, though in somewhat altered particulars and intensity of dedication. Washington had to accept the role if it hoped to stabilize these countries on reli-able capitalist foundations, to rehabilitate their compromised property-owning elites, to halt social disintegration, to make the world, in the words of Woodrow Wilson's much-misunderstood but hard-headed phrase, "safe for democracy."

Trade figures show that the American strategists succeeded

TABLE 5   U.S. Industrial Growth

Federal Reserve index of manufacturing production (1947–1949 = 100)		Total capital of all manufactures (in billion 1929 U.S.$)		Total steel ingots and castings produced (in million long tons)	
Year	Index	Year	Amount	Year	Amount
1929	58	1929	63.3	1929	56.4
1939	57	1937	55.3	1939	47.1
1943[a]	133			1944[b]	80
1946	90	1948	77.9		
1955	140			1955	104.5

[a]This was the high point during the war.
[b]The high point during the war, this figure was not exceeded until 1950.

TABLE 6   Index of Total Farm Production[a]

Year	Farm output	Livestock and livestock production
1939	80	85
1944	97	105
1946	98	101
1955	112	120

[a]1947–1949 = 100.

in blasting open the hitherto blocked channels of exchange, contributing materially to the revival of these countries' economies. From 1950 through 1960 the volume of world exports doubled. By 1971 the monetary value of world goods trade was three and a half times greater than at the start of the 1960s; for world exports in manufacturing there was a threefold increase from 1960 to 1971, a rise going well beyond the record expansion of the third quarter of the previous century. America's share was a quarter of world exports of manufactures in 1960, which by 1974 fell to a fifth. The significance of this upward spurt in the expansionary cycle is not lessened by the fact that a part of American exports was financed by aid programs, many of which required recipients to buy goods from this country, carry insurance with American underwriters, and transport all or part of the shipments in American vessels. In the first desperate years this country's substantial transfers of money and goods patched up the leaking

TABLE 7   Gross National Product and GNP Per Capita (in 1929 U.S.$)

Year	Gross national product (billion$)	GNP per capita ($)	Implicit price index (1929 = 100)
1929	104.4	857	100
1939	111.0	847	82
1945	180.9	1293	118
1946	166.8	1179	126
1950	187.1	1147	151
1951	199.9	1295	165
1955	230.8	1396	172

vessel of world capitalism when it was in danger of foundering. These transfers, so far as all economic and military grants went, amounted for the years 1946–1952 to $35 billion; in 1953–1961, $48 billion; for the entire 1946–1976 period, $192 billion; with grants making up over three-quarters of the total.

2

After the war the economic columns of European newspapers and periodicals were bulging with analyses of the famed "dollar shortage" (which lasted for over a decade until the European boom was well launched). This was the monetary expression of the Europeans' productive weaknesses: they were unable to import adequately, or to earn dollars to pay for what they did import. Governments reacted by controlling and rationing payments and maintaining import quotas. America's attempt to push Britain to early convertibility of her currency led to a fiasco that reverberated across the continent. This mistake was part of the learning process for our economic mechanics who finally grasped that they had to shore up the European economies if their grand design of a free-trade world was ever to get off the drawing board.

The position of the United States was historically unique for a world leader. All through the 1950s and 1960s the U. S. balance of payments ran deficits, in some years considerable ones.* Yet this country experienced none of the money crises and budgetary upsets that plagued Britain during these same two de-

*Great Britain had a balance-of-payments surplus and no persistent, aggravated price inflation for the entire century from Waterloo to Sarajevo.

cades. The dollar was accepted as the world reserve currency and everyone had complete confidence in it. It was not as good as gold, but better than gold, since dollar deposits would draw interest. The United States held large gold stocks, but that was not the important thing. The world's bankers understood that America's fundamental economic position was strong, that her trade balances were favorable, that the deficits in international payments were due by and large to the heavy costs of maintaining the imperium: troops stationed abroad, 340 bases in thirty-six countries, doling out generous grants and loans to bolster sagging economies and strongmen-on-the-make, and extra expenses in regional wars.

While the "dollar shortage" was acute, the Europeans were only too glad to welcome this outpouring of paper dollars (larger than U.S. earnings on merchandise exports and foreign investment) with which the United States was financing her overseas military and economic expenditures, and soon capital exports as well. These dollars in effect were IOUs on our assets. With the merry-go-round whirling, our deficits were furnishing world monetary liquidity by building up foreign dollar reserves; and the European monetary authorities, so long as they remained agreeable, were making loans to the Americans. As Shonfield put it, "The United States acquired massive valuable business investments, yielding a high rate of profit, and paid for them by increasing its official liabilities to foreign governments, which carried a low rate of interest. It seemed an excellent stroke of business."

All was well while the American deficit was looked at as a passing disturbance. By the mid-1960s, however, the Europeans had rebuilt their economies, their foreign trade was in full swing, and they no longer believed that the United States would or could right her imbalances. The central banks had accumulations totaling some $30 billion and were uneasy about accepting more. America's dominant position could no longer be sustained. Our trade surplus was progressively declining, inflation at home was rising, our national managers were resorting to the printing presses to meet growing deficits. The dénouement was inevitable and in 1971 the Bretton Woods system fell apart, in the midst of what Shonfield called "the most serious crisis in international economic relations." In that fateful year the U.S. trade balance went into deficit for the first time since 1894, and the hoard held abroad had mounted to $53 billion. The dollar was thereupon devalued and its convertibility to gold, already unofficially discontinued, was now formally dropped. To add to the disarray the Nixon directorate made warlike moves against competitors by placing a 10 percent tax on dutiable imports.

In early 1973 there was another full-blown crisis, the dollar pile-up abroad had rocketed upward by another half, the dollar was again devalued, and the era of an orderly international monetary system with fixed exchange parities was at an end. Its working life had been short, far shorter than the period of pre–World War I ascendancy of the pound. Now all countries floated their currencies against each other, which in practice became a system of floating blocs, with some currencies attached to the dollar, some to the German mark, some to English pound sterling. This institutionalization of monetary anarchy reflected the inability of the managers overseeing the economies of the OECD world to find a new framework for the changed economic universe that emerged in the 1970s.

By the late 1970s America's trade position was in recurring deficit and there were a number of runs on the dollar similar to the runs on the pound in the 1960s. This naturally led to feverish discussions, written and oral, concerning the causes, with attention centering on American productivity decline. Some compared our plight to Britain's. On this particular proposition the analogy is a faulty one. It would be like comparing an ace baseball pitcher no longer in his prime with one who has dropped down to the minor leagues. British labor productivity had been falling behind those of Germany and America from the turn of the century. American labor productivity has been for many decades and still is the highest in the world. If our recent declining rate of productivity growth is a reality, not a statistical fortuity, then Germany and Japan and others will overtake us fairly soon—or have already done so. However, in 1979 the Japanese worker was said to be producing 66 percent, and the German worker 88 percent, of the output of the American worker. Volkswagen executives, when opening their assembly plant in New Stanton, Pennsylvania, stated that they had made intensive surveys which showed that American workers were more productive and stayed on the job longer than their German counterparts. So America's industrial decline in the past half-dozen years cannot be explained on grounds of inadequate labor productivity. Other things have to account for it.

One proposition to note as a shaper of capitalist economies is militarization. Our huge arms budgets beginning in 1950 with National Security Council (NSC) 68 spiraled upward over the years to emit the government's strongest institution—the Pentagon-directed military-industrial complex. The United States has emerged as the world's foremost exponent of military technology and the biggest exporter of arms. Although it has systematically put its weight on the side of greater militarization of all its allies, the other powers are discreetly following a good distance behind. They have resisted blandishments to assign the same percentage of their wealth and skills to an economically unproductive enterprise.

Seymour Melman, professor of industrial engineering at Columbia University, originated the argument that America lost leadership in numerous industrial fields because of its obsessive preoccupation with military technology. In a nutshell his thesis is this: The military sector of the economy has grown disproportionately large, the bulk of research and development funds are directed to military and related fields, and there is a systematic neglect of the needs of civilian industry, with capital and talent irresistibly drawn to the major powerhouse of activity and influence. The result is a massive deterioration of efficiency in industry after industry—a proposition that Melman backs up with an array of data. He provides reports and figures to demonstrate that in the 1960–1970 period there were sizable increases in high-technology imports; that this country had lost its long-standing leadership in machine tools; that by 1968 over two-thirds of metal-working machinery in American plants was older than the working equipment in German and Japanese counterparts; that productivity growth was consequently trailing Europe's and Japan's. The public basked in the belief that military spending constituted a huge government public works project ensuring the full utilization of capital and labor. Unfortunately there was little awareness of the indirect costs of a permanent war economy: diversion of human and physical capital from economically productive to nonproductive use, a declining trade position, growing obsolescence of some leading industries, and deterioration of the infrastructure. It also happened to be a machine for inflation powered by billions in the military sector turning out goods lacking use value for consumption or further production, but making claims on civilian goods and services.*

Galbraith picked up the theme recently in his remarks in a symposium in Seattle on the medical consequences of nuclear weapons and nuclear war.

> During the 1970s we spent annually around $100 billion on our defense establishment for a total for the decade of roughly $1,000 billion in constant 1976 dollars. Capital in this magnitude can be used for arms; it can be used for private capital investment; it cannot be used for both. . . . We used from 5 to 8 percent of our gross national product for military purposes. The Germans during this decade used between 3 and 4 percent—in most years about half as much as we did. The Japanese in these ten years devoted less than 1 percent of their gross national product to military use. . . . Our investment in fixed nonmilitary and nonresidential investment ranged from 16.9 percent of gross national product to 19 percent. That of Germany ranged upwards from 20.6 to 26.7 percent. The Japanese ranged in these years from 31 percent to a towering 36.6 percent. The investment in improvement of civilian plant was broadly the reciprocal of what went for weapons. Can anyone looking at these figures suppose that our military spending has been a source of industrial and economic strength? Can anyone doubt that it has been at a cost to our industrial eminence and to the prestige and influence that go therewith?

3

This leads to another major proposition not caught in the nets of statisticians' standard productivity charts. Analyses of America's place in the world arena, and comparison with other countries, are out of plumb unless they take into consideration the fact that there has been a shift in industrial organization. Alongside the American home economy her businessmen have created a second American economy whose plants and offices

---

*Melman's positive argument is imbedded in a larger thesis of questionable value on the dominance of a new military state capitalism over the entire economy. It would take me too far afield were I to attempt to deal with it. His cogent proposition, which I have summarized, is also somewhat attenuated by his determination to ascribe to Pentagon Power all manner of unrelated ills and trials. But his explanation for the decline of America's technological preeminence and loss of trade, removed from its rickety, overextended framework, rings true.

are scattered around the globe. This other economy is right now about two-fifths the size of the home economy, give or take a few percentage points. Vernon explained, "Practically every one of America's largest firms have developed a substantial overseas network of subdivisions and branches," with the output of these facilities equal to 40 percent of the home output. "In banking, U.S. leaders have been writing as much as half of their business overseas." The fifty major U.S. companies are doing the same or close to it. Multinational corporations' (MNCs) growth rates in industrial sales, investments abroad, profits from overseas enterprises, have been and will continue to be very much higher than at home. Foreign affiliates' sales accounted for a quarter of world marketable output in 1968, and this jumped to over two-fifths by mid-1975. Jack Berman pointed out a decade ago the consequences of this faster growth of MNC sales than of gross national product. He estimated that by 1990 half the GNP of the non-Communist world would be attributed to multinational companies, 70 percent of it American.

Fortune lists sales of $1219 billion for 1978 for the 500 largest U.S. industrial companies, a 12 precent increase in each of the last three years, 5 percent when adjusted for inflation, with assets totaling $899 billion. Business Week's all-industry composite of 1200 companies, including banks' operating revenues, lists sales of $1833 billion in 1978. This can be properly evaluated in the light of total world activity: the gross national product of the non-Communist world stood at some $4600 billion in 1975, with $4000 billion in the developed market economies alone. Even in the depression year of 1982, sales of the 500 were 37 percent higher at $1672 billion and assets 45 percent greater at $1309 billion.

Although there are estimates of 25,000 foreign affiliates controlled by 3500 U.S. corporations, most of these are MNCs only in a narrow technical sense, and their affiliates are simply sales or promotion branches. Four hundred of Fortune's top 500 comprise the authentic MNCs, and 85–90 percent of investments and sales are on the books of the top 200. What clothes an MNC with the purple of true majesty as against the fair-sized but undistinguished company with branches in one or a few countries across its borders? Not just the number of its affiliates and the number of countries these are located in. The MNC has moved beyond the parochial to a global outlook; its strategy is set by integrated, worldwide determinants, not a mere extension of its home-market needs.

With an additional economy at major corporations' disposal, one larger than that of any one foreign industrial power, it stands to reason that the home economy is being altered, constricted, parts of it pulled into various grotesque shapes. It is immaterial for purposes of understanding what is going on whether the huge amounts of capital that have been sent abroad would have or could have otherwise been profitably invested at home. They were not—they were instead employed in acquiring or setting up an empire of subsidiary plants and establishments in the five continents. The effects at home have been momentous, and will be discussed shortly.

We are at the point where we have to make a detour into (1) the internal character and evolution of the U.S. economy that makes possible or calls for expansion overseas; and (2) the political repercussions of the overseas movements internationally, and then back at home. Regardless of who controls the large corporations—managers, institution and family insiders, or bank-managed voting trust funds—the corporations are the major directorates of the economy of our time. If any future conflicts develop between business and government, it is the high-positioned executives overseeing their affairs who will devise the strategies and issue the marching orders of their camp. We have to know how the corporate mainsprings work if there is to be a proper economic grounding of the circuits of extended statism.

Truism number one of our economic situation is the concentration of enormous capital accumulations in corporations. Truism number two is that the corporate leviathans are getting bigger and fatter at a faster rate than ever before. In 1968 *Fortune* magazine's 500 largest nonfinancial companies gulped down two-thirds of all industrial sales and three-quarters of all profits. The top 200 controlled the same percentage of total corporate assets as did the top 1000 companies in 1941, over 60 percent. According to a projection of Dr. Willard Mueller, then chief economist of the Federal Trade Commission, 200 corporations would own two-thirds of all manufacturing assets by the mid-1970s, the same proportion owned by the top 500 in 1962. Later, appearing before a Senate committee at the end of 1969, Dr. Mueller stated:

You may recall that I testified before this committee in 1965 that, should postwar trends in aggregate concentration continue, by 1975 the 200 largest manufacturing corporations would control two-thirds of all manufacturing assets. Unhappily, we have reached this level ahead of schedule. Today the top 200 manufacturing corporations already control about two-thirds of all assets held by corporations engaged primarily in manufacturing.

In their study of concentration in American manufacturing in the late 1950s, Professors Kaysen and Turner consolidated industries into 147 categories, 58 of which were defined as highly concentrated (eight firms accounted for half or more of sales; the twenty largest, three-quarters or more), and another 46 defined as concentrated (eight firms responsible for a third of sales; the twenty largest, less than three-quarters). Using the Kaysen–Turner criteria, Averitt found that in 1963 among forty-two subgroups, the four largest firms produced 52 percent of the value of shipments while the eight largest produced 67 percent; twenty-nine of the forty-two industries were highly concentrated oligopolies. In leading cases like the electrical industry, two giant firms dominated; in farm machinery, three; in transportation equipment (excluding private), four; in chemicals there was a relatively large number, seven chemical companies and six non-chemical companies.

In the normal year of 1979 the 500 had sales of $1445 billion (some deflating needed to take account of price rises), a jump of 18.6 percent over the previous year, representing three-fifths of the entire gross national product. Their assets climbed to $1035 billion, a jump of $137 billion over the previous year. Corporations with assets from $250 million to over $1 billion held almost 74 percent of all manufacturing corporate assets. The gilded 500 enjoyed a median return on equity of 16 percent and employed approximately sixteen million people, a jump of 400,000 over the previous year, over three-quarters of all jobs in manufacturing.

The consequence of this capital concentration is obvious. With few exceptions the major markets are under the authority of three, four, half a dozen, sometimes up to a dozen, giant corporations. They make the decisions for the entire industry, with one or two of them assigned the role of price leaders. The firms may compete fiercely, but the competition is in advertising, packaging, image creation, name-brand inculcation, but not in prices on goods and services of comparable quality. This has been designated "imperfect competition"; it can also be described as quasi-monopolistic control.

It is common knowledge that this country has antitrust laws and that the Supreme Court in the past has ordered the dissolution of monopolies. Examples are the old Standard Oil Company, American Tobacco, National Packing, or the more recent divestiture of DuPont's control of General Motors. None of these has reintroduced an era of Brandeis-like competition between sturdy, modest-sized concerns. What the antitrust laws and their largely ceremonial enforcement accomplish is to constrain big corporations to limit market control and price administration to oligopolistic arrangements—which the courts accept. The companies achieve their expansion not by the old exclusivist techniques of cornering the market, but by vertical integrations, foreign operations, and conversions into conglomerates.

In his *New Industrial State*, published in 1967, Galbraith elaborated the view—still a minority one among economists—that intertwined with the need to control prices is the need to control what is sold at those prices; consequently management of demand and conditioning consumer behavior

> is, in fact, a vast and rapidly growing industry in itself. It embraces a huge network of communications, a great array of merchandising and selling organizations, nearly the entire advertising industry, numerous ancillary research, training and other related services and much more. . . . Effective control of consumer demand requires management not only of how income is spent but also of the amount of income that is available for spending. . . . Measures to maintain a desired level of aggregate demand are part and parcel of the task of industrial planning. . . . It would be quixotic for the mature corporation to seek control over its prices and then leave purchases at these prices to the random fate of taste and accident. . . . The need to control consumer behavior is a requirement of planning. Planning, in turn, is made necessary by extensive use of advanced technology and capital and by the related scale and complexity of organization.*

*Galbraith's concept is more complex than this quotation might indicate. It involves making a distinction between physically and psychologically based wants, together with a declining marginal utility of income. A discussion of this is outside the limits of my inquiry.

Like the pre-1914 discovery of the new middle class, the movement to control the consumer and to minimize this aspect of market irregularity—flying in the face of the (Alfred) Marshall orthodoxy—was first noticed by Marxian revisionists and schismatics, in this latter case by Werner Sombart, professor of political economy in Berlin. The analysis was pursued in the Weimar Republic period by members of the Frankfurt School, although Horkheimer and Adorno were interested primarily in the cultural impact of the new huckstering. In this country Veblen was the first to point out that the major purpose (in his words) of quantity production of customers under the surveillance of publicity engineers was to eliminate market uncertainty. A decade later E. H. Chamberlin at Harvard and Joan Robinson at Cambridge shook up the economics profession with their close-grained analyses of the new type of monopolistic competition.

Specifically, control of consumers is not identical with control of prices, and it can never be as stable and secure. In the nature of the endeavor, and despite the enormous sums spent for analyzing age groups, ethnic groups, income groups, there is inevitably an element of guesswork in reaching conclusions and making decisions. Vastly expensive errors of judgment based on faulty market analysis occur time and again because of unanticipated changes in public tastes, introduction of new products, changed circumstances, and economic downturns. Competing advertising campaigns may cancel each other out. Moreover the public, in sheer self-defense, sometimes tunes out altogether—becomes numb and oblivious to the psychological missiles ceaselessly thrown at it. But for all practical purposes the large corporation can now plan its production for several years ahead with what is considered reasonable assurance that within manageable fluctuations it can engineer a specific level of demand.

What then remains of the free competitive market? On the national level is the "other" economy, what Robert Averitt called the dual economy. The first is one of huge corporations, directed by high-powered and highly compensated executives, working out of expensively furnished offices, occupying vast expanses of floor space in steel-and-glass skyscrapers of our metropolitan centers. This is the decisive section which has the lion's share of assets, investments, sales, profits, income, power. There is another economy, the economy of the beauty parlor, the shoe repair shop, the corner garage, the furniture store, the restaurant, up to and including numerous small manufacturers of novelties, consumer rubber and leather goods, apparel, subcontractors supplying large firms with components and parts, as well as individual practitioners in the professions. This economy is labor intensive, competitive, subject to violent oscillations, prone to bankruptcy or being swallowed up through purchase by big corporations.

Notwithstanding its hazardous character for the individual entrepreneur the institution goes on, and in one sense prospers. The number of small firms has gone up since the 1940s with population growth, although the small-business totality is responsible for a decreasing amount of output and sales. In human terms, small business remains a major fixture of the economic landscape. The citizens as consumers have more dealings with these businesses than with the corporate giants. Certain trade associations struggling for concessions for their small- or middle-size business constituents have influence in state capitols. Professional associations have a major say in matters affecting their fields. Then, too, the number of employees involved is telling. In a study of thirty-one million workers in all industries in 1958, 23 percent worked for companies with fewer than twenty employees. If we consider companies with 20–249 employees, there was an additional 26 percent. In certain sectors, like wholesale trade, 43 percent was in the first category, 47 percent in the second; in retail trade, 47 percent was in the first, 23 percent in the second.

This is a sphere, however, in which weightiness is not determined on a one-man, one-vote basis. The overwhelming number of these businesses make up clusters of tiny satellites, lacking autonomous powers, revolving around the major planets. For the representative year of 1973, a good year before business failures and bankruptcy filings multiplied in the mid-decade recession, we find the following: Of some 1,900,000 income tax returns of active corporations, those with assets of under $100,000 to $1 million, accounting for 93 percent of returns, had 6.7 percent of all assets and 10.5 percent of net income. Firms with assets of $100 million and over, covering only 0.2 percent of returns, held over 70 percent of total assets.

It is from the businessmen of the second economy, with negligible or no ability to regulate their own markets much less control the general course, subservient to the will of major banks

and corporations, and long since deprived of levers for independent decision-making, that media practitioners derive their antiquated concepts of how the economy works. It is with this lesser
economy in mind that they discuss ailments and therapies. That
is what makes so many of their presentations fanciful or irrelevant. For any meaningful discussion of our economic problems,
the world of the large corporation and the oligopolistic market it
has created has to be at the center of our focus.

4

Let me add a final word on the structural evolution of the
corporation. An expansionist destiny was written into its genetic
makeup. From the beginning of the Industrial Revolution accumulation of capital led to increases in the size of the firm. Larger
size transformed a single-function establishment directed by one
or several owners into a complex, multisectored organization
functioning through an elaborate division of labor and integrated
by a hierarchically positioned managing personnel. Alfred Chandler, the economic historian, recorded the main stages. The small
local or region-oriented one-man ownership or simple partnership gave way through intermediate forms to the great national,
integrated, multifunction corporation. One way was for a company to expand and push out rivals by its own efforts, or through
acquisitions, or mergers, or all three. The enlarged company then
integrated by cutting out middlemen and setting up its own national marketing network. In another strategy, a number of manufacturing companies joined in a horizontal combination—trade
association, pool, trust, or holding company—consolidated at a
later stage their individual operations into a unified establishment oriented to the national and at times the continental market. The consolidated firm then integrated by reaching forward
into marketing or backward into purchasing, or in time, where
the products permitted, into variations of both.

The internal structure of the enterprise, Chandler shows,
changed to conform to the strategy:

Expansion of volume led to the creation of an administrative office
to handle one function in one local area. Growth through geographi-
cal dispersion brought the need for a departmental structure and
headquarters to administer several local field units. The decision to

expand into new types of functions called for the building of a
central office and a multidepartmental structure, while the developing of new lines of products or continued growth on a national or
international scale brought the formation of the multidivisional
structure with a general office to administer the different divisions.

This last structural innovation was pioneered after the First
World War at General Motors and DuPont. It has remained, with
variations and refinements, the model for large corporations with
differentiated products. Alfred P. Sloan, Donaldson Brown,
Henry Haskell, Edgar Clark, and their associates in both corporations who were responsible for working out the new structure,
were all systematizing bureaucrats, a new breed of methodical
organization men who followed the previous generation of empire builders. These were not the speculators and adventurers,
the Cookes, Goulds, Astors, and Vanderbilts, but the promoting
breed who carved out the dominant corporations—William C.
Durant, Coleman DuPont, Henry Ford, Walter P. Chrysler, Willard H. Dow, Paul W. Litchfield. They lacked the temperament to
draw up organization charts, and certainly would have resisted
accepting any limitation on their authoritarian rule.

What their more administrative-minded successors felt
called upon to replace were contradictory organization procedures which proved deficient in coping with crises. They concluded that the overcentralized structures, departmentalized by
function, that had been bequeathed them left the corporation
unequal to the task of adapting to rapid technological and market
changes. The solution they devised was to combine operational
autonomy with strategic centralization. Separate divisions were
set up by product, not function, and given completely autonomous power under a single head. At the same time strategic
decision-making, long-range planning, and basic policy decisions were centralized in a top leadership freed of administrative
routine and provided with a staff to carry out its assigned responsibilities. The organization schema, adopted by others in the
intervening years, became the general standard for major corporations with variegated product lines, a schema that has proven
sufficiently supple to be successfully employed under changing
circumstances in the postwar era.

To recapitulate: After the Civil War industrial enterprises

concentrated on manufacturing. They were single-function: they bought what supplies they needed; they worked up their finished products; they sold them through commission agents, wholesalers, and brokers. Once the corporate heavies emerged, dominating their national markets, commanding huge assets, trained personnel, technological skills, and patents, there followed integration into marketing or purchasing or both. Obviously this is the schematization of an evolution in which no two corporations, even in the same industry, followed identical lines of development or moved at an identical pace. Some combined or skipped stages and anticipated later strategies. Others, whose growth came from a simple expansion of their existing few products sold to the same type of customers, remained in the subspecies that they had embodied in an earlier period.

After integration came product differentiation as illustrated in the meatpacking industry. By the 1890s the "Big Five"—Swift, Armour, Morris, Cudahy, Schwarschild & Sulzberger—pushed up from the commercial wars to monopolize the market. Each firm then, as related by Chandler, "turned to developing goods that could further employ the vast resources it had collected. To beef, these firms quickly added a full line of meat products, including lamb, veal, and pork. To make better use of their branchhouse network, they began to market poultry, eggs, and dairy products. To obtain more profit from their 'disassembling' and other processing operations, they went into leather, soap, fertilizer, and glue businesses."

This insatiable urge of the corporation to control its total market situation, this lust for pushing out without let-up into new lines and regions, originates not in a Nietzschean will to power (although it amounts to the same thing in practice); it originates in its excess capacity in a volatile market. The struggle is never-ending, and the threat of getting done in is ever-present, confronted as the corporation is with periodic recessions and shifts in market requirements. It was this that goaded busy executives to expand into derivative, related, and for that matter, unrelated branches of industry. The urge for diversification is even more aptly illustrated in the case of the DuPont Company. From the time of its consolidation in 1902 until 1918 the firm was augmenting the output of a single line of products of explosives. It moved forcefully into diversification because it had built up an enormous increase in capacity in the course of the war, as well as for the manufacture of raw materials. The new department set up was called the Excess Plant Utilization Division.

The way the company executives went about their search for new lines, and the kind of new products they developed, is representative of the recent evolutionary phases which erupted into the multinational phenomenon. While the original DuPont product was explosives, from the vantage point of the company's researchers and engineers it was viewed more rigorously as a branch based on the technology of nitrocellulose chemistry. Diversified expansion was scientifically, but no longer materially, related to the original product as with the meatpackers. Some years earlier, when plagued by excess capacity, Irénée du Pont, then in charge of planning, had researchers concentrate on three industries whose products had nitrocellulose as their basic ingredient—artificial leather, artificial silk, and pyroxylin products including photographic film. This led to the purchase in 1910 of one of the leading firms in the artificial leather business, the Fabrikoid Company. In the war years, with production rocketing, the company leaders grew more concerned about the enormous capacities which DuPont was building up to meet what would be a temporary demand.

At this point the diversification strategy was given a place of honor on the executive committee's agenda. The artificial leather line was expanded and the entry into pyroxyline was hastened with the purchase of the Arlington Company, one of the largest celluloid producers in the country. DuPont also moved into dye-making. With the assistance of German dye chemists recruited by the State Department, a new dye manufacturing operation was set up. To make a long story short, within the short space of several years DuPont purchased additional key companies. Thereupon it moved further into vertical integration by buying up still more manufacturers of basic products feeding these new lines of production. By 1921 DuPont product divisions included, in addition to high explosives and military and commercial smokeless powder, dyestuffs and pharmaceuticals, pyralin articles and sheeting, paints, varnishes, pigments, dry colors and heavy chemicals, Fabrikoid, rubberized articles, films, and Parlin solutions.

The goad is excess capacity. To utilize this excess capacity the company moves into new products and markets. To facilitate this diversification it buys up new companies and expands its investments in plants and equipment. This diversification takes it far afield, since what is related in the chemist's laboratory may and generally does require unrelated manufacturing technologies. It may also require diverse selling techniques, since some products are necessarily sold to manufacturers, others directly or indirectly to the consumer. The new strategy calls forth a new organization schema embodying divisions by products rather than by function, towered over by a governing central planning executive staff.

At a more recent stage of maturation diversification leads to expansion into conglomerates—the merger within one corporation, and under one central management, of totally unrelated industrial enterprises. Tax-law metaphysics, risk reinsurance, stock market vagaries, and fast killings for brokers all play their part in the continuing conglomerate merger boom. Some of the publicized amalgamations originated in the ability of high-stepping promoters to exploit tax-law loopholes and the arithmetic of profits/earnings ratios in stock pricing. Whatever the ingenuity and adventurism at work, however, bankers and promoters could find no opportunities to display these virtuosities of marriage-brokership if new technological and scientific advances had not laid the groundwork for the conglomerate phenomenon. The momentum slackened apparently at the end of the 1960s after old-line Wall Street houses upset the attempt of Leasco Data Processing Equipment to gobble up the Chemical Bank. But conglomerate acquisitions and mergers, though reduced in the early 1970s, continued running high, as Table 8 shows. In the second half of the decade there was a renewed burst of activity, with the value of acquisitions at the level of a decade before. Between 1979 and 1982 companies spent $170 billion to acquire other corporations, with conglomerates the predominant resulting companies.

Some of the conglomerates are less than textbook models of organizational logic. They bring to mind that many mergers set up at the turn of the century, the work of promoters, not engineers, were examples of stockjobbery. Watering and overcapitalization of securities of merged enterprises was the rule. A government study in 1900 of 183 industrial combinations disclosed that over $3 billion of stocks and bonds was issued for companies with a capital worth less than half that amount. In the case of Ling-Temco-Vought, one of the ranking conglomerates, the

TABLE 8 Mergers and Acquisitions in Manufacturing and Mining

	1969	1970	1971	1974	1976	1977	1979
Total no. of acquisitions	2307	1351	1011	602	559	590	519
No. of conglomerate mergers	114	79	51	38	63	69	87
Value of assets of acquired firms with $10 million or more in assets (billion $)							
Conglomerate mergers	8.1	4.7	1.9	3.0	5.2	6.7	11.6
All mergers	11.0	5.9	2.5	4.5	6.3	8.7	12.9

	1965–1969	1970–1974	1975–1979
Total no. of acquisitions	8213	4749	2717
Value of assets of acquired firms with $10 million or more in assets in all mergers (billion $)	38.5	17.9	43.5

SOURCE: *Statistical Abstract 1977* (Washington, D.C.: U.S. Bureau of the Census, 1978), p. 569; *Statistical Abstract 1981*, p. 537.

common stock equity in 1969 was 7 percent and the rest of the capital was long-term debt or the minority interest in constituent firms. Half of net earnings were engrossed by fixed charges. Whatever stockholders earned in the years ahead, the corporate marriage brokers did handsomely right at the creation. Morgan Stanley earned a fee of $14.6 million for the Shell Oil/Beldridge Oil deal and Salomon Brothers earned $6.5 million for the Elf-Acquitaine/Texasgulf deal. Even on the lower rung, Lehman Brothers pocketed $3 million for the Nabisco–Standard Brands coupling. For the brokers, it was a lucrative game. Nevertheless tho turn of the century merger boom and the current conglomerate boom represent more than stock-market manipulations of the Moore brothers in one case, and James Ling and Roy Ash in the other case. The promoters realized early which way corporate winds were to blow and stepped in to hasten economic Manifest Destiny along. After the promoters came the bankers and lawyers, with the administrators, treasurers, and engineers not far behind.

The new conglomerate structure heralds a new stage of diversification. It is an exploitation of central managements' newfound ability to control divisions of disparate industries by putting to work the instrumentalities of advanced technology. The conglomerate firm enables corporation directorates to amass enormous capital resources for new acquisitions, speculations, and overseas expansion. It enhances the power positions of the favored few. It mitigates risk and uncertainty by spreading commitments over a number of different industrial markets reacting to varying cycles, rhythms, customer groups, and profits sources. Historically, it represents the fusion of advanced data processing with huge capital accumulations and modern managerial controls. This brings us to the multinational corporation, to which I now turn once again.

5. Multinational Corporations

1

The modern corporation, firmly held in hand by a policy and control directorate, came out of the Second World War bloated with liquid capital and extended facilities. It was necessarily on the lookout for new opportunities and fresh markets. It had learned in the course of diversification how to coordinate a sprawling empire. It was habituated to working up multifarious products in plants strung across a 3000-mile-wide country and beyond. It was adept at applying cost accounting, interdivisional billing, and for that matter the more subtle techniques of creative bookkeeping. At its central office were assembled technicians trained in cost-effectiveness analysis, computer routines, managerial control, long-term planning. In six years of government-financed and war-induced expansive markets corporations had taken giant strides in perfecting new processes and products, as well as concepts for new products. Technologically, organizationally, financially, the quasi-monopolist majors were ready for the plunge abroad.

This was not the first time that Americans appeared as latter-day *conquistadores* to the Europeans. At the turn of the century when the United States was still a major importer of capital, there were some 75–100 American subsidiaries producing in Canada and Europe. Though many of them were merely assembly and sales outlets, and in extractive industries, oriented toward their home markets, the American presence created profound uneasiness. Their go-getting proclivities, brash salesmanship, serial production techniques, scientific management—the entire American Gestalt represented a threat. According to an economic historian of the period,

> The European press . . . from the 1880's on, resounded with complaints against the "American menace," or the "American invasion," and with proposals for concerted action to deal with it. . . . In 1897, Count Goluchowski, the Austrian foreign minister, in a circular letter to other European countries, proposed that the countries of Europe combine to take concerted action directed against American commercial competition.

The proposal was premature. The relationship between Europe and America was first turned around when this country changed from a debtor to a creditor nation at the end of the First World War. Were it not for the unexpected intrusion of the Great Depression a decade later the multinational phenomenon would probably have erupted in advance of the technological innovations of the 1950s. In the 1919–1929 decade our direct investments doubled in Canada and Europe where the bulk of investments were located, and increased two and a half times in Latin America. By 1929 more than 1300 companies in Europe were either owned or controlled by American capital. American-attached enterprises were leading in oil, electrical, automobile, rubber tires, and office machinery, as well as public utilities. In 1922 the value of total U.S. investment in Canada outstripped the British, as it already had after the war in Mexico, Cuba, and parts of Central America. Worldwide British overseas investments were still a fifth larger than America's in 1929, but U.S. investments were growing much more rapidly.

The outcry against this second American invasion was more frantic. Was the United States the modern Macedon, destined to become the old world's master? The press of England, France, and Germany was full of alarms. Ludwell Denny, a noted American publicist at the time, wrote a book at the end of the decade, *America Conquers Britain*, that was considered a brilliant forecast of things to come. The pervasive fear led the British General Electric Company in 1928 to deny voting rights to foreign shareholders when Americans were buying and soon held 60 percent of the stock. The discriminatory scheme, called by the London *Chronicle* "financial Bolshevism," was only withdrawn under direct threat of American retaliation and pressure by the London Stock Exchange. Earlier, in 1924, in true Marxian anticipatory style, Leon Trotsky was predicting that the existing Anglo-American trade war over markets would end in a war of arms "on a scale never seen before"—and many agreed that it looked that way.

The prospect vanished when the New York stock market crashed and the Great Depression took the stage. Output in manufacturing fell by half and international trade by 60 percent between 1929 and 1932. Accordingly all available funds were needed at home. Where here and there American corporations went against the tide by adding to their overseas investments, it was because they had to do so if they were not to abandon their markets in the face of ever-higher tariffs being erected everywhere, and their inability to remit profits because of newly enacted exchange controls. But the headwinds were blowing in the opposite direction. From 1933 to 1939 there was a net inflow. In 1940 the total book value of direct investments was somewhat lower than in 1929.

After the war, as we have seen, the main American transfers abroad came from the government as grants, loans, and military subsidies. By the early 1950s the financiers and managers decided that the old powers had been set on their feet again, hence that Western Europe was safe for investments. Something else had taken place to give buoyancy and added dynamism to direct investment abroad—the revolution in transportation, communications, and control. The jet engine compressed distance. Telex, television, and cable telephone broke the barriers of space. The computer opened the door to hitherto unmanageable intricacies. Routine data for directing global operations could be transmitted by wholesale lots and retrieved almost instantaneously. The executive could now travel from New York or San Francisco to London, Geneva, Rome, Rio de Janeiro, or Tokyo within a matter of a day. Staff managers at company headquarters could consult with branch managers and coordinate operations scattered over continents with greater ease and rapidity than they could in the past when company plants were located in several cities in their own country.

With that the spigot was unloosened and the golden nectar began to flow again. By the 1960s it was well past the $3-billion mark annually. With the 1970s it had passed the $4-billion mark. In the crucial investments sector of manufacturing the rate of increase was in the range of 10 percent annually from

1950 to 1970, twice the growth of U.S. exports of manufactured goods over the 1960s. Between 1967 and 1971 total world direct investment increased from $108 billion to $165 billion; the American accumulated share grew from $60 billion to $86 billion, better than half the total. In the mid-1970s American accumulated direct investment stood at $124 billion, Britain's at $40 billion, the rest of the world at $76 billion; in other words the proportions remained roughly the same. At the end of 1980 the book value of American direct investments stood at $216 billion, a 74 percent increase in six years (total private assets abroad were over two and a third times greater). But Raymond Vernon calculated that real worth is twice book value. A knowledgeable finance writer figured investments at three times the book value. In either case this is a gargantuan enterprise, and it is still gathering speed.

Let us pause at this point to ask what the writer of a reasonably organized textbook would have asked at the very beginning, namely, what exactly is the present-day multinational corporation? How does it interlock with its own national and host countries' economies? What advantages does it have, if any? Of the dozen or more definitions to be found in the texts on multinationals, I have pasted together the following:

> Multinationals are oligopolistic firms with differentiated products, whose structure has been determined by an inner dynamic for vertical integration and horizontal combination. They own enterprises in countries outside the one in which they are headquartered, which account for a substantial portion of the MNCs' total production, sales, and resources.

The definition may be considered overly wordy, certainly inelegant, and it is not recommended for inclusion in inspirational remarks at public festivities. However, it contains the elements that I consider important to identify the latter-day mutants of an older species. To begin with it is the oligopolistic mammoth that becomes a multinational enterprise. All oligopolies are not multinationals, but all true multinationals are oligopolies. Some leading firms, because of the nature of their products and for specific market reasons, are content to till their plot in the national gardens and not to lust after foreign acquisitions. They are satisfied to export such wares for which there are foreign markets in classic style. No second-string firm, however, can take on the burdens or pursue the hoped-for lush pickings of the international enterprise.

Since it is a continuation of what went before, what is the difference between the multinational of today and of yesterday? For one, there is the massiveness of the present establishment, the immense size of the holdings. True, the book value of American direct investment in relation to gross national product is not so very much higher than it was in 1929, but this is a case where percentages do not tell the story. Portfolio investments were still far larger in the 1920s than direct investments, a proportion that altered drastically in the 1950s, and with it the entire concept of investments abroad. Furthermore we are calculating a percentage of a GNP that is as large as that of the rest of the OECD world combined. The American corporate establishment abroad in the 1920s was the pygmy precursor of the post-World War II colossus.

Not so many years ago, before the dollar was laid low and the Japanese and Germans were breaking down the ramparts of the American market, there was a third outburst about the American conquest memorialized in Servan-Schreiber's Le Défi Américain. The data he used may appear superannuated now, but American holdings remain substantial in all of Western Europe, including Germany, England, and France; and what is decisive, they are in technically advanced groups, or those singled out for rapid growth prospects. Canada is an economic semi-colony of ours; American investors control over half of all manufacturing. The investment was recently estimated at about $40 billion, four-fifths of total foreign capital in the country. In Britain's other former dominion, far-away Australia, American holdings nosed out Britain's two decades ago, although the latter's stake is the largest single foreign commitment of British industry. Donald Brash, an expert on the subject, wrote that "most Australians would have difficulty naming a breakfast food, a cosmetic, or a toilet article not produced by the local subsidiary of some American company."

When the Common Market was formed in 1957 there were great expectations that an integrated European industrial complex would develop, in time rivaling the American one. Individual incidents were repeatedly seized on to predict the coming interpenetration of European national investments. These expectations were not fulfilled. What did take place—in part in reaction to the American threat, in part an endemic thrust of the modern corporation to control its markets—were the great merger transactions (already referred to) in the main European countries through the 1960s and beyond.

Through the 1960s when American direct investments increased spectacularly in the Common Market areas, Shonfield wrote, "There was no corresponding international movement of capital among the EEC countries themselves. In spite of the urgings of the European Commission and the widespread feeling that there should be a European counterweight to the influx of American companies, there were few transnational mergers or takeovers by large European-based corporations." Instead of European commercial banks coordinating or supervising an integration of Common Market industries, Kindleberger noted that it was United States banks—Morgan Guaranty, Chase Manhattan, First National City, Bank of America—that were represented in the several EEC countries. A *Fortune* magazine writer quipped, "It has become a cliché in banking circles to say that the only really European banks nowadays are American." The long colorful tradition of great national states, for many years world powers, with their separate languages, legal systems, tax laws, cultures, and elites, was inimical to attempts at unification.

As a palliative, transnational consortia were set up from time to time. A few of them—CERN in nuclear research, French-German-English collaborative production of tanks, missiles, helicopters, and the A-300 airbus—have worked out. But they are essentially temporary formations handicapped by divided authority and the inevitable high costs of ad hoc arrangements. The classic illustration is that of Unidata, supposed to have been Europe's collective reply to IBM. The partner firms— Siemens in Germany, Philips in Holland, and CII in France—all maintained their own corporate personalities and strategies. As an effective challenge to IBM it was a nullity. Of course the time-honored cartels are still there. In the fifteen years of the EEC's existence, charges of illegal cartel agreements have been brought by the EEC or national authorities against many major producers. They often break up and are as often reconstituted— but these are for allocating markets, not for extending them. The changed climate of the 1970s will be considered later in the chapter in another connection.

2

The next thing to observe about the present multinational is the changed character of investments. At the start of the 1960s almost one-half of U.S. investments outside Canada was in the LDCs, but by 1971 this was reduced to a quarter. There was the decided shift to the industrialized world. The then book value of direct investments in developed nations was $53 billion as against $21 billion in the LDCs. Estimates at the end of 1980 were $157 billion in advanced countries, $53 billion in poorer countries. Roughly the same proportions obtained for the foreign assets of the seven industrialized countries combined—the U.S., Britain, Germany, France, Sweden, Canada, and Japan.

Coming into advanced economies like Germany's or Britain's or even Canada's, the multinational subsidiary firm has to conduct itself in an altogether different manner than in Bolivia or Zaire. The manager is dealing with a relatively stable, reasonably legitimate, culturally efficient government. A complex infrastructure is in place. The labor force is on an educational par with the one at home. Business is an honored and influential calling in the polity. Government officials will not attempt any raiding expeditions on behalf of themselves, their relatives, or cronies; by the same token corporation officers have to keep to the rules. (Assuredly this does not exclude multi-million-dollar bribes to government procurement officials in Japan, Italy, or elsewhere.) There can be no suggestion of the near-sovereign powers wielded in the past by private companies in colonial or backward regions.

The reasons for the increased flow of foreign capital to other developed countries are neither arcane nor unprecedented: availability of more skilled labor forces; richer, more diverse markets; superior ability to use subordinate bodies for stragetic purposes; greater security. Holdings in advanced countries are not a substitute for holdings in underdeveloped countries. There are different kinds of resources and markets to exploit; the two supplement each other. Neither is this a new departure. At the height of her empire in 1885 Britain held half of her private-corporation foreign holdings in the United States, in 1914 a larger investment in the United States than in all of South America, or in India.*

*Not that investments in Europe are shellproof in times of strife and disorder. Before the war France held Russian government bonds worth approximately £500

Conditions in Third World regions are also not what they had once been. Enterprises cannot be run like Gould's silver mine concession at Costaguana in Conrad's *Nostromo*. The peoples of the so-called Third World, from one end of the globe to the other, no matter how indigent, backward, disease-ridden, exploited, and brutalized by corrupt rulers, are conscious of their nationhood and aspire to national improvement. Some of the indigenous middle classes often may be more interested in their own enrichment than in populist melioration; many of the entrepreneurs still constitute an essentially *compradore* class. Even in these cases the elites are more self-assured and have greater negotiating reserves than their forebears. Many have been to foreign schools and are better educated in modern business methods, bureaucratic procedures, government and military administration, they have better connections and sources of information; they are more independent. The new breed of lawyers, promoters, bureaucrats, militarists, have risen to the top on the wave of awakened nationalist movements in which they were participants or conspicuous beneficiaries. Numbers of them were politically to the left when students, and continue to be influenced by leftist intellectuals. The international competition between corporations of the industrialized world has provided them with the means to maneuver between rival salesmen, including those of the Soviet world.

External nationalist pressures in league with MNCs' internal needs changed the nature of corporate operations. Multinational affiliates are concerned not only with raw materials but with delivering finished goods. In Brazil and Argentina, for instance, U.S. companies—Singer, Sperry-Rand, Ford, GM—in the 1960s transformed their long-time sales, service, and assembly operations into full-fledged manufacturing facilities. New American-

million. Why political concessions exacted from the czarist government were supposed to be worth the risk for private investors on 4 and 5 percent bonds, no one will ever know. A war or revolution—and both were distinct possibilities— would bring certain default. In any event the Bolsheviks did repudiate the loans, and not a penny of the £500 million was ever recovered. Czarist Russia may be considered a Third World country of that period. But American investors rushing to buy up in wholesale lots German government bonds in the 1920s were not much better advised. The Dawes loan of 1924 to Germany, underwritten by J. P. Morgan, was oversubscribed ten times by Americans. In the words of Kindleberger, "it was the spark that ignited foreign lending": first, similar bond issues to Krupp and other German firms, then loans to Japan, France, and Latin America. Half of all foreign government bonds issued from 1925 to 1929 were in default by 1937.

owned complexes arose in food processing, chemicals, pharmaceuticals, electrical supplies, office equipment, household goods. This is the design of the new model in sections of the underdeveloped world, a far cry from past investment schemes in banana republics. Since U.S. manufacturing companies in Latin America sold roughly 89 percent of their output in the host countries, the multinationals required a growing market for their products and an urbanized labor force to produce them. Even in the case of the MNC "export platforms" in Southeast Asia—Taiwan, South Korea, Hong Kong, Singapore—favored for their ability to provide unskilled and semi-skilled labor at low costs and to guarantee low tax payments, the old relationships are vastly altered. These offshore facilities are not only producers of primary materials, extractive or agricultural, but also manufactured .parts, components, partially finished products, complete subassemblies in some cases, for the consumer electronic and electrical products industries; or commodities of old-time labor-intensive industries—toys, shoes, wearing apparel—for which the platform dispensaries have become major sources of supply.

One can sum up the multinationals' evolution this way: The American corporation operating overseas had been nationally oriented. It was an entity with differentiated products that had integrated forward and backward. The branches overseas were extensions of its prehensile limbs to perfect integrative functions, to ensure control of its raw materials and essential inputs, to round out its marketing network so as to distribute the goods that could not profitably be sold at home. In contrast the new multinational corporation is internationally oriented. In some cases it sells more products abroad than at home, and takes in more profits from foreign sales than from domestic sales.

It does not matter whether the percentage goes over the fifty mark or whether it is below it. The MNC directorates operate as global staffs. Where they set up shop and how they distribute their plants; where they secure their required inputs; whether they purchase some of their raw materials or buy up the mines, latifundia, and primary establishments; to what extent they contract out certain aspects of their enterprises to purchasing or marketing satellites, and whether these are at home or abroad; whether they shut down operations in country X to shift them to country Y or shut down operations in country X in order to roll over to another line of manufacture; what markets they seek to capture and in what countries—all this and more is within the decision-making province of top managers working out of home country headquarters.

The MNC's starting point internationally can be a technological, managerial, or marketing advantage; the need to get under rising tariff walls or to ward off a native or international competitor so as to maintain its oligopolistic position; or the ability to produce more cheaply for the foreign market than it can by exporting from home. The product-cycle theory was never an explanation of all the motivations for all MNC ventures. But whatever the immediate goal, and even when corporations have reasonable assurance that they can market successfully abroad, they still must have the necessary organization to be able to make such an ambitious move, and the capital or the ability to raise the capital, to bear the expenses.

Companies with great surpluses of funds in their treasuries, and blocked from expanding in their own industries at home, may still move into new industries by becoming conglomerates. Actually the two processes proceed together. True MNCs are not limited to just one industry any longer. They dispense a broad range of products. It is no longer a subject for merriment that an owner of movie houses like Loews goes in for manufacturing watches. Cartoon characters in magazines for sophisticates no longer archly observe that ITT does not confine itself to electrical equipment but has branched out to hotels and sandwich spreads. Even GM, overwhelmingly committed to one product, the automobile, is a conglomerate. It has a large multiplant electrical division manufacturing refrigerators and other electrical household goods; it is in the locomotive business, as well as the banking business financing its automobile sales. It has just unloaded its earth-moving equipment division. Diversification is now the hallmark of the large corporation everywhere. In a mid-1970s Harvard study of 376 MNCs based on a classification system of 158 product lines, 180 U.S.-based MNCs had 207 standardized lines inside their principal industry and 656 standardized lines outside their principal industry. For 135 European and British-based MNCs the same headings read 169 and 425; for 61 Japanese-based MNCs, 54 and 133.

Hence when a corporation moves abroad it may be protecting its oligopolistic position not just in one industry but in an array of industries. Local acquisitions and expansion into conglomerates cannot be a substitute for expansion abroad when sizable companies are concerned. Additional product lines may require the formation of additional foreign affiliates to safeguard their international flanks. The modern oligopolistic, multiproduct, transnational-equipped corporation can no more retreat behind its market ramparts at home without courting disaster than the French could stand successfully behind the Maginot Line. Any attempt to become a rentier with portfolio investments abroad would undermine its entire position, as with those creatures in the natural world in which structure is at war with function—a prelude to the extinction of the species.

In most instances of large acquisitions, mergers, or movements overseas, though the initiating party may have a ready stock of disposable cash, the scheme is financed and generally organized by bankers. These transactions today run to such large sums that corporate titans require reinsurance and equalization of risks in their ventures. Companies that invest heavily abroad borrow heavily abroad. For every dollar that moves from the United States to foreign manufacturing subdivisions, something like three or four dollars is raised by these subsidiaries outside the United States. The Tariff Commission study noted:

> The foreign affiliates of U.S. firms are largely independent of their parent enterprises for financing. Most of their financial life is conducted abroad, and net flows of funds between parents and affiliates are but a small piece of an enormous volume of moving funds.

Vernon's guess was that a subsidiary received from its U.S. parent resources and rights worth a quarter of its total assets; and the rest came from profits earned by the subsidiary and plowed back into the business, profits transferred from other subsidiaries, and moneys raised from banks and capital markets outside the United States. Perhaps 30 percent of these assets are generated by the subsidiary itself, and 45 percent acquired by borrowing.

3

We are dealing with a manifestation of late capitalism that is no less central to the system than was the rise of the national corporation in the previous century. Although property ownership and profit-making remain mainstays of the economic order, the MNCs are substantially altering dispensations in one area after another.

The MNCs dominate export-import trade, hardly surprising since they are the same companies that dominate the U.S. economy in general. Foreign direct investment, not traditional trade, is now the fulcrum of international exchange. By the end of the 1970s the total value of output of enterprises controlled by parent organizations outside the producing country exceeded the total value of all world exports, $330 billion as against $310 billion. The sales of American subsidiaries were estimated to be from two to three times the value of U.S. exports of manufactured products. Other data going back to the late 1960s showed the total value of eleven OECD countries' production associated with foreign direct investments to have been 40 percent higher than their total exports.

Accompanying this, even at home in 1970 American MNCs dominated export channels since they shipped 62 percent of all manufactured products. Long before the MNCs' emergence, imperial powers tied trade to loans, grants, investments, force majeure; but trade itself, however guided, went through regulation channels. The MNCs have further transcended the market mechanism as the oligopolist corporation has done with the price mechanism. In carrying through their transactions they often bypass traditional export-import firms to make their own managements the principals of international trade exchanges.

The MNC is both buyer and seller. The pattern of a lot of its trade is not set in the marketplace but by administrative decision. Not only does the MNC manager buy and sell products within his own empire, within limits he can determine the price to suit his company's internal needs and allocate overhead costs in the same way; he can decide when to physically transfer funds and in what currencies; he can decide whether to buy the goods from a company's plant in this or that country, or whether, in conformity with complex internal calculations, it will suit his purposes to buy parts from a native concern and sell similar parts manufactured by his own company to others in different countries. The need at the end of a fiscal year to show a profit in line with or better than that of the competitors limits but does not eliminate supramarket arbitrariness. A substantial profit is required of the MNC as a totality, not necessarily of all its individual affiliates. Hence official statistics that the United States' share of world exports declined from this figure to that figure in some decade do not have the cutting edge that they would have had before the MNCs took the stage.

Industrial and banking circles have exercised great power through the different historical stages of capitalist nation-states, at some periods overwhelming power. The MNC phenomenon, with its tendency to speed up capital concentrations and its spread over transnational geographic areas, has augmented traditional business power by weakening the controls of nation-states over their activities. That political leaders have been willing partners in undermining their own prerogatives does not gainsay the fact that the power balance has shifted somewhat in the making of certain decisions. In any ensuing crisis, under prevalent arrangements and laws, the forces of government have less ability to chart or modify an economic course. According to Nye, "There are currently some 200 large multinational enterprises or clusters of corporations which operate simultaneously in 20 or more different nations and are joined together by common ownership and management strategy. The three billion dollars of value added annually by each of the top ten multinationals is already greater than the gross national product of some 80 member states of the United Nations."

Even the seasoned governments of strong industrial states are at an obvious disadvantage when dealing with the leviathan corporation. It is the disadvantage of a pluralistically divided, internally warring creature with diverse impulses and contradictory mechanisms in confrontation with an integrated, concentrated organism, perfectly structured for specific pursuits. The nation-state may know many things and the multinational corporation may know only one thing, but the things the nation-state knows are not always consistent or energetically maintained and the thing that the corporation knows it knows very well. One MNC director related, "It is the job of governments to make the rules, and ours to find the loopholes."

Here are several illustrative items from recent Western history. In 1964 and 1965, when the devaluation of the British pound was thought to be imminent, there was a wave of high dividend payments among the foreign-owned subsidiaries, and a number remitted over 100 percent in their earnings by dipping into accumulated profits—in the case of one subsidiary, over four times its profits. There was another such profit-grabbing spree in the months leading up to the crisis of November 1967. The same thing occurred in France in 1968 and 1969. Vernon mentions that the foreign affiliated concerns can accommodate themselves to any government's restrictive legislation with minimum effect on their basic strategies. American firms doing business abroad can funnel their earnings into foreign tax havens, thereby protecting them from the home tax collector. They can also bring them home with the assurance that U.S. taxes on such earnings will not be onerous. Robbins and Stobaugh discuss such techniques as shifting accumulated funds which may originate from interest on inside-corporation loans, from dividends, or from licensing royalties or fees for technical assistance.

The lead-and-lag operation referred to, familiar to all students of MNCs, carries the power-of-attorney over the stability of foreign exchange markets. In the crises over the German mark during the early 1970s U.S.-owned subsidiaries in Germany added to the pressure for revaluation by building up their mark holdings. Again during both the 1964 and 1967 devaluation scares in Britain MNC headquarters had their European subsidiaries defer payments to their British subsidiaries by as much as six months, while remittances from Britain by affiliates of Canadian companies rose substantially. U.S.-owned United Shoe Machinery moved to safeguard its positions by hedging in the forward exchange market against devaluation as well as having its various subsidiaries defer payments to the British affiliate. Canadian-owned Massey-Ferguson did the same thing. During the pressure on the French franc in 1968 the MNCs moved out of francs into Deutschemarks, Swiss francs, or dollars to the tune of $1 billion. One major U.S. company reduced its holdings of francs from $10 million to $100,000 while others borrowed francs and sold them for other currencies. Another sold 100 million francs forward, equal to its total assets in France. The MNC treasurers may have nothing more in mind than to protect their companies from unwarranted losses due to spasmodic monetary oscillations. The sheer weight of these unregulated transactions, however, often determines the movements of the exchanges. What is new is the scale and reach of the MNCs.

TABLE 9   U.S. Banks' Expansion Abroad

	1960	1970	1977
No. of overseas branches	124	532	730
Assets/liabilities of overseas branches (in billion $)	3.5	52.6	174.5 (1976) 260.0 (1979)

4

The MNCs' institution building and international integration was completed with the creation of their own banking system astride the nation-states. Americans led off the invasion of foreign shores in the wake of their MNC bombardment. The figures on overseas subsidiaries in Table 9 tell the story.

A patrician selection of 130 from the 15,000 banks of all sizes and varieties strung across the United States joined the exodus. Of these, possibly two dozen account for the bulk of assets, deposits, and transactions, as well as purchases into established European banking institutions. Before the pendulum began to swing the other way, America's international bankers resembled an exclusive order of nabobs. Between 1970 and 1976 the top ten commercial banks posted 30 percent annual rates of growth in their overseas earnings, from $167 million (17½ percent of total profits) to $825 million (over half of total profits). Two of them, Citibank and Chase Manhattan, relied on overseas earnings for three-quarters of their total profits.

The same dynamic was at work that propelled manufacturing corporations. The extraordinary urge for international banking started in the 1960s. The MNCs needed all sorts of services, and the banks had to follow close on the heels of their corporate customers if they were not to lose the trade to competitors. In the process, international banking was revamped. The MNCs had bred a new generation of corporate treasurers impatient with the leisurely styles and time-frames that bankers were accustomed to. The treasurers had to move swiftly across money markets, and could not have days elapse before their transaction in one market was recorded in central bookkeeping. They demanded streamlined operations, and their demands had to be respected. The bankers also responded to the growth of the Euromarkets. To get in on this profitable, fast-moving business they had to strip for action, and that meant having active branches on the scene.

One thing led to another and by the 1960s there was a boom in multinational branching by U.S. banks. Not only have the numbers and assets of branch banks rocketed, but most of their deposit liabilities are time deposits. In other words, they are up to their necks in the Eurocurrency market business. Like MNC conglomerates they are offering variegated services as consultants; investment counselors; promoters of deals, acquisitions, and mergers; purveyors of credit and monetary information; advisers on international money management. The MNC treasurers have a lot of decisions that have to be made and made rapidly. A basic MNC will now work through a "lead" bank in which it maintains large balances. It will have accounts with several other banks. Each of the firm's subsidiaries will have similar banking relationships. The managers have a choice to use the firm's internally generated funds, to use the parent's domestic capital markets or local capital markets, or loans from the international market. There are also at least half a dozen markets to choose from in deciding where to hold balances and in what kind of accounts.

Clearly this is a field for a few dozen supers only; presidents of ordinary-size local or county banks cannot even aspire to enter this rarefied circle of blue bloods. In 1973, according to the Federal Reserve, nine Wall Street banks made more than a quarter of all commercial and industrial loans and about half of all the money they lent went to global corporations. George Budzeika of the New York Federal Reserve calculated that about 90 percent of the entire indebtedness in U.S. oil and natural gas, two-thirds in machinery and metal products, and three-quarters in chemical and rubber was held by these same nine banks. "It is difficult," concluded Budzeika, "to control large banks whenever demand for credit is heavy. The growth and profits of these banks—their very viability—depend on their ability to satisfy the credit demands of their customers. These banks, therefore, are strongly motivated to find loopholes in control measures and to press credit expansion to a greater extent than may be deemed advisable by monetary authorities."

The banking giants, consequently, for all intents and purposes are a law unto themselves. The international spread of banking combines facilitates the international spread of the producing corporations. The evolutionary drift shifts economic decision-making to substantially uncontrolled private sectors. To that extent, private decisions for business expansion or contraction can and often do cut across and render ineffectual central-bank raising or lowering of interest rates.

This takes us to the inner sanctum of the recently created international monetary market. The Eurodollar market is an off-spring of this country's long-standing balance-of-payments defi-cits and the flooding of international markets with dollar IOUs. Growing amounts of American debts held by foreigners in inter-est-bearing deposits led to the spectacular re-creation in the 1960s of an international market in short-term capital. The flood of money from this source found its way into the so-called Euro-banks, which are simply foreign banks or branches of U.S. banks accepting dollar deposits and making dollar loans. The Euro-banks, centered in London but also spreading out to Zurich, Paris, Luxembourg, Hong Kong, Singapore, and Nassau, were one of the inducements for American banks to set up branches abroad. (Eurocurrencies, including Eurodollars, are short-term time deposits in currencies other than that of the country in which they are held. Eurobonds are debt securities underwritten by an international syndicate and sold in countries with curren-cies other than that in which they are denominated.)

The important thing to keep in mind about this novel devel-opment is that large amounts of international bank funds are being created outside the control and reach of either the U.S. government or the Federal Reserve system. The Euromarket is a private club eluding all national or international controls. When, for example, the Johnson administration tried in 1965 and again in 1968, wisely or unwisely, to restrict capital outflows in order to staunch the deficits in the balance of payments, the program hit a void. The MNCs went through the motions of living up to the regulations while borrowing money from the Eurocurrency market and extending their lines of credit with European banks. The international corporation proved beyond the reach of the nation-state, but not because nature or evolution was bypassing the liliputian cavortings of governments. "These governments," Shonfield remarks in astonishment, "never tried to act together to impose some minimum standards on this monstrously robust and unruly offspring of the international society that had been fathered on them." From time to time proposals to control the Euromarkets are adumbrated by central bankers and government functionaries, but thus far these have come to nothing. Their implementation would require a high degree of cooperation between the powers—which is lacking—and a populist thrust in the countries' internal politics, also lacking. (When the Federal Reserve Board at the end of 1981 authorized banks to set up international facilities in this country, it did not alter basic relationships. The decision, in compliance with American bankers' solicitations, freed them of reserve and insurance requirements in their foreign transactions. They can now do from home offices what they had been doing from their branch offices abroad. This may in time shift the primary location of the by-now $2-trillion Euromarket depository from London to New York. This $2-trillion figure represents ten times more international indebtedness than existed ten years ago.)

Alexandre Lamfalussy, then of the International Monetary Fund, demonstrated that by the late 1960s the ratio of liquid assets to national currency reserves in the leading Western industrial countries had risen disproportionately. In four countries—the United States, Japan, Britain, and France—reserves had fallen to less than 10 percent of the national money supply. This was skating on very thin ice, and the danger was all the greater because domestic circulation was rising and the amounts of mobile funds in private hands had reached astronomical figures. The U.S. Tariff Commission calculated that short-term dollar assets deployed by MNCs and private banks reached $162 billion in 1969, $212 billion in 1970, and $268 billion in 1971, all unbelievable figures, and that the lion's share of this huge packet of liquid capital was held by American MNCs and private banks. The 1971 total was more than twice the value of all international reserves held in central banks at that time, reserves that the central banks rely on to defend their national exchange rates. As the Tariff Commission investigators show, referring to the $268 billion, "A movement of a mere 1 percent of these, or $2.7 billion, in response to exchange rate weakness or strength is quite sufficient to produce a first-class international financial crisis."

As of September 1978 the estimated size of the entire world Eurocurrency market was $795 billion gross and $450 billion net (again, twice the size of reserves that central banks around the world keep to protect their currencies). Since the market came to life in the 1950s, growth has averaged about 25 percent a year.

Eurocurrency bank credits, $66 billion in 1978, were more than twice that by 1981. The Eurobond market, which in a few years dominated the entire foreign bond market, has had an equally spectacular career. New issues, a mere $164 million in 1963, shot up to $3 billion at the end of the decade and $18 billion in 1977. The international foreign bond market handling the traditional type of issues has also come up strongly: only $389 million in 1963, issues were listed at $16 billion in 1977. Not only the MNCs but European government-owned enterprises have become major borrowers in both markets, responsible in some years for a quarter of total Eurobond issues. In 1969–1971, years in which the British government was presumably guarding the national portals by maintaining a full panoply of exchange controls, it was encouraging or directing the heads of public enterprises to turn to the uncontrolled Euromarkets for their financing. Nationalized industries in other countries were also major customers.

James Meigs, a corporation economist, brought the subject down from the statistical heights to the sphere of personalities: "If you want to find all those evil speculators, don't look for them on the Orient Express. They're on the 5:15 to Larchmont." In a similar vein, the *Wall Street Journal* jeered at President Nixon for blaming the recurring monetary crises on "international money speculators." The paper's correspondent wrote from Englewood Cliffs, N.J.:

> Well, it appears a nest of these rascals is in operation right here on the Hudson River Palisades. The Gnomes of New Jersey, it seems, are busily engaged in bollixing up world financial structures with such weapons as Hellman's Mayonnaise, Skippy Peanut Butter, Bosco and Shinola.
>
> This is the headquarters, right out in the open, of CPC International Inc., the 82nd largest industrial company in the US and a major multinational manufacturer and distributor of food and industrial products. CPC (it used to be the Corn Products Refining Co.) has operations in 39 nations; of its 44,000 employees, 25,000 are abroad. And it does business in dozens of currencies. In the course of a year, CPC engages in monetary transactions across national borders amounting to many millions of dollars, marks, francs, yen, pesos, cruzeiros, baht and kip.

Two consequences of the rise of a private international money market should be noted. First, the integrator is no longer the national financial system but international markets that stand outside of, and are uncontrolled by, national authorities. Second, it is increasingly hard, if not impossible, for any national central bank authorities to move counter to international capital market trends. In the words of the Tariff Commission investigators, "even if a country's exchange parity is not in such serious disequilibrium that an exchange rate modification is called for, a perverse movement can force such a change because of an economy's vulnerability to massive highly volatile flows of short-term funds." The violent lurchings of funds across the exchanges in response to small changes in the cost of loans in different countries, or in anticipation of changes in currency parities, demonstrate that the financial and industrial mastodons have brought not stability, but unruliness, to the international economic scene.

5

Hymer and Rowthorn, in an essay of a dozen years ago, anticipated that extensive European mergers would result in heavy investment overseas, first outside the United States, then in the United States itself. They predicted intensified activities as both U.S. and foreign corporations battled to capture worldwide market positions in an effort to protect themselves from each other's challenges: "In the coming competition between European and U.S. corporations, the markets of the third world will be an important battleground, because the stakes will be not only the limited markets of Africa, Latin America, and Asia, but oligopoly equilibrium in the developed world itself." Fred Bergsten, writing a few years later when growing rivalry was evident, was concerned that the international investment fury "could replicate to an unfortunate degree the evolution of international trade policy in the interwar period."

With the 1970s a sizable countermovement was unmistakeably under way: European and Japanese capital was entering the United States in rising annual consignments. When the media became aware of what was going on, the public was deluged with the mixture of news accounts and dire forecasts reminiscent of the uneasiness exhibited by the European press during the several American invasions. What did it all add up to when we read that the Japanese were taking over the Hawaiian tourist industry, that British Petroleum had a majority interest in Prudhoe Bay Alaskan oil reserves and had won control of Sohio, that Royal Dutch Shell had absorbed multi-billion-dollar Beldridge Oil, that the French state-owned Elf-Aquitaine oil combine was the new owner of Texasgulf, Inc.? Should housewives have grown concerned when they learned that an old reliable like A&P supermarkets was now run by German interests or that the world-famous cosmetics dispensary Helena Rubenstein was in the grip of a Japanese soap manufacturer? Was it socially significant that American youths could now gorge themselves on Keebler cookies, Stouffer pastries, Nestlé's chocolates, Good Humor and Baskin-Robbins ice cream, and relieve themselves with Alka-Seltzer, at every step of the way adding to the sales totals of foreign multinationals? Should we have blanched when we read that the Deutsche Bank had opened business offices in New York City; announced plans to start a large finance company in alliance with Fiat, the Italian auto maker; spent over $100 million to purchase Pennzoil Plaza and Shell Towers in Houston; and offered half a billion dollars for one tower of New York's World Trade Center?

Private foreign assets—including all bank deposits but less direct investments—had risen to $240 billion at the end of 1980, a spectacular increase of more than twice that of five years before. More than two-thirds of the world's 500 MNCs outside the United States now have subsidiaries here. Foreigners hold more than a quarter of all American government securities, and 5 percent of Wall Street's 1⅓ trillion-dollar capitalization. The book value of their direct investments has risen from $28 billion five years ago to $66 billion, and their affiliates spent about a third of all new outlays on plant and equipment in this country. Since their investments are concentrated in specific industries, foreign-owned companies rank among the three or four largest in such fields as agricultural chemicals, building and construction supplies, phonograph records. Outside multinationals have also penetrated substantially into chemicals, pharmaceuticals, electronic equipment, retail trade, real estate. By now Agfa Gevaert (photo supplies), Massey-Ferguson (farm tractors), Michelin and Dunlop (tires), Saint-Gobain (building materials), Bayer, Hoechst, Ciba-Geigy, Hoffman La Roche, and Sandoz (pharmaceuticals), Sony, Panasonic, and Hitachi (televisions and tape recorders), Electrolux (vacuum cleaners), and Nestlé (candy and food products) have become household names alongside the automotive spectaculars, Volkswagen, Toyota, and Honda.

It is in banking, however, that the foreign invasion has cut deepest and is symptomatically most telling. The large European banks, it will be recalled, were bulging with dollars in the 1960s. Many treasurers, on the watch for suitable outlets, established footholds in the lucrative American market. When the European counterinvasion started in the early 1970s they had to move more aggressively for the same reason that impelled American banks to go abroad a decade earlier: to furnish loans and services to their migrating multinationals lest the business be snatched from them by enterprising locals. Multiplying at the rate of 30 percent annually from 1972 on, 122 foreign banks were doing business at the end of 1978, working out of some 300 branch outlets, commanding assets of $116 billion, and controlling 6 percent of all commercial banking. They were the fastest growing segment of the banking industry.

Their secret weapon was price cutting, relying on somewhat smaller returns than the 15–20 percent profits that American bankers were accustomed to. The foreigners' progress rose spectacularly in 1979–1980 when four huge takeovers by British interests were approved by government authorities. Hong Kong and Shanghai Banking acquired a 51 percent share of Marine Midland with assets in excess of $12 billion. National Westminster bought outright the National Bank of America with assets in excess of $4 billion. Standard Chartered swallowed Los Angeles's Union Bancorp. This was followed by the largest bank transaction of all, costing London's Midland Bank $820 million for a 57 percent share of the San Francisco–based Crocker National Corporation, the fourteenth largest bank in the country. By the first quarter of 1981 foreign-controlled houses held 12 percent of commercial bank assets and issued 19 percent of all business loans, which in the two foremost banking centers, New York and California, ran to 40 percent and 35 percent.

This is a sizable penetration, and naturally U.S. bankers were deeply resentful that foreigners were doing here what Americans had done abroad a decade earlier. The result was that Congress passed the International Banking Act in 1978 which, it was claimed, would equalize competitive positions between foreign and domestic banks. The law gave the Federal Reserve the authority to impose standard reserve requirements for both national and state branches of foreign banks that have $1 billion or more in worldwide assets. Whatever the act's provisions may mean for the future, they have not affected the pace of foreign branch lending thus far; neither did they temper the zeal of the comptroller of the currency for approving major foreign acquisitions in the next two years. One of the act's largely overlooked terms may prove of greater importance for banking legalities: state governments were elbowed aside to give the Federal Reserve the principal authority over foreign banking operations.

The outcry against foreigners' buying up American banks was only part of the general hubbub. The line on the fever chart rose perceptibly during the oil crisis. There was talk that oil-exporting countries might use their enormous profits to seize control of important sections of American industry, and that once ensconced in positions of power they would manipulate economic and political levers for their own national purposes. Media excitations led to some nationalist repercussions. There was the incident of a prominent Saudi Arabian businessman forced to relinquish control of the First National Bank of San Jose because the stockholders and customers were up in arms. In a second incident another Saudi investor, after securing a controlling interest in Detroit's Bank of the Commonwealth, tried to buy into the Community National Bank of nearby Pontiac. He was pressing his luck. The newspaper accounts of the purported transaction were fiercely antagonistic. He had to break off negotiations when union pension fund officers decided not to make their fund available, thus removing a part of the capital needed for the tender offer.

However, such incidents were isolated ones and the media Paul Reveres soon turned to other matters. There was no mystery why high-tension journalism could not be sustained and why laws enacted were less than stringent, more concerned with disclosing data than interfering with activity. American companies are vulnerable in the highest degree to retaliatory attacks. If they keep the foreigners out, foreigners can keep Americans out. Moreover whatever wounds individual businessmen might be nursing, the danger of foreign control was remote—entirely imaginary as a matter of fact.

Alarmist accounts that Arab princes or Brazilian nabobs were buying up securities to subvert Washington's global strategy are strictly the stuff of spy films. Arab governments have lent some credence to the melodramatic view of money matters with misguided attempts to combine business with anti-Israel politics.

By and large, however, and even in the case of wheeler-dealers from the Near East, investors are concerned with two things: high returns, and safety of their funds. The hard-bitten managers of the multinational companies are preoccupied with the same two things, and in addition they have to safeguard their international market positions. These strictly business interests may intertwine at times with prevailing political questions. When they do, foreigners talk the same language as Americans—aside from the foreigners' opposition to discriminatory regulations against themselves In short, profits, not plots, are on the newcomers' minds.

The United States is the world's largest and richest unitary market. It is still the capitalist paradise. Profit opportunities are many and better shielded than elsewhere by both legal fiat and social folkways. Rich investors are worried these days about leftward tendencies in Europe, fearful that the world has become a hotbed of unrest. Against a background of danger and violence the United States represents an oasis of stability and safety. As a leading German investor put it, "the last capitalist will die in the United States." There was concern in banking circles that funds would stop coming in from oil-producing countries after President Carter froze Iranian assets at the end of 1979. Nothing of the sort happened. A special report issued by Chase Bank's World Information Corporation a year later explained that Arab oil scions were constrained by market realities to place a large proportion of their export capital in this country. In fact the prediction was made that the more turmoil in the world, the larger will be the flow of Arab funds to this country.

There is something else. Like the Europeans twenty years earlier, Americans welcome the infusion of fresh capital and technology. City and state officials have been acting like purchasing agents of banana republics in offering extravagant inducements to lure foreign companies to their territories. The governors of Pennsylvania and Ohio were not above entering the fray to decide in which state Volkswagen would locate its American assembly plant. Pennsylvania's victory in the contest did not come cheaply. Before Volkswagen's executives would set up shop in New Stanton, they were weighed down, like Oriental potentates, with lavish gifts. These included a $40-million state loan, interest payments set at a nominal 1¾ percent for twenty years, a $30-million public bond issue to build a rail spur to the

plant, another $10 million for workers' training and plant reno-
vation, and a five-year moratorium on local property taxes—all
told, a regal offering estimated to have a monetary value of close
to $100 million. The Pennsylvania transaction set a record at the
time (1976) for welfare munificence, but it was not unique. Like
the campaigns of southern Chambers of Commerce early in the
century to attract New England textile manufacturers, there was
a cutthroat competition to win the favor of investors from
abroad.

The countermovement into the United States, substantial in
numbers and still in progress, is for all that weaker than has been
America's outward thrust. Portfolio investments in private and
government securities are estimated at a third of American comparable investments abroad. American banking affiliates around
the world have more than twice the assets of foreign bank subsidiaries in this country. In direct investments—the decisive
proposition—the book value of American-controlled multinational enterprises abroad is more than three times greater than
that of the foreign counterparts here. According to recent estimates, foreign-controlled companies hold 2–3 percent of total
American corporate assets and contribute approximately 3 percent to our gross national product.

Comparative figures notwithstanding—and it should be
kept in mind that total foreigners' investments and holdings in
countries other than their own are larger than those in the
United States alone—does the foreign presence in America
mean that the oligopolistic equilibrium has been restored or is
on the way to restoration? One has to come to an agreement
first on what an oligopolistic equilibrium means quantitatively.
This is a conundrum akin to past disputes among political scientists over the true dimensions of the European balance of
power, whether the spirited activities of country X or country Y
represented an attempt to restore an impaired balance or to
upset the existing true balance. Rather than venturing into me-
taphysical realms we should look at what is happening after the
invasions and counterinvasions.

Writing on the same subject as Hymer and Rowthorn, and at
the same time, Vernon surmised that European attempts to reestablish an "oligopoly of equilibrium" would work out pacifi-
cally, "approximating the kind of unspoken half-truce that is
characteristic" in national markets. More recently he reversed

himself: "In spite of the strenuous and unremitting efforts of leading multinational firms in many lines to develop some measure of stability and security among themselves, there is very little evidence that they have succeeded. On the contrary, in most lines the evidence suggests that the prospects for stability in the market are somewhat less secure than they were, say, a decade or two ago."

This is an understatement. The economic story of the past decade has been one of rising international strife, the more menacing because it is part of an attempt to unload on others the deleterious effects of shrinking markets and unemployment. It has been the story of the abandonment of fixed exchange rates, of currency and interest-rate manipulations, of the use of the dollar for national advantage, of the mobilization of Europe behind its own leading currency to better square off against the Americans, and of the jousting among the Europeans, in turn, for the vantage ground. Monetary struggles are not encapsulated in their own enigmatic spheres. They signal economic struggles for favored positions. The anarchy of the money markets is a monetary expression of the anarchic scramble across the borders for each other's customers. As we shall see, the multinationals have been prime disorganizers of the home economy. How could they be expected to organize the international economy rationally?

6. Politics and Economics

When we shear away old encrusted ways of making value judgments, are we not up against an elemental proposition that economics has forged ahead of politics? There are those who believe that both the rise of the multinationals and of the Eurocurrency market demonstrate that industry and finance have outgrown the national procrustean bed, that progress in communications and transportation has created an interdependence that makes national boundaries obsolete. They insist that the international institutions that businessmen have been constructing are simply Darwinian responses to changed environmental needs. Sidney Rolfe, a business analyst, argues that the true power of the multinational corporation resides in the fact that it is the first major institution to understand and act on the reality that "history is not of the essence here, evolution is"; that "what the world faces is *le défi international* rather than *le défi Américain.*" This thought has been expanded by business theorists and boosters to include an ongoing struggle between multinationals and nation-states.

Peter Drucker, high priest of management organization, explains that the multinational, a necessary response "to the emergence of a genuine world economy," is "fundamentally autonomous, has its own dynamics, its own demand patterns, its own institutions. . . . The territorial political unit and the economic unit are no longer congruent. This understandably appears as a threat to national governments." John Fayerweather, economics professor at New York University, develops the same theme of an

128

inherent conflict between the multinational firm and the nation-state. He is sanguine, however, that victory lies with the forces of light, "this new global institution to serve the welfare of people of all nations." The reason he is sanguine is that the MNC represents "progress," and "progress" has won out over the centuries against those who would impede its triumphal march. He offers the illustration of the Catholic church in the Middle Ages, whose emotional hold on peoples "through religious dogma" was no less forceful than that being exerted by nationalism. But despite all, "new ideas did take root, and ultimately the entirely new system of knowledge and education took over throughout Europe."

Christopher Tugendhat, a British financial writer, later a Member of Parliament, now part of the EEC directorate, made the same analogy, although for him it is the companies that represent the past Catholic church and the kings who felt their national sovereignties endangered by its international organization. Eventually the conflict was resolved, he explains, when some countries broke with Rome while others negotiated treaties with the pope. That is what he favors: the countries have to strike a bargain for "a new industrial concordat between themselves and the companies." Courtney Brown, then dean of the Columbia Graduate School of Business, agrees that the multinational is the harbinger of a new world order. Since the "conventional political nostrums" have proved "insufficiently creative, and in many cases, misdirected," people all over the world "are awakening to the realization that they must look to the . . . practical men of affairs." Another contributor to Brown's symposium, Emile Benoit, then a professor at Columbia University, in a more sophisticated vein also holds that the tension between the world of petty, quarreling national groups, and the other world "intrinsically linked for good or ill by modern technology—is the central drama of our era," and that the two cannot coexist for long.

If we turn to Brown's men-of-affairs directly we find them adumbrating the same themes put forward by academics and business writers, in papers and speeches probably drafted in many cases by the same academics and business writers. The major proposition enunciated by all respondents is the inadequacy of the present nation-state. William Spencer, president of the First National City Corporation, says, "The political boundaries of the nation-states are too narrow and constricted to define the scope and sweep of modern business." The stricture is repeated by others: "badly adapted to our complex world" (George Ball, chairman of Lehman Brothers International); "we are being pushed [to a world economy] by the imperatives of our own technology" (John Powers, president of Pfizer). From this, others move rhetorically to an inevitable struggle between the antiquated nation-minded state and the forward-looking internationally oriented corporation. Exclaims Drucker, "We need to defang the nationalist monster." Jacques Maisonrouge, head of IBM's Europe division, offers Brown's invidious comparison between the "fragmented political world and its ancient quarrels and rivalries" and international business dispassionately and constructively "building new complex economic structures linking and crisscrossing national economics." Which leads some to the next audacious step: in the words of A. W. Clausen, then president of Bank of America, "an international corporation that has shed all national identity"; or Ball's "ultimate solution," the "supranational corporation which will not owe its charter to any nation-state and which will be equally resident—and equally nonresident—in any country in which it operates."

This astonishing "business internationalism" very likely represents a none-too-subtle hint to government bureaucrats not to preoccupy themselves too much with regulating the corporate leviathans lest the latter shift their allegiance elsewhere. It is an empty threat, if threat it be; an unserious ideology, if ideology it can be called, when corporate officials swear at government bureaucracy with one breath and call for fat handouts from the public treasury in the next breath. For purposes of discussion, however, let us treat the remarks made on this score as a thesis earnestly propounded and conscientiously thought through. On the face of it it is apparent that this particular attack on the nation-state lacks historical depth. The nation-state is the instrumentality which over half the globe fuses diverse ethnic groups, religious communities, tribes, and the like, into cohesive entities that will unitedly work to create a viable economy. Nationalism in these parts is still the battle cry that it was in Europe in 1848.

Even in the Western world, where overripe nationalism led to two devastating world wars, nations have been unable to cut the Gordian knot of parochial sovereignties and rivalries. The destruction of the Greek city-states, debilitated by fratricidal conflicts and forcibly united by an empire builder; the unification of feudal fiefdoms into national units made possible by bourgeois

infiltration and monarchical coercion—these often-cited analo-
gies from the past have proven to be without application to present-day predicaments. Neither peoples nor governments have
proven capable of transcending the boundaries of national language, laws, customs, and historical conditioning, the catas-
trophes of the past three-quarters of a century notwithstanding.
This does not rule out the possibility that the political map may
be redrawn in the future in a new historical thrust powered by a
unique combination of old elements. But for the period ahead we
have to reckon with the existing system of nation-states as they
have evolved from the more distant past or after two world wars.

The other assertion that will not withstand critical scrutiny
is that because advanced nation-states have many anachronistic
traits, and because multinational corporations are engaged in international business and have established business connections
crisscrossing the continents, they are therefore carriers of a
higher social order. Regardless of their pretensions, or executives' effusions at businessmen's banquets, the MNCs are not
international companies but national companies doing business
internationally. That is not the same thing. Stephen Hymer had it
right in his two-decades-old doctoral dissertation which he cor-
rectly titled "The International Operations of National Firms: A
Study of Direct Foreign Investment." Changing their names from
American Brake Shoe to Abex, United States Rubber to Uniroyal,
Standard Oil of New Jersey to Exxon, may help the MNCs to
create a more international image, but it does not alter their
national underpinning.

Kenneth Simmonds, in his essay "Multinational? Well, Not
Quite," explains that the American firm tries hard for obvious
reasons to get the brightest and the best foreigners to manage its
overseas enterprises. The cost of keeping Americans abroad is
very high, and the MNC needs a person or a group of persons
who know the native language, culture, customs, etc.: "Once it
gets this talent the American firm spares no effort in grooming it.
But adequate grooming for management of a subsidiary is a different thing from preparation for headquarters management. Subsidiary top management is normally a castrated top management
with the truly entrepreneurial function removed." In a study of
the 150 largest U.S. industrial corporations in which one-fifth of
total employment is foreign, only 1.6 percent of top management
could by any stretch of the imagination be called foreign. For 71

corporations with especially heavy foreign activity, and where foreign employment jumps to a third, the figure of foreigners in top management stayed at 1.6 percent. Simmonds quotes an ex-manager from an article that appeared in the British *Sunday Times*: "I know of no British senior Ford executive who any longer believes that there is a real future for a Briton in Ford."

When *Business Week* conducted an inquiry into why able young Europeans were leaving U.S.-owned subsidiaries to work for locally owned companies, the magazine reporter was told by a Belgian that Europeans are subject to a form of discrimination he described as "White Negroism." Identical criticisms have been leveled at multinational corporations of other national origins. Howard V. Perlmutter explains "tokenism" and "window dressing" by the fact that people in authority are at the cultural level where the "multinational view [is] a screen for ethnocentrism. Foreign affiliate managers must, in order to succeed, take on the traits and behavior of the ruling nationality. In short, in a U.S.-owned firm, the foreigner must 'Americanize'—not only in attitude but in dress and speech—in order to be accepted." In the few instances where nationals of two countries make up the ownership as at Shell, Unilever, or Nestlé, the nationality principle still governs by apportioning the directorships between the two groups.

The national composition of MNC top managing staffs, taken alone, explodes the pretension that the international company in name is an international company in fact. Actually the presence of a number of carefully sifted, American MNC-oriented foreign nationals—and the policy is to permit a few more of them to step into the inner sanctum—does not negate the national character of the enterprise any more than the employment of a former mine union official in the top management of a coal company demonstrates that firm's labor-relations liberality. The former unionist has been satisfactorily socialized, as we can be sure foreign nationals are when they are accepted into the board rooms. Were the MNC to break away from its national moorings, it would be lost in limbo.

It would appear that business executives' lofty rejection of the nation-state is of the same genre as traditional business cant excoriating "government bureaucracy" and "government spending." This has not interfered with corporation bureaucrats' working hand in glove with government bureaucrats, or with the free movement of individuals from one bureaucracy to the other. The Founding Fathers bequeathed a tradition that government has to be kept at bay; their checks-and-balances were designed not only to prevent the mob from taking over, but to prevent an official-dom from imposing a tyranny. The business creed that govern-ment is inherently evil is a derivation from this tradition. It is put to use too inconsistently, arbitrarily, and selectively, how-ever, to rate as even an elitist ideology.

2

The American multinational is an institution chartered under American laws. It needs the tax bounties, the protection, the sustenance, of the country's police powers and diplomatic "presence." Without these it would be as helpless as a homeless waif. It could not function for a day, any more than could the national corporation before it was strong enough for the leap overseas. Talk of chartering the MNC by an international organ-ization like the United Nations or the OECD, or locating on an island of its own, belongs to the realm of the Freudian uncon-scious, not of the reality principle. There can be no true interna-tional corporation—even were the present-day MNCs capable of becoming such—until there is an international sovereign or quasi-sovereign authority under which they can function.

Nor is the proferred analogy between the multinational of today and the early proponents of science and knowledge an apt one. The businessmen who staff and direct the multinational corporations are not carriers of a new culture, much less of a new world order, any more than the transition from William C. Dur-ant to Alfred P. Sloan was on a par with the transition from Thomas Aquinas to John Locke. As one goes through the materi-als laying out the new business ideology, what is striking is its parochialism. This is not the ideology of or on behalf of a new society. It is the ideology of a privileged class explaining that it is doing good, that its behavior is praiseworthy, that its role is socially beneficial. The essence of the position is that there is a new good capitalism that is a break from the old bad capitalism, that corporate managements are now mindful not only of their responsibilities to earn profits but also of their responsibilities to the broad public for ethical and constructive behavior.

It is not lack of sincerity or good intentions on the part of business leaders that makes declarations of this nature empty of content but the nature of the entire environment in which the business corporation works and has to work. The corporation is not set up for social service pursuits. On the contrary its personnel have been painstakingly selected for its single-minded pursuit of marketplace success. The company's rating on the stock exchanges would plummet, its abilities to raise finances for expansionary or modernizing projects would wither, it could not survive in today's gladiatorial arena were it seriously to undertake to shoulder broad social responsibilities. That is not how the organism is structured; we might as well ask the lion to warble like a thrush. It is one thing for a corporate official to be assigned to donate modest sums (and take tax breaks on them) to hospitals, community charities, or for the support of a symphony orchestra or repertory theater. But managers can change the corporation's essential motivations, strategies, behavior, or role only when the society itself has changed essential social arrangements and its system of rewards. Until and unless that happens one can more readily expect a change in rhetoric than in conduct. As Edward Mason, past president of the American Economic Association, saw it, the motivations of corporate managers are materially no different under the gospel of social responsibility than under the gospel of growth rates and profit maximization. He wrote, "Despite such phrases as the 'permanent revolution,' the 'managerial revolution,' the 'capitalist revolution,' and the 'new era,' some doubt persists that the contemporary economy is as different as all that from the American economy of 1900. It has been pointed out that the share of industrial assets, employment, and value accounted for by the largest firms today is about the same as their share fifty years ago. . . . Moreover, a look at certain broad indexes of economic behavior does not reveal any startling or revolutionary break in long-term trends."

The authenticity of the challenging message of the Balls and Clausens is belied by the sociology of the multinational corporation, and it is belied by the sociology of the business class as well. None of the lyricists of the multinational corporation as international evangelist made the pretense of representing managers as zealots for the more spacious society. Actually one could scour the earth from end to end without discovering less likely candidates for the roles of structural reformers. The very idea of country-club denizens and their wives demonstrating with banners against the confinements of the nation-state would be a subject for cocktail-hour hilarity. By a Darwinian selection for their natural propensities, and by meticulous training, corporation officials from the topmost to the lowest levels are conformists and conservatives. All investigators of this subclass are agreed on that broad characterization. The one well-known contrary opinion was that of James Burnham, who several decades ago described the managers as a band of Nietzchean achievers intent on imposing their own distinct property forms on society; but it is generally recognized that his was a work of imagination, not of description.

The conditioning of the suborder starts right in the classroom. The university business school exudes the atmosphere of the large corporation, shares its assumptions, extolls its value judgments. As is common knowledge, the corporate organization in which the young neophyte aspires to find a place is not a democracy or a near-democracy. In its internal arrangement it resembles an unlimited monarchy. The top manager is the autocrat. He may be operating under the general policy direction of a select board of oligarchs and court functionaries, which in some cases he controls (in conjunction with his allies). Decisions are made at the top and issued to the managers in the echelons below in the form of decrees to be carried out, not dissertations to be discussed. The disposition of the managerial force, as in the military, is rigidly hierarchical. This is also the principle employed to mark off gradations of authority, and the track for advancement.

Upon graduation the student does not have to brace himself for a leap into this forbidding environment; as William H. Whyte wrote, he simply transfers. The technical training and indoctrination in the "management view" is continued in special company-organized centers. When they have completed their courses, according to the editors of *Fortune*, "the students are ready to be what the corporation wants them to be." No pejorative inference should be drawn from these young people's pliability. In the main they fall in with the corporations' goals and procedures as a matter of course without violating their consciences. They had been socialized to think along these lines when they opted to enroll in the business schools. If by chance a stray heretic manages to move past the fine-meshed portals, one of three things will happen quickly: (1) he will get out; (2) he will be told to leave; (3) he will swallow his pride and decide to play the game in accordance with the rules because he wants to make a place for himself in the corporate world.

What the corporation recruiters now seek is a smooth, adaptable person; they avoid the willful, "inner-directed" individual who will want to make waves and probably disturb the organization's even routine. "We used to look primarily for brilliance," said one president. "Now that much-abused word 'character' has become very important. We don't care if you're Phi Beta Kappa or a Tau Beta Phi. We want a well-rounded person who can handle well-rounded people." In the light of these requirements it is hardly surprising that in their analysis of the selection and makeup of corporate functionaries, Clark Kerr and his associates came to the conclusion that "members of the managerial class are prone to become conformists rather than leaders in the larger affairs of society."

Given the enlargement of the corporation, the reduction of secondary managers' responsibilities to routine tasks, and the hierarchical organization, the corporation has become no less (and possibly more) bureaucratized than government (William Miller took note of this development years ago). And the two characteristic traits of bureaucracy that concern us here are conformity and political conservatism. On the first, Chester Barnard, formerly president of the New Jersey Telephone Company, wrote in what is considered a classic in business managership, *The Functions of the Executive*, that " 'Learning the organization ropes' in most organizations is chiefly learning who's who, what's what, why's why, of its informal society"—in other words, the operations of its "invisible government." Yet the procedures, for all their value, "lead to excessive compatibility or harmony . . . resulting in 'single track minds' and excessively crystalized attitudes; and in the destruction of personal responsibility." That is one aspect of it. The other is that the bureaucracy, viewed as a social caste, insists on accommodation and orthodoxy, idealizes orderly routine and administrative tidiness, makes a fetish of loyalty to superiors and moving through prescribed channels. When a group of General Electric trainees was asked what they would do if a brilliant person like Steinmetz were to apply to them for a job, they expressed grave doubts that he could fit it. "I don't think we would put up with a fellow like that now," one said.

Bureaucracy breeds conformism because safety and advancement for the individual lie in adapting one's activities to the rhythm of the machine; danger, and at the ultimate, self-destruction, await those who would interfere with the established way of doing things. From the ranks of the select who have what it takes to fit in, and their further winnowing in the scramble for place and status, emerges a dedicated, disciplined, reasonably competent directorate and line staff. In its totality what has been crafted is a slickly functioning apparatus, and in the case of important corporations, an awe-inspiring one in terms of its jobholders' ability to manage the company's multifarious activities. But, as recent events at General Motors and Ford demonstrated, at the expense of creativity and foresight. The business functionary has become habituated to a life of insular calculation. Like dealers in the futures market, it is a calling that makes its practitioners too narrowly instrumentalist. Robert Merton described it this way: "The bureaucrat's official life is planned for him in terms of a graded career, through the organizational devices of promotion by seniority, pensions, incremental salaries, etc., all of which are designed to provide incentives for disciplined action and conformity to the official regulations. The official is tacitly expected to and largely does adapt his thoughts, feelings, and actions to the prospect of his career. But these very devices which increase the probability of conformance also lead to an over-concern with strict adherence to regulations which induces timidity, conservatism, and technicism."

That is one reason why senior members of law firms and banking houses are prominent as would-be elder statesmen of the business community. Because of their need to analyze the positions of a number of their clients' firms, and to devise a variety of services to satisfy their requirements, they can extend their vision to encompass a broader terrain of relationships and problems. They are accustomed to giving advice when political variables, legal determinants, and power calculations have to be weighed in making critical decisions. Not having to invest their energies and time in only one firm, some leaders in these professions can overcome the parochialisms associated with exclusively managerial pursuits. Thomas Lamont of the house of J. P. Morgan won wide acceptance as a model statesman of this type several generations ago. Henry Stimson, James Forrestal, John McCloy, Averell Harriman, and Robert Lovett, in or out of government, to one or another extent filled similar roles in the war years. Today, Ball, Clausen, and Felix Rohatyn (of the house of Lazard Frères) aspire to assume the mantle. Whatever their individual talents or acuteness of vision, these business statesmen are too embedded in business power structures to be able to move very far from accepted doctrines. Where they intimate a vaguely drawn alternative schema, it is accepted by their colleagues like an enjoyable, spirited Sunday sermon which can safely be forgotten on going to work Monday morning. The business statesmen are not heralds of a new era; they are accredited establishment "devil's advocates."

The politics of the business bureaucracy, particularly in the sizable corporations, tends to conservatism; sometimes deep-dyed reactionism. The record of the main contingents of the upper-tier business community in obstructing, resisting, denigrating the Welfare State is too well known to require documentation. Their subsequent grudging toleration of it was tactical, not fundamental. They remained the financial mainstays of the conservative parties both here and abroad. When political winds veered and the opportunity arose for the conservatives to stage a comeback, they gleefully moved to turn the clock back to the 1920s under their newfound spokesmen, Ronald Reagan in this country, Margaret Thatcher in England. Political conservatism or reactionism is the natural expression of a wealthy, property-owning class in a one-vote-to-one-citizen parliamentary society which is segmented because of extensive economic inequalities. To bridge the gap between political democracy and economic oligarchy an unceasing ideological onslaught is unavoidable. The beneficiaries of the unequal arrangements are instructed with good reason never to surrender any forward ideological position lest the system be subverted from within. Hence their representation of multinational corporations as revolutionary artificers is not one of their more credible creations.

The political characterization of the business elite should not be taken to mean that it is a seamless entity mobilized unitedly on behalf of or in opposition to every proposition of importance that comes to its attention. During Roosevelt's first administration the Harrimans, Kennedys, Baruchs, Strauses, and Astors supported the New Deal because they were convinced that the system would be safeguarded by championing indicated reforms and eliminating blatant abuses, that it was positively dangerous to remain inert and immovable and, like King Canutes, ordering the onrushing waves to halt. What is involved is a difference of approach among rulers that has persisted throughout contemporary history.

Although Democrats remain a decided minority in upper industrial and banking circles, and the southern breed of the order is more reactionary than are many Republican stalwarts, the party is the beneficiary of financial and moral backing from various businessmen in all sorts of fields of endeavor. Whatever the precise character of their liberalism, they avow their adherence to the cause, and help to sustain the liberal side of the two-party system. It is one of the historic achievements of the parliamentary polity that an administration is differentiated from the state, and that administrations can be changed without calling into question existing property rights and economic modalities. However, through periods of populism as well as stand-pat-ism, the North Star of the predominant business elite points to undiluted conservatism.

3

The managerial caste yearns for stability, regularity, social predictability, time-honored traditions; yet the effects of its economic activities, like the activities of the bourgeoisie since the start of commercialism, are anything but conservative. The MNCs, prime movers in a drama whose final act remains to be written, have already twisted the country's economy, making it harder for federal and state governments to administer the Welfare State. One important effect of corporate international organization has been to aggravate the American turn from manufacturing to service industries. The secular tendency is an old story. Up until 1920 the shift to services was the counterpart of the migration from agriculture to industry and the growth of cities. The bulge in services came primarily from the construction of great transportation networks, building up of residential areas, utilities, distributive facilities. After 1920 industrial employment was still rising absolutely but service employment was growing faster.

A more pronounced shift came after the Second World War. By 1947 twenty-six million people were connected with goods production and twenty-five million were in secondary service positions, including transportation, communications, and public utilities, as well as government. The divergence from the earlier part of the century was now more pronounced. For the next two decades service employment doubled while goods-producing employment went up 10 percent. The gap partially closed in the 1970s, but service-producing divisions are still rising more rapidly than primary divisions. At the end of the 1970s less than a third of the workforce was engaged in manufacturing, mining, construction, and farming, and over two-thirds of the workforce was in transportation and utilities, trade, real estate and insurance, professional occupations, and government.

The threefold spurt in government employment in thirty years was the result of the commitment to welfarism and militarism. The juxtaposition is not a novel one. Since the time of Bismarck and Lloyd George the two have often been yoked. The term "welfarism," as used here, refers to more than the system of government props and minimum standards—unemployment insurance payments, handouts to the indigent, medical care and pensions for the elderly, etc.—that most people identify with the Welfare State. In its wider application the term covers the vast array of government obligations, social services, licensing and regulatory procedures, ranging from free public school education and subventions to private universities to recognition of labor unions and outlawing race discrimination. As is recognized, staffing the required offices, bureaus, departments, commissions, and institutes calls for a large workforce directed by administrators and lawyers who are highly paid, all of which necessitates the outlay of large amounts of tax money.

Left to their own devices in the postwar decades, many agencies proliferated endlessly in accordance with the law of bureaucracy. Funds were inevitably squandered by making municipal political organizations, which operate on feudal principles of patronage and mutual allegiances, the dispensing authorities. As in the case of the military, waste is built into these structures. (Periodic disinterested efforts to prune away dead limbs and to clean out pestholes can only be welcomed in the interests of keeping welfarism functional. It is another matter when opponents wield the axe to wreck social services under the guise of renovating them.) The welfarist bureaucracy may administer the projects in its care efficiently or inefficiently. The regional bureaucracies may be reasonably honest or thoroughly graft-ridden. Nevertheless without these services, whether minimally or effectively projected, the modern industrial state, which already functions badly, would start to disintegrate, and not just at the edges.

The other major claimant to the public treasury, and one responsible for the bloated government apparatus, is the military. This requires no special elucidation at this point. It suffices to mention in passing that when a country undertakes to build a world imperium it must build a large military establishment to safeguard it—and that that will further tilt employment statistics to the service sectors. The essence of the matter is that the advanced industrial, mass society has developed distinct, organic styles and needs, making it a voracious consumer of services. The growing market for restaurants, hotels, recreation and entertainment emporiums was a coefficient of postwar affluence and mass consumption. In response to related stimuli, ever-larger numbers of workers went on the payrolls of educational institutions, hospitals, health care centers, and public relations counseling offices.

This organic evolution of late capitalism was given a strong push by the multinationals. They have created and nurtured a full-blown economic establishment outside the territorial boundaries of the United States that employs a fifth the number of workers in manufacturing at home. We do not know everything that is going on, but we have sufficient pertinent data. We know that manufacturing exports have been overtaken by manufacturing production in American-controlled foreign subsidiaries whose sales abroad are at least twice greater than these exports from home. Components and parts for numerous industries are imported from American-controlled plants, and these cheaper imports have choked off production of these items at home as surely as English textiles at one time wiped out the maufacture of native cottons in entire provinces of India. The effect has been like a hammer blow propelling the American economy toward secondary, in some cases parasitical, pursuits. Daniel Bell has written that the United States is becoming a rentier society. Hopefully, this is not to be the final point of rest, for were it so, this would be a decaying society.

The massive migration is creating big problems for this nation-state. Government has been stripped of powers over certain banking operations and capital distributions. Government decisions calling for deficit financing can be peremptorily abridged or reversed by MNC treasurers' votes of "no confidence." These have already been discussed. An accompanying torment is a relatively declining tax base. This can occur in hidden form when a formally rising gross national product is overloaded with unproductive, non-use-value items like military hardware, junk items like public relations extravaganzas, or the waste of human labor and resources for synthetic would-be services. The government can tax such businesses and the individuals drawing salaries and wages from them, but in the totality of economic enterprise these become charges on the costs of real production goods, consumer goods, and services.

As with the turn to services, data on the shrinking tax base has to be examined for its long-term implications. The share of corporation taxes in federal revenue collection declined from 23 percent in 1965 to about 14 percent ten years later. This is a major decline even though absolute money receipts rose by half. How much of this is on profits repatriated from abroad? An American-owned capital plant in foreign countries, with a book value in 1980 of $216 billion, encompassing a workforce of four to five million in manufacturing, generating annual outputs in excess of half a trillion dollars, pays the lion's share of its taxes to host countries, not to the home country. In a 1975 study of the question, Hufbauer and Nunns, two experts from the Treasury Department, showed that in 1972 (a typical year) the MNCs paid approximately $1.2 billion in taxes on foreign income into the U.S. Treasury and $12.5 billion to foreign tax collectors. Because the U.S. "has principally exported capital and technology and imported labor," it collects far less in taxes on international income than do foreign governments. "In a sense the United States has exported a high-yield tax base and imported a low-yield tax base." The disparity on what the government collects on income at home and on international income is accentuated because further exclusions and allowances are permitted to encourage certain activities abroad. Thus in these calculations tax preferences account for an estimated additional $1.2 billion in uncollected tax revenues.

These are conservative figures. Prof. Peggy Musgrave's estimates are higher. According to her calculations, if taxes and undistributed earnings of American-based companies abroad were treated in the same way as they are at home, the burden for the taxpayer would be lightened to the extent of $3.4 billion. Stanford G. Ross, former assistant tax legislative counsel of the Treasury Department, testified that the tax laws "are tipped in favor of foreign investment," and that major reforms are called for. Everybody in the field admits that our tax laws, with their tax credit and tax deferral provisions, provide incentive for capital expansion abroad. Called by Peter Drucker "the greatest engine for monopoly ever devised," they put a premium on capital retention and make the corporation, not the individual, the foremoot repository of national oavingo.

The nation-state can make a case that the corporations, in pursuit of their activities abroad, call on American embassies for representation, or what is usually the rule, the American presence gains them respectful attention. Their technological prowess, a major selling point in their international dealings, has been advanced in large part by federal government subsidies for research and development. But when it comes to furnishing revenue to this same government which is the author of these beneficences, the MNC affiliates are beyond the reach of the tax collector. At present, government agencies are willing dispensers of the bounty, cheerful coadjutors in the expansionary game. But if and when a breed of politicos made of sterner stuff comes on the scene, it may look with jaundiced eyes on American businessmen paying out huge sums to foreign governments when local public authorities are up against fiscal and political insolvency.

The havoc that can be wrought because of a declining tax base has been dramatized in the last few years' budgetary crises in one city after another. The result has been curtailment of public services, spreading urban rot, increasing crime in the streets. This is an unintended payoff for the mass flight to the suburbs in the postwar years, to be followed by the exodus of many business offices and industrial plants. To the federal tax collector it was a matter of indifference whether textile plants were located in New England or the Carolinas, whether masses of people chose to live within city limits or in the suburbs. It is a different story when the question is whether Ford or Texas Instruments operates major plants in the United States or in Europe or Latin America.

It is becoming harder for this government (and governments of the other developed countries) to raise needed revenues because of business and consumer resistance while at the same time demands on it are growing apace. Federal expenditures rose from 13 percent of GNP in 1945–1950 to over 22 percent in 1966–1970. State and local spending rose even more, from 6 to 12 percent. All government spending remained at roughly a third of GNP in 1976–1980. This is in line with the long-standing trend in all advanced countries. The crisis of our cities, now a cliché of the popular press, is the social expression of an ongoing fiscal crisis which is due to the structural gap between the state's expenditures and its revenues. The state is caught between the mutually contradictory duties of preserving traditional income disparities and of maintaining the infrastructure, services, and welfare props of a modern society.

There are those who discount the importance of the taxes-foregone argument since inflows from investments abroad have been greater since the late 1960s than new capital outflows. Although corporations sent some $29 billion overseas in the 1960s, $42 billion, plus an additional $12 billion for royalties and fees, was returned—for a net inflow of over $35 billion. In 1980 alone there was a $27-billion capital outflow and a net investment income on international transactions of $33 billion. So where is the loss? Those who argue this way do not comprehend the interlocking variables in a complex situation. True, this inflow is a helpful addition to the credit column of this country's balance of payments, and is of moment for financing military and diplomatic commitments around the world. However, the benefits are largely private but the costs are largely public: (1) these repatriated funds yield smaller taxes than similar funds earned at home; (2) a dollar of exports produces some fifteen times the credit in the balance of payments than a dollar in foreign sales; (3) in order to yield the present big annual inflows, enormous amounts of capital had to be invested abroad over many years; (4) above all, by not investing at least some of this capital at home, by investing it abroad instead, there were harmful spinoffs like obsolescent plants, abandoned plants, declining productivity, lopsided economic developments and specializations.

4

The tilt toward service industries relates to the sociology of employment trends—whether, as time goes on, this country becomes a technology supplier, a supervisor, organizer, and packager of other people's primary manufactures. Of more immediate concern is the number of jobs the economy is generating. With unemployment and underutilization of plant capacities again major American problems, thoughts have naturally converged on MNCs, the fear that heavy investment abroad means underinvestment at home, that the expansion of jobs for foreigners means the contraction of jobs for Americans.

Trade union officialdom has made the MNCs and exports of technology the culprits responsible for a host of evils ranging from the growing unemployment to the decline of American economic preeminence. Relying on a special study that it commissioned in 1971, the AFL-CIO claimed that 500,000 jobs were lost between 1966 and 1969, and by exrapolating from this figure, that 900,000 jobs were lost in the five years 1966–1971. An extension to more recent years would increase the total sizably. The claims rest on conclusions that 700,000 job opportunities were foregone in the enumerated three years because of the rise of imports that displaced American products, while jobs attributable to exports increased by only 200,000.

Employers' organizations and academics sympathetic to their point of view countered with figures to prove a diametrically opposite case. In a document submitted to the Senate by the National Association of Manufacturers, the writers called attention to six major studies that purport to demonstrate that U.S. foreign direct investment "is a net creator of domestic jobs which otherwise would not have been created," that MNC affiliates were directly responsible for producing 600,000 new jobs over five years' time. This figure is arrived at by estimating the exports "saved" by investments abroad which would otherwise have been "lost" to foreign competition. This includes MNC exports to affiliates for capital equipment, further processing, and resale, and creation of additional jobs for managerial, technical, and clerical support requirements.

These divergent estimates cannot be reconciled. Essentially both the union and employer papers are exercises in advocacy. It is as if a group of historians were occupied in reconstructing a history of Europe for the past five centuries on the proviso that Columbus and his successors had not discovered the American continent. In that case, would England have gained precedence over Spain a century earlier, or at all? Who knows? The investigators who put together the U.S. Tariff Commission's monumental study brought out the alternative assumptions that have to be made to arrive at conclusions that the MNCs either "lost" or "won" jobs in the United States.

In Option 1, direct investment abroad is treated as an addition to the foreign government's domestic investment and as a reduction in the U.S. home investment. This loads the argument in favor of the MNC critics: as one country's investment rises, the other one's falls. In Option 2, foreign investment causes no diminution of home investment but is a substitute for domestic investment in the host country. This loads the argument the other way. The foreign investment in this case takes the place of the investment that the foreigner would otherwise have made. There is another possible alternative, Option 3. In this modification of Option 1, host country investment rises absolutely, but would have done so had the MNC not come along, while investment at home is unchanged. It is further assumed in this "as if" world that U.S. exports can entirely replace production that is lost because of affiliates' sales. It is also necessary, to maintain the symmetry of the argument, to work in the favorable employment effects of foreign-owned MNCs in the United States. In attempting to estimate the major impacts of all the variables in industry after industry, our statisticians calculate that in Option 1, over the five-year period there would be a net job loss of 1.3 million, in Option 2 there would be a job gain of half a million.

It is an impossible assignment to be asked to trace the thousands of transactions initiated by MNC headquarters and the hundreds of thousands of transactions of their subsidiaries in order to determine which of these options is closest to reality— and most of this information, in any case, is unavailable to the researcher. It is an undisputed fact, however, that we have been struck with trade deficits for the first time since the nineteenth century, and that corporations constituting the motor of the American economy now rely on their foreign properties for a third or more of their sales and profits. Without getting mired in numbers games, it can be demonstrated that magisterial corporate activities abroad have introduced serious distortions into the home economy with baleful consequences for masses of people. According to Robert Gilpin, "Reliance on foreign investment means neglect of domestic investment opportunities and social needs. Resources flow abroad to facilitate corporate growth rather than to improve America's cities, decrease her dependence on foreign sources of energy, or seek out other domestic investment opportunities. As in the case of Great Britain in the nineteenth century, the emphasis on foreign investment and the search for new markets for old products tends to abort the reinvigoration of the American domestic economy and its technical infrastructure."

When the American MNC prodigy first descended on the world's economies, the many critics centered attention on its prejudicial activities in host countries. There was the Gaullist reaction codified by Servan-Schreiber for industrialized Europe. There were and are similar complaints in Canada. Both leftist and Third World analysts buttressed with new data the thesis of neo-imperialism. Most American students of the question, sympathetic or hostile to the critics, assumed that the headquarters country in any case was the beneficiary of the grand enterprise, and they continued assuming that after labor unions raised their outcry against job losses. Part of the perception of the postindustrial society, part of the reasoning for the coming preeminence of the "knowledge" industry set in motion by its originators and mentors, the scientists and engineers, had its origin in an MNC-induced worldview.

This country, or this country at the head of an alliance of several advanced industrial countries, was to be the general staff of world technology and industrial allocation, gradually moving the standardized, more labor-intensive activities characteristic of an older, cruder stage of industrialization to the world's peripheries, all the while dedicating itself to the production of advanced mathematical systems to energize, enrich, and service the multifarious undertakings of the brave new world-to-be. Paul Samuelson warned that it was not a realistic perspective, that the rest of the world would not permit this country to become a rentier living on investment returns from abroad. Long before that issue was joined, it became clear to many that the program for a service-and-rentier economy is the sure prescription for America's disintegration as an industrial power—with all that that signifies for its internal dispositions, prospects, and plans.

7. Unfinished
Business

1

The unique feature of present developments in the industrialized capitalist world is this: while nation-states have grown somewhat weaker in relation to the private corporate kingdoms domiciled in their territories, they are expansionary integers with constantly added accretions of strength in relation to society as a whole. The statistical manifestations of the expansionary state are familiar since they furnish the fuel to conservatives for public handwringing and repeated and well-publicized predictions of disasters unimaginable in the offing. It will suffice to run over some of the main items, many of them already referred to in my exposition.

First, the nationalizations in Western Europe. These have been extensive in England, France, Italy, Austria, and Finland, comprising anywhere from a fifth to two-fifths of productive investments, with fewer but still considerable nationalizations in Holland, Belgium, and the Scandinavian countries. In France and Italy the public sector includes big sections of bank and credit institutions. (This does not include recent nationalizations in France under Mitterand. The new laws authorized the acquisition of additional banks and industrial groups, raising industrial sales in the public sector from 16 to 29 percent of the total.) Were these nationalizations parts of a masterplan to socialize the economy, or decisive sections of it, there would be ample justification for conservatives' alarm. But this is a case where the propertied want to eat their cake and have it too. *The Economist* put it squarely in one of its more cynical moments:

That is the paradox of a time when the private sector, no longer content to sit and watch the waves of government intervention lap about its knees, has started to shout for help. No meeting of businessmen these days is complete without a ringing affirmation of the market system, competition, entrepreneurship and private ownership seen, with good reason, as the best way of securing these things. Yet at the same moment no government office is complete without its queue of corporate executives seeking government guidance, clamoring for government protection against disruptive (i.e., competitive) imports, haggling for government handouts.

The nationalized industries or enclaves are used to absorb industrial losses, to take over at public expense bankrupt or no-longer-profitable enterprises, to improve productivity of private companies, to run public clinics for rehabilitation of run-down or disease-ridden patients. There are also legal and administrative inpediments to the nationalized corporations' abilities to show earnings on a par with those of private corporations. That is part of the explanation why private managers and their political allies can point with glee to the low returns in public enterprises.

Public corporations, as presently constituted and run, are impregnated with the capitalist spirit. In outlook, sense of values, company strategy, group associations—in every way that counts—their managerial personnel are wedded to the ongoing capitalist system no less than are the entrepreneurs and managers of the private sector. They are permitted by social democratic governments, no less than by conservative governments, to carry on in that spirit and by those rules. Indeed given the totality of welfare states' relations they could not function otherwise. They have no difficulty, when opportunity beckons, of participating, whether as a minority or majority holder, in private industrial syndicates, as is the case of the French public-owned coal concerns, Houillères du Nord and Houillères du Pas de Calais, or of Renault, the nationalized auto concern, or of becoming typical multinational corporations with regulation capitalist-run affiliates abroad, as is the case with Renault again, or Elf-Aquitaine, British Petroleum, and Volkswagen.

That being so, why are conservatives raging? The conservatives see nationalizations as representing a trend which, if permitted to continue, will in time threaten both their mode of operations and their privileged positions. Nationalized enterprises, though conducted on capitalist lines, are controlled by a managerial elite that is beholden to the state. This elitist caste supervises an enclave of state capitalism. True, these managers are loyal enough to the existing private corporate fiefdoms, and approve as a matter of course their seignorial prerogatives and exactions. But this can change under other social and political circumstances—and the ever-alert upper-classmen want to ensure that the opportunity is blocked to any shift of that kind of allegiance and perspective. They are being farsighted.

State capitalist trends are not confined to nationalizations. They show themselves even more revealingly in the expansion of all divisions of government. Using the period of the 1960s and 1970s (in which there may be secondary elements of discrepancy), the percentages of the entire labor force in public employment were in some cases three or more times greater than the workforce in the nationalized enterprises (see Table 10).

Which brings us to the favorite target of abuse, high taxes. They are, in truth, very high. As of 1975 total taxes as a proportion of GNP stood at 46 percent in Sweden, 37 percent in Britain and France, 35 percent in Germany, 32 percent in Italy, and 30 percent in the United States. These tax figures, derived from OECD data, understate the extent of government managership of the national product since expenditures often run higher than collections. Computations of actual government spending as a proportion of GNP show larger figures for all major countries: Sweden, 53 percent; Britain, 45 percent; Japan, 42 percent; France and Italy, 40 percent; and Germany, 39 percent. According to Department of Commerce figures, total federal, state, and local expenditures in the United States in 1977 added up to 36.5 percent of GNP. The federal debt (in constant 1972 dollars) almost doubled in 1960–1978 from $151 billion to $293 billion, the interest on which ran over 10 percent of outlays. To this must be added state and local shares of government debt which have been rising more rapidly than the federal part, as shown in Table 11.

Unlike private businesses, the federal, state, and local governments cannot make use of their borrowings to generate profits. They must rely on economic expansion to enlarge their tax bases if surpluses are to be run up to pay off the debt. This is highly unlikely even in periods of prosperity because the predisposition is for tax reductions, not debt retirement. The costs of selling government securities and servicing the debts go up in a period of inflation, and the public debt itself exerts added pres-

TABLE 10   Public Employment as Percentage of Total Employment

Country	Nationalized enterprises	Total public sector including central, local, and military
Britain	12	28.5
France	12	21
Germany	9	21
Holland	8	17
Italy	11.5	18.5
Sweden	10.5	30
United States	3	19
Japan	3	13

sure. The liberal apologia of some years back that (1) there is really no problem to an internally held debt since government securities are held by individuals and corporations as assets, and (2) that government debts have risen far less substantially than private debts, is irrelevant though factually accurate. That it is a tributary stream to the inflationary pool is of some interest; and what is particularly relevant in the present context is that management of a growing part of national wealth extends the role of government as arbiter of national decisions and destiny. Though in the present stage government manages fiscal and monetary funds to assure the viability of private enterprise and to buttress its profit-making apparatus, and the individuals doing the managing are reliables of the corporation and banking worlds, the ground may be prepared (in the event of certain social and political compulsions) for transfers of authority from one entity to another entity.

To the extent that anything is certain in social matters, the continuation of high taxes is one of them. Whoever in the past coined the maxim "as sure as death and taxes" was unknowingly the prophet of our era. Their continuation, indeed their probable increase, is guaranteed by processes inherent in our industrial societies.* If we recall that it was depressions and wars that led

* The current Reaganite flurry about transferring some taxes from the federal to already-overextended state governments and reducing other federal taxes will prove to be another millionaire clubman's will-o'-the-wisp.

TABLE 11   Debt of All U.S. Government Divisions

Year	Amount (in billion $)	Federal % of total
1950	281	91
1960	356	80
1970	514	72
1976	871	72

to the inflation of government, and that welfarism and continued militarism were the yeast for its continued rise, we have to conclude that big government has a shining future, since the causes that brought it into being will reassert themselves.

The intrusion and preponderant position of government in research and development exemplifies creeping state capitalist encroachments in another sensitive sphere. Critics of the system, left-wing and otherwise, often cite these data to demonstrate how the state uses public funds to underwrite private profits. What may be of greater moment historically is that a government bureaucracy, rather than private corporate bureaucracies, are setting priorities and allocating funds. The facts are startling, although well known.

In 1955 in the wake of Soviet Russia's Sputnik launching the word went out that we could not afford to be bested in the science competition, that the decks were to be cleared of any and all impediments for science and technology magnification. By that time the United States was already spending more for R&D than it had at the high point of the war. Then came the deluge. The outlay in 1955 was $6 billion; in 1960, $14 billion; in 1965, $20 billion; in 1970, $26 billion; in 1978, $47 billion. In real dollars outlays trebled from 1955 to 1977. Spending for space research and technology went up from $600 million in 1960 to $6 billion in 1965, before leveling off in the next years to $4- to $5-billion averages. This country was outspending the other capitalist industrial nations in the 1960s by ratios of ten and fifteen to one, three times that of all of Western Europe combined. Even when proportioned for population comparisons there were four times as many researchers here as in France and Germany, more than twice as many as in Britain and Japan.

It is unnecessary to expatiate on the maximal position of science and engineering knowledge in economic innovation and advancement, or on the centrality of the application of research to major areas of industrial activity. America's economic hegemony, in the quarter century that we had it, was linked to our leadership in science and scientific application—and it was the state that had to take the lead. Two-thirds of all R&D expenditures were funded by the federal government through the years of tempestuous growth (the same proportion as in England, even higher in France). Following the principles that govern in these matters, the bulk of the work that these government subsidies engendered was performed within private industries, another eighth in blue-ribbon universities, over half in the case of basic research. But I am pointing to the human agencies managing the funds and parceling out the contracts. Here the position of government was and remains pivotal.

2

Now let us talk about the military component. In 1966 Robert McNamara, then defense secretary, counted during the previous decade 149 armed struggles, either native wars against colonial powers or armed uprisings against domestic regimes or wars between two newly minted underdeveloped nations. Another study listed eighty wars between 1945 and 1967, all but eight of them involving Third World participants on both sides. The next decade saw an intensification of these so-called regional conflicts with the Vietnam fury in the van. The nations spent in this decade a fifth more for their military establishments for a grand total of $400 billion. While the NATO and Warsaw Pact powers accounted for three-quarters of the total, the bitterly impoverished nations threw onto the gaming tables close to a quarter of world military expenditures.

The combination of readily available arms throughout the world, some quite advanced, in the midst of clashing nationalities, and the unsettling conditions attendant on traditional societies reaching out for modernity, is a guarantee of lethal explosions to come in the wake of the many that have already taken place. Time and again these bush-league conflicts suck in the superpowers and their allies, if only as arms suppliers, contractors, and advisers. Though for them the stakes may be marginal or nonexistent, *realpolitik* dictates the need to forestall the rival entente from establishing its own bases which may conceivably be used against the opponents. This makes for more work for the foreign experts, the need to hire still more staffs to look after logistics, draw up position papers, sign contracts for matériel. Selling military supplies to the benighted is only part of it. There is the seemingly unstoppable race of the two superpowers to devise ever more fiendish weapons of destruction, and to arm themselves and their allies in a manner that but a few decades ago could only have been the final mobilization for war. At a minimum it is an assurance that the armed peace of the NATO and Warsaw Pact powers—if it holds—will require extensive supervision by many states, especially the superpowers.

As to the economy, we have entered a period of decline. It is idle to make predictions of how the wheel will spin in the years ahead, but several things are already clear. The first is that the great prosperity and growth in the twenty-five years after World War II came about because of the confluence of special favorable circumstances, economic, technological, social, and political, not because wise men had learned how to inoculate their societies against the business cycle. In the euphoria of the fat years some Keynesians made that claim or one close to it; with the lean years the claim has been orphaned. American Wilsonianism— the Bretton Woods monetary system, the World Bank, U.S. grants and loans, General Agreements on Tariffs and Trade (GATT)— contributed to the expansionary élan. Wilsonianism, however, was expediting a movement in play; it cannot reverse an ebbtide.

Second, it is clear that prosperity and growth produced a by-product that threatens, like some side effects in medicinal therapy, to be more dangerous than the disease it was intended to cure. The prosperity brought in its wake a case of inflation so persistent that it did not fade away in the face of deep recession and widespread unemployment throughout the Western world. In the flourishing 1960s many in government and business thought that a little inflation was not such a bad thing, that it was a small price to pay for greasing the wheels of prosperity. But attitudes changed in a hurry when it was realized that the frolicking kitten had overnight turned into a raging tiger. For a decade in the case of some, for up to two decades in the case of others, governments of the capitalist world have tried a variety of remedies, including faith cures, to rid themselves of the disease—and they have demonstrated that they do not know how. Those who have managed to even moderate the fever have been able to do so only by expensive tradeoffs with growth. This new fact of the postwar period—stagflation—is the ragged banner ushering in a period of economic trials and dislocations.

The big modern states turned into Welfare States in order to purchase mass acceptance and social peace. In all industrialized countries larger shares of rising government budgets are going to pay for social security benefits—and the demand not only for their continuation, but for their liberalization, appears insatiable. Where will it all end? Three well-known academics, the Frenchman Crozier, the American Huntington, and the Japanese Watanuki, studied the entire question in a comprehensive sociological context in the mid-1970s and codified their findings in a report to the Trilateral Commission on the governability of democracies. The conclusions they came up with are profoundly pessimistic and antidemocratic.

Our political systems, we are told, are overloaded with participants and demands. This fosters irresponsibility and the disintegration of consensus. In the past democracies were only partially open, sometimes only theoretically open. To operate effectively, the democratic political system requires some degree of public apathy and noninvolvement. Now with the breakdown of authority and the loss of trust in leaders of established institutions and government, the traditional elitist schema of screening and holding down the number of participants and demands has collapsed. We are suffering from too much participation. The populace makes incompatible demands. It clamors for more action to resolve pressing needs while resisting more social controls to fulfill them. The impossibility of maintaining controls by the old precepts of fragmentation, stratification, and enforced social divisions and barriers, has led to a crisis of governance. We are choking on an excess of democracy, causing the democratic distemper. Domestic problems have become intractable problems. The public has developed expectations which are impossible to meet. Overloading the political system with demands which extend its functions while undermining its authority can lead, unless curbed, to democratic suicide.*

This was the high-level analysis and message. Numbers of publicists on the middle level were quick to draw the obvious conclusions, exhorting their readers to mend their sinful ways: "Don't overload the government circuits"; "We must lower our expectations"; "Nobody owes you a living"; "More welfare = more budgetary deficits = more taxes = more inflation = national bankruptcy." This type of argumentation has enormous appeal to certain sections of the population in certain circumstances. It has figured in amassing the electoral majorities that entrusted governments to the conservative parties in England and this country. Yet this so-called middle-class revolt against the expanding state and its voracious demands—if indeed it has any deeper meaning than a routine changing of the guard—is bound to be a wasted effort.

The industrial society has created its own necessities and standards. They can no more be conjured away then the need can be exorcised for owning an automobile to travel to work when public transportation is lacking. Or to buy high-priced, mass-produced bread when neither the facilities nor the time exist to bake bread at home. Or to demand that the state provide health care and insurance when the extended and stable family that presumably used to look after its own has long since been demolished by the forces of industrialism and urbanism. Or to hold the state responsible for providing jobs for all when private enterprise fails to satisfy this critical need. The thrust for equality, functional rationality, economic security, a voice in matters affecting one's life, is part of the foundation of democratic, industrial society. It is not a faucet that can be turned on and off at will, extolled when government campaigns or industrial desideratums call for an active, trained workforce and disqualified

---

* The same cluster of ideas has been publicized in the United States by the neoconservative circle around such magazines as *The Public Interest* and *Commentary*, and is associated with their more prominent spokesmen, Daniel Moynihan, Daniel Bell, Irving Kristol, Nathan Glazer. Most of their themes—the crisis in authority, cultural anarchy, "overload" on government, the need for discipline and unity at home in the face of dangers from abroad—have been staples of conservatives from the time of Edmund Burke. It is difficult to say whether Crozier–Huntington and the neoconservatives borrowed from one another since both filled their ideological pitchers from long-standing conservative wells.

when the demands of this same aggregation of animated matter becomes inconvenient for some.

For one, the sellers and hucksters of the advanced industrial societies, which have become the consumer societies, cannot permit their definitions of the good life and the successful individual to be tampered with. Industry is dependent on a mass market. While a few pundits may write about lowering our expectations, hundred of millions of dollars are spent annually to mobilize an army of market researchers, dramatists, lyricists, actors, and singers to instruct us to raise our expectations and to keep them raised, that life without an automobile, a trip to the tropics, a late-model color TV, is a life that is hardly worth living. These manufacturing and selling activities are the important ones in determining our expectations and shaping our way of life. Since great expectations are built into the fiber of this industrial society, neither scolding nor admonishments will change the reality of man among the machines.

Professor Crozier, to justify his proposition that we have to reverse gears, can write that the tremendous economic gains made by all groups in the past twenty years had the opposite effects of what was expected: instead of relieving tensions, it exacerbated them—but his scales are out of balance. He is like the charity-giver who is chagrined that he has not been awarded the medal that he thought was his due; or the disillusioned liberal whose hopes for progress are dashed because the Welfare State manufactured new problems faster than it was able to solve old ones. The prosperity and growth of the postwar decades has not given birth to the happy, grateful wards that one can meet in a Fielding novel, but they moderated class conflicts and channeled them in directions not inimical to the system. In the United States, once concessions were made to antiwar and black protesters, the rebellious students and their families resumed their customary private pursuits and black spokesmen entered traditional electoral politics or secured employment in establishment institutions. As the saying went at the time, the system was working. It was not the re-creation of the era of Harding and Coolidge, much less McKinley, but in a precarious world, pitching and tossing like a sailing vessel on stormy seas, for the traditional elites to maintain their hold was achievement enough. Only a doctrinaire would demand more. One cannot sensibly demand that social stability be equivalent to the peace of the grave, or that reforms bring social stability for all time.

Crozier–Huntington and their intellectual friends have isolated an important contradiction in our late capitalist societies. But their solution of shaming people into going back to their prewelfarist stations and humble abodes so as not to overload government circuits is a nonstarter. The contradiction will not be resolved by schoolmasterish exhortations. Whether it is eventually resolved by forcibly pushing back millions to a less civilized state, or integrating them in a more rational and equitable one, it is a fact that one more promissory note is at hand that will be falling due, whose recipients will be demanding full payment.

There are those who insist that "collectivism" in any form is anathema to the American genius, at variance with our entire culture. Eugene V. Rostow, not unexpectedly, is among them. Edward Mason, in his presidential address to the American Economic Association in 1962, made the same point as Rostow on more practical grounds. The French type of planning will not be accepted here; Americans, particularly American businessmen, will not agree to government's having authority of that kind, since "the really revolutionary changes in the role of government and in the relations of various groups to government produced by the great depression and the war have not yet been fully accepted in this country." Professor Mason went on to argue that, in contrast to Europe, a wall separates government and business decision-makers in the United States.

He must have been aware, although he did not refer to it, that at this very time discussions of planning abounded in this country (stimulated by the French experience and press exaggerations of French accomplishments), and so many conspectuses and drafts were drawn up as to make plans for planning a minor foundation industry for a passing moment. Gerhard Colm, chief economist of the National Planning Association, thought that the common feature of these various plans had similarities to the European variety, and that they were "beginning to have significant impact on the performance of the American economy"—a proposition as shaky as Mason's contrast of Europe and the United States, although Colm too was of the opinion that the French model was not for us because of "the more individualistic attitude of entrepreneurs."

Both Mason and Colm were acquainted with many American businessmen, and without a doubt read their minds accurately. Nor did they overstate businessmen's influence in these matters. What was missing in their analyses was historical breadth. Businessmen's preferences are only one element in the making of big national decisions, and at some critical points in history stiff-necked businessmen are constrained to agree to things they would not ordinarily accept. French industrialists had as little enthusiasm for national planning in 1946 as American industrialists had in the 1960s or have today. Yet confronted with the possibility of losing their properties altogether, they gladly accepted "French model" planning à la Monnet, and would probably have swallowed stronger medicine if they had to.

We are all knowledgeable about American individualism and know with what pugnacity it is usually asserted by business spokesmen. But people forget how their equally self-assured fathers and grandfathers appeared in the early 1930s when temporarily tamed. Shaken and bewildered by the thunderbolts of the Great Depression, discredited in the eyes of the public, they enrolled, with banners flying and drums rolling, under the Blue Eagle into a much more authoritarian organization than Monnet's. Although worthless as an economic rejuvenator, the National Recovery Administration (NRA) was successful in enlarging the scope of government bureaucracy in economic matters beyond what it had been thought possible. Charles Evans Hughes's Supreme Court, guardian of the old order, put out of business the sprawling organization that in any case had become unmanageable by then. The government absorbed the attack and kept growing rather than shrinking, by extending its authority through other agencies. A revamped and rechristened Agricultural Adjustment Administration (AAA) was to reorder the entire agricultural sector and enshrine government subsidization and supervision of agriculture as a principle of the Welfare State. The Tennessee Valley Authority (TVA), the huge complex on the Tennessee, Ohio, and Mississippi Rivers for flood regulation and electricity generation created by an act of Congress at the height of populist strength in 1933, survived the attacks of private utility corporations and the later encroachments under President Eisenhower. The sole half-socialistic program of the New Deal, it survived to become part of the accepted economic order of things. The Securities and Exchange Commission, set up to regulate equity markets and corporate issues of stocks and bonds, calls for more thorough supervision than any Labour government in Britain or social democratic government on the continent has yet proposed for its own equities markets. In short, the temper of business movers and shakers can shift very rapidly when it is brought up sharply against the realities of national resolve or incontrovertible social need for change.

The entire machinery of modern industrial democracies, with its intricate nervous system, it special-purpose organs, its many complex parts that have to function in perfect accord, an end product of several centuries of trial and error, can be compared, as a literary metaphor, to the fashioning of a new species by a Darwinian process of selection. According to this reading many of the welfarist demands that seem to some to originate solely in unrealistically swollen expectations, so that no sooner is one claim appeased than two others are put forward, are in actuality organic responses. They represent the attempts of *homunculus* to survive in overcharged, overdemanding, impersonal societies. They cannot be brushed aside unless democracy itself is throttled—and probably not even then.

This is not negated by the fact that people resist higher taxes while demanding more welfarism, or want government budgets reduced and government services increased. Popular demands are sometimes contradictory; sometimes linked sets of demands are mutually exclusive. The key to some inconsistencies is that one group of people takes the lead in resisting taxes while another group of people is out front calling for social reforms. Those in the swing group may support now one, now the other, depending on their own circumstances and the political atmospherics, to make up at any one time the "voice of the people"— the electoral majority. The ebbs and flows of electoral politics are the variables; the swelling of the political apparatus is the constant. The state's growing encroachments and usurpations are clinched by the periodic breakdowns of our epoch.

My purpose in listing a few of the important items of the New Deal legacy is not to cast doubt on or to downgrade the power of the business corporations in postwar America. It is very real, substantial, and pervasive. The shamefaced nationalizations or half-nationalizations that have been put through in recent years, like the establishment of Amtrak in a bankrupt railroad field, or of the Defense Supply Agency in the Pentagon, with its staff of 55,000 to negotiate contracts and oversee performance on the part of private suppliers, are faithfully anchored to the principle of underwriting profits and socializing losses. But that these nationalizations had to be put through at all, albeit in shamefaced fashion, and emasculated by means of stipulations under which they have to operate, is testimonial enough to the growing need of state ownership even with the present unfavorable attitudes.

The inchoate nationalizations, or similar ones as with Ruhr-kohle AG in Germany, or the more explicit government arroga-tions of authority in the Industrial Reorganization Corporation in England and the Institut de Dévelopment Industriel in France, are symptomatic of the drift. By themselves the Western European nationalizations, and the lesser ones in this country and in Germany, can be viewed as the institution of overdue structural adjustments to make the dwelling more livable, the socialization of losses to make the profit system more profitable; just as it can be said that in past periods, popular education, the broadened ballot, etc., although introduced in response to populist clamor and over the opposition of prestigious stand-patters, reinforced the system and readied the nation for industrialized mass society. Considered in the historical context of the postwar years, what the state power now does and is expected to do, and the probable calls for more government intervention in the days to come, the nationalizations as well as the other accoutrements of the Welfare State have to be seen as signposts along the road to a more comprehensive statization.

3

If political systems were subjected to many buffetings in the fat years, how will they come through the lean years? If state power grew faster in the half century since the Great Depression than it had grown in the two centuries from the start of the Industrial Revolution, what can we anticipate when industrial societies enter a period of stagnation, and the clamor grows more shrill for sharing the decreasing bounty? Walter Dean Burnham writes "that the American dream is about over." What he means is that the epoch of abundant raw materials and pell-mell growth is coming to an end, that "the costs of the transition to something else will be agonizingly high," and that "if the political system is not to blow up under the strain, these costs will have to be apportioned with some pretense of equity." With that, I will embark on a discussion, brief though it will be, of the constricting environment and physical limits to industrial expansion. I enter this domain with great trepidation, for I am aware that the cemeteries are filled with the bleached bones of the many prognosticators from Malthus on who were certain that we were close to the saturation point because of geometric population increases or scarcity of land or exhaustion of minerals, and that one after another their prognoses were proven to be mistaken. But I am not a neo-Malthusian and my thesis does not rest on a constricting-environment explanation. All the same the ecological factor cannot be passed over. It has already asserted itself in world economics, politics, and perceptions, even if in a different way than that anticipated by environmental alarmists.

Malthus alerted the economists to the problem. His essay on population, first published in 1798, created a sensation, its propositions forming the bedrock of classical economics. His well-known ratios of geometric population leaps in contrast to limited mathematical food growth attainabilities frightened a whole generation with its prospects of mass starvation. Ricardo molded the Malthusian dogmas into formulas, and in their popularized versions they became shibboleths in the early Victorian period like Freudian catchwords are in our own day. This classical political economy saw its culmination in Mill's "stationary state," an evolution made inevitable by what were accepted as two immutable laws, the law of population and the law of diminishing returns.

Marx and Engels never took Malthus's population law seriously. They related population to the accumulation of capital, and saw overpopulation and the maintenance of an industrial reserve army neither as a law of nature nor the destiny of mankind but as a specific feature of capitalist industry. They believed that every historic mode of production has its own population laws. In outlook, and as a tradition, Marxism was and remains hostile to all forms and offshoots of Malthusianism. Malthusianism accepts limitation as an ineluctible dictate of nature, scarcity as man's fate. Marxism is the doctrine of abundance, of potentially inexhaustible plenty, of the ability of industrial society, once it casts off the incubus of capitalist relations, to abolish want and deprivation. Marx and his successors never doubted that just as the bourgeoisie, with its superior forms of organization and technology, was able to unleash the productive forces "slumbering in the lap of social labor" and accomplish the many prodigies described in the Communist Manifesto, so the proletariat, standing on the shoulders of these predecessors, would be able to usher in a society that would inscribe on its banners "From each according to his ability, to each according to his needs."

The population theories of the classical economists became discredited toward the end of the century as birth rates declined in the advanced European countries and as scientific and technological advances, and the opening up of new virgin lands, magnified agricultural production. Western nations were far from stationary. Political leaders were not bashful in trumpeting the message of dazzling economic prospects and ever-rising affluence. Liberalism became as one with Marxism in bringing into focus vistas of continual industrial expansion. The two debaters saw the right answer in conflicting forms of social organization, but neither of them exhibited concern that the wells of nature might one day run dry. There were occasional warnings that too-rapid population growth would eventually outstrip supplies or that mineral riches were being unconscionably pillaged, but these warnings were answered airily that we could safely count on modern science and engineering to tap new resources, come up with new techniques, discover new uses for hitherto unusable substances, to furnish industry with the raw materials it required.

There was a conservation movement in this country under both the first and second Roosevelt; Gifford Pinchot, its intellectual leader, originally chief forester in the Agriculture Department and twice governor of Pennsylvania in the 1930s, figured prominently in both efforts, as did other Progressive Era personalities. The concerns of the conservationists, while bearing a resemblance to those exercising the present generation of environmentalists, originated in a different world as regards class sponsorship, tone, ideological bent, and programmatic objectives. For one, the air of frightened foreboding was absent in those earlier, optimistic days. Man's abilities to destroy had not yet attained the demonic thoroughness of our nuclear age. When in the early 1970s environmentalism became a popular cause in this country, and to one or another extent throughout the industrial world, it seemed to the committed that not just a prudent use of resources, but life on this planet, was the issue. We were witnessing one of those sharp reverses of outlook, not unusual in the history of ideas, brought about in this case by the puncturing of earlier expectations.

Let us recall that David Riesman in the 1950s, articulating an opinion held by an entire intellectual community, wrote that the bare economic problems had been solved or were on the way to solution, that society had to concentrate on working out new living styles in which leisure rather than the drudgery of work was to be the dominant theme. In a few years talk of Triple Revolutions was heard from both technologists and leftists, with Utopia, it was announced, a practical possibility for the living generations. Herman Kahn, unerringly responding to popular intellectual currents, published studies about the year 2000 replete with listings and projections of super per-capita incomes, short working hours, long vacations, a "leisure-oriented" Eden, and not just in the United States. But the Green Revolution did more to enrich select numbers of landowners than to solve the problems of impoverished peasant masses. The Cybernetic Revolution petered out following established rhythms in technological innovations, so that instead of continuous booming we hit the recession-prone 1970s. The Nuclear Revolution, which was to provide unlimited and dirt-cheap energy to meet any and all industrial and personal needs for centuries to come, turned into a mixture in which the sweetness was to the gall in a ratio of one to ten. The oil crisis of 1973 commingled and brought to the political surface variegated, widespread feelings of vulnerability.

Environmentalism as a popular cause grew out of the American insurgencies of the 1960s which then spread throughout the world, and in the process kindled all manner of movements of discontent. It demonstrated the internationalization in our time of political and cultural concerns. There is the ability of the electronic media to direct world attention on specific events, and the homogenization of tastes and attitudes—both offshoots of the technology of late industrialism. When the counterculture of the decade exhausted itself, groups of radicalized young people, organizationally unattached, took up the ecological cause.

Not surprisingly, present-day debaters—environmentalists and expansionists, alarmists and philistines—go over the ground of argumentation that was plowed by earlier Malthusians and anti-Malthusians. The data are updated; the underlying approaches are not dissimilar. In one well-known projection worked out several years ago by a group of computer scientists at MIT, Malthus's ratios are advanced again, now decked out with flow diagrams, computer printouts, system dynamics models, and bearing the seal of approval of the Club of Rome: Population, industrial production, other variables, have been growing exponentially; much of the physical environment, however—cultivatable land, minerals, ability of the earth to absorb pollution—is finite; some combination of these physical aspects sets a limit to population and industrial increases; the choice is to radically reorganize our social institutions very soon or face an unmanageable crisis not too much later. Carl Kaysen, then director of the Princeton Institute for Advanced Study, presenting the case of the opposing school of thought, questioned the premises and rejected the conclusions: resources are properly measured in economic rather than physical terms; the problem is one of cost limits, not physical limits; not just population but technology is advancing exponentially; in the workings of the economy adjustment mechanisms play a crucial role, and as in the past can be sufficiently powerful to determine required shifts in use of resources, population movements, patterns of consumption.

I will now take up these matters of ecology from the point of view of how they affect statist trends.

4

I will pass very rapidly over the danger of nuclear war and the conclusive effects that a release of nuclear-tipped bombs and missiles in the possession of the two superpowers would have on the environment. Not that I am as convinced as Louis Halle and those who think like him that nuclear war between the major powers is permanently ruled out. But it has to be assumed, as a matter of pedagogic convenience if for no other reason, that mankind will not blow itself to bits or poison the planet to make life impossible: hence that the social sciences, that questions of government organization, of economic arrangements, remain important and worthy of discussion.

Heilbroner has adumbrated another fearsome possibility, that some underdeveloped nations will be able to get hold of or produce their own nuclear weapons, and will be tempted to use them as instruments of blackmail to force the industrialized world to make a massive transfer of wealth to them—since that is the only way the poor nations will obtain major redistributions. Strictly speaking this is not an environmental but a military matter, and in any case is unlikely. If the threat of one's own annihilation is a deterrent for the big powers to unloose nuclear weapons on their opponent, it is a stronger deterrent for a marginal power that may have only one or two low-level atomic bombs in its arsenal. Such a temptation may cross the minds of political desperadoes, but the vagrant thought will be immediately followed by the age-old calculations that govern warfare. A poor nation may outlast a strong one in a defensive fight on its own territory—Vietnam showed that—by displays of incredible perseverance and enormous expenditures of lives, provided it has the help of a powerful patron; but it is courting certain annihilation if it raises the threat of nuclear blackmail. Hara-kiri is not unknown among individual warriors; governments do not consciously practice it. And if a depraved ruler were to defy logic, cross the dread boundary line, and do the unthinkable, it would constitute an episodic calamity, not the new pattern of north-south relations.

Another worrisome problem is that man-made heat emissions will eventually bring us to an ecological Armageddon. An inevitable by-product of industrial expansion is the additional heat that is being generated and added to the atmosphere. The amount of carbon dioxide in the air is constantly increasing, and will probably increase still faster as additional countries industrialize. The multiplying effects can, in the matter of a few generations, produce climatic changes leading to extinction of the species. According to a 1979 report prepared by a group of scientists for the Energy Department, "Carbon dioxide from unrestrained combustion of fossil fuels is potentially the most important environmental issue facing mankind." The sense of the report is that if industry continues to burn carbon-based fuels at present rates, the amount of carbon dioxide in the atmosphere will double in thirty-five years, and the globe's temperature will increase by an average of two to three degrees, and very much more at higher latitudes. This could result in a rapid melting of the icecaps, a fifteen-foot rise in sea level, and other major changes in the climate that might play havoc with agricultural production and turn rich regions into dust bowls. Two years later a team of seven atmospheric scientists connected with the National Aeronautics and Space Administration (NASA) published an even more alarming study. They predicted that on the trends of the past hundred years, even if fuel burning increases at a relatively slow rate and there is only a moderate rise of five degrees Fahrenheit in the atmosphere, in another century the climate would approach the temperature of the Mesozoic, the age of the dinosaurs.

Were most of these estimates valid we would have to question the logic of continuing with industrialism at all. But there is no way to deal with this intelligibly as a problem of sociology or practical politics because the atmospheric scientists are uncertain about too many essentials. They are in basic disagreement among themselves. Prof. Charles Cooper, director of the environmental center at San Diego State University, points out that any conclusions concerning the impact of global climatic change "must necessarily be highly tentative and speculative; some may be wholly wrong." Consequently his demand is a modest one: "Man has apparently become a major geological and geophysical agent in his own right, able to influence the physical and biological conditions of the future, deliberately or inadvertently, in a way not open to our ancestors. There is an urgent need for intensified research to limit some of the uncertainties which now make informed political choice almost impossible."

The three environmental propositions of greatest relevance for our discussion are population growth, exhaustion of raw materials, and pollution. The first, exponential population growth, is not an internal problem for the developed countries. In the industrialized world the great fact of demographic history has been an adjustment of birth rates to death rates and to available economic standards. There is no need here to delve into the various causes for this, even if we understood them all, but it is a sufficiently fundamental feature of advanced society for us to be able to state categorically that the population explosion is essentially the problem of sections of the underdeveloped world. There it is linked with economic stagnation, illiteracy, malnutrition, and disease. There Malthusian checks are the equalizers as populations press against inadequate food supplies.* Social pu-

* According to a 1979 report prepared by the United Nations Fund for Population Activities, the population growth rate is declining in many developing countries as well as in the industrialized ones. Some of the major projections in the report are:

trefaction and political precariousness are major reasons for the rise in one country after another of military regimes of quasi-populist or pseudo-socialist pretensions.

When I included two paragraphs on the shakiness of Third World finances in my first draft a few years ago, I was only interested in explaining that the underdeveloped countries were sitting on mountains of debts to Western banks, that in many cases these amounted to untenable proportions of their total wealth, and that some economists doubted that a number of these countries would ever be able to clear their accounts. I recalled that a more localized credit shock wrecked international banking in 1931, and that analysts could no longer wave away the argument that the capitalist world was subject to critical disruption originating at the extremities of the system.

One year along and these propositions became truisms and clichés. When Poland in 1981, in the grip of political crisis, could not meet payment on her $24-billion external debt, this was airily accredited in the Western press to the predictable mismanagement of Communist bosses. When the following year Mexico, with an external debt of over $80 billion, had to confess insolvency and admit that unless emergency funds were made available it would have to default, and it was clear that a long line of debtors would be similarly clamoring for relief in the next weeks and months, banking officials and finance writers admitted to the existence of an international banking crisis. The avalanche of debt that was threatening the entire global economy, they explained, made it necessary for the major governments to rally round and bring their checkbooks with them. Keynes reportedly had said that if you owe your bank a thousand pounds, you have a problem; if you owe it a million, the *bank* has a problem. That is the situation today.

As of the end of 1982 foreign debts of Third World countries, not counting the debts of OPEC oil producers and of the East European bloc, ran $600–650 billion. The debts of five Latin

By the year 2000, nine-tenths of the two billion additional world's inhabitants will live in the Third World, where 20 percent of the population already suffers from severe malnourishment, 30 percent does not have access to clean water, 40 percent either has no job or no regular employment, and 50 percent of those over fifteen are illiterate.

The world's urban population doubled between 1950 and 1978 and will double again by 2000. This is "bound of have radical-to-revolutionary implications for national economic and social structures."

American countries, mainly to American banks and institutions, added up to $260 billion. Mexico, Argentina, Chile, and the Philippines have foreign debts equal to half their GNP; for Singapore the figure is two-thirds; Argentina and Chile are burdened with interest charges equal to about 90 percent of the value of their exports. And this is not the end of the bad news. The boom in lending to weak countries came at the same time that multinational corporations grew accustomed to financing huge programs of expansion by extensive borrowings, and some of their promissory notes are no less shaky in economic downturns than loans to the Third World. Harold Lever, a former financial officer in several British governments, noted in an article appearing on the Op-Ed page of the *New York Times* that the venturesome operations of the world's big banks was only made possible by using their subsidiaries in the unregulated Eurodollar markets—"They have built a structure of debt that must surely be the largest and most remarkable financial house of cards ever created"—and that it was bound to collapse.

The first rescue operation of Western bankers and government officials—agreed to in innumerable executive luncheons—was to increase the lending pool of the International Monetary Fund (IMF) to $98.5 billion from $66 billion. Even before the formal enactment and its approval by the constituent governments, the bankers, assured of the generous impulses of their Treasury and Central Bank officials, proceeded to restructure the debts of Mexico and other mendicants. The rescue operation straightened out the books for the time being, but it was a strictly limited resolution of the crisis at hand. The great banks remain manacled to their insolvent clients whose creditworthiness is more likely to deteriorate than to improve. Moreover the terms of the rescue missions are based on familiar IMF Victorian economics known under the rubric of austerity programs. The governments of the poor countries, in return for winning time, may be storing up for themselves economic breakdowns and social conflicts less negotiable than the banking crisis they have just finessed.

The bankers are well aware that the structure of their international system is precarious, and that the prudent thing is to provide a firmer foundation. A number of schemes are being bruited about ranging from Felix Rohatyn's super agency affiliated with the IMF that would trade long-term low-interest bonds for the debts that have piled up in the bank portfolios, to the proposition of Mackworth-Young, chairman of London's Morgan Grenfell, also calling for a super agency that would trade non-interest-bearing bonds backed in this case by the Central Banks for numbers of their flea-bitten loans that they list as assets on their books. The schemes differ in details but they have one thing in common: through one or another neat technique the bankers propose the socialization of their losses or of most of them. They would retain control of their enterprises, they would continue to take the profits, but they would unload the bad debts on the taxpayers—an unequal bargain. Fortunately the plans are in the stage of cocktail-hour exchanges. Kindleberger of MIT, grown wary over the years of thinking big, was prepared to settle for short-term solutions. He said, "The important thing is to hang in there. When you're riding on the back of a tiger, the thing is to hang on to the tail, just hang on."

The next item on the agenda is the question of dwindling resources or exhaustion of raw materials, so that at some point industry's maw can no longer be adequately stuffed. With this is linked the question of air and water pollution, the turning of extended areas into uninhabitable wastelands. In time, if the noxious detritus is permitted to accumulate, the threshold of human tolerance may be crossed. That is the nightmare haunting environmentalists.

The practical question is a more complex one. Whatever may be the reality in the distant future, in our time and our children's time matters appertaining to natural resources and pollution are of an economic and sociopolitical, not ecological character. Scientific and engineering knowledge is available to replace depleted resources by new findings, synthetic substitutes, alternative technologies—although sometimes we may have to make do with second best. Similarly we know how to clean up the worst of the befoulments and poisonous sinks left us as a dolorous legacy of two hundred years of industrialism, and the standards that have to be set to prevent industry from continuing to contaminate entire regions—this time with redoubled thoroughness and speed.

The fact that scientists and engineers know how will avail little if social and economic arrangements do not permit its use, any more than knowledge of how to limit population can be put to use in the face of antipathetic customs and contrary individual needs. The environmental factor takes on the importance that it does because it has dramatically announced itself to humanity at a time when economic and social crises are approaching on their own trajectories. This means that the nation, while having to come to grips with chronic unemployment, continual inflation, accumulating decay, and the consequent social disorders, will have to do so in the more forbidding climate of heavier costs and fewer options.

The common penalty attached to giant salvage operations, major conversion schemes, or large-scale redistribution of investment and manpower allocations is high cost. More often than not they will entail basic diversions of labor and materials from production for goods and services that have proven ability for providing rich returns to private businesses in favor of undertakings in untested fields in which risks are too great and profits too uncertain to have appeal for private investors. Many socially indispensable undertakings are inherently unsuited for drawing off large profits. This is well understood by staunch free-enterprisers in the case of libraries, symphony orchestras, even post offices (although for post offices there are not a few, in both business and politics, who see no reason why the postal service should be treated differently from telephone communications or television entertainment). What will be on the national agenda in a crisis, however, is not subsidization of an ailing industry or a public service industry, or several of them, but a fundamental reshaping of economic activity. Structural reforms will be in order which will eliminate the economic sicknesses of late capitalism. At the same time the changed arrangements should make it possible to wipe out the pestholes of social pollution, the spreading violence and crime, the decaying cities, the breakdown of civilized relations.

It is no part of my purpose to look into or to make arguments on behalf of one or another technology, like developing a cost-efficient coal conversion program, or to present a brief for developing mass transportation within cities and to and from cities, or to advocate an integrated national program to give young people training and jobs so that they will have a purpose in life and become imbued with zeal for public service. My purpose is to indicate that neither political nor economic authorities are presently set up to cope adequately with even the present, more easily manageable crises. My additional purpose is to infer that, as now constituted, they will be completely out of their depths in coping with a situation in which a number of components are combined, making for a comprehensive crisis.

Now capitalism as a system of power arrangements, profit compulsions, and group privileges is not suited to deal with a systemic crisis. For certain operations corporate strategists in a market-oriented economy show superb aptitudes. When it comes to fusing technology and production or production and marketing, once these are susceptible of yielding good profits, we all know what prodigies the businessman can display. Even under war conditions, after holding up production until corporate leaders got what they wanted in the way of lifting restrictions on profit-making and of tax write-offs, and after bringing the country to the brink of disaster with contrived shortages of rubber, aluminum, and steel, the dollar-a-year men proved both willing and able to gear up the economy into the powerhouse known the world over as the "arsenal of democracy." They did so well that they came out with enhanced prestige, beneficiaries of popular esteem. At the time they had not grasped that they were helping to raise up the spectre of immense government which they had inveighed against a few years before and were to inveigh against a few years later.

Yet these same wizards of organizing production were singularly inept in devising constructive proposals to overcome the devastating crisis of the early 1930s. They offered the nation instead their fears, obstructionism, trained provincialism, and private greed. They kept their power but were on the way to losing their legitimacy. The state, in the administration of Franklin Roosevelt, was constrained to take over jurisdiction of many duties and preoccupations which up to that moment were thought to be outside both the province and capability of the government officialdom. Once the nation is thrust into an era of repeated downturns and crises, churned by monetary disarray and debt accumulations, the economy skewed by multinationals' helter-skelter integrations, the society racked by social antagonisms arising out of economic dislocations and turmoil, government will be constrained to move more forcefully to assume an internal sovereignty far in excess of what was attempted by New Dealers.

8. The State in Ascendance

1

Part of the thesis of this book is that the afflictions periodically besetting late capitalism are due to become more acute and less manageable. These complications are aggravated by the three developments referred to that did not have to be reckoned with in the crisis of fifty years ago.

First is the emergence of ex-colonials as independent states. The industrial powers have to treat these countries' rulers deferentially and employ costlier techniques than was their custom or need in the imperialist heyday. Beyond that, the instability of most of these regimes threatens the stability of the rich nations. Second is the rise of the Soviet Union as the second world superpower. Western analysts often lose perspective by focusing all their attention on that country's detestable dictatorship and undeniable economic weaknesses. What is of equal importance in an analysis of the world balance is that a large section has been torn from the capitalist communal body. Consequently the organism, for all its dominant position, suffers from an irreparable disability. This shows up at certain critical junctures as in America's inability to subdue Communist North Vietnam, or in the arms race in which absolute superiority is beyond its grasp. One cannot blink away the facts that the existence of another superpower representing an antithetic social system constricts capitalism's range. Third, energy depletions and environmental impediments are raising costs and clogging circuits to production growth. Market-oriented free enterprise traditionally advanced the economy in helter-skelter fashion, assuming little responsibility for its defilements of large areas or improvident depletion of natual resources. It was routine behavior to unload on governments the responsibility for building complex infrastructures required by industry out of public tax money. In earlier stages before technology had attained its devastating efficiency, capitalist élan carried the national enterprise forward despite the wastes and debaucheries. That stage is no more. The prodigality of the past has caught up with us. Society has passed the point of no return in permitting natural resources and public funds to be treated like inexhaustible treasure troves.

The era of crises points to the inescapable need to shape the national economic undertaking. This can be envisioned only with the introduction of central planning. As the preliminary, the central planning authority will put an end to the higgledy-piggledy economic arrangement with various projects careening uncontrolledly at cross purposes. It will be entrusted with the responsibility of reopening the production circuits for renewed growth. In reality by bringing coherence and rationality into the industrial and fiscal spheres, it will check the outright chaos that threatens to envelop the public order. The planning process will be elaborated in the succeeding pages once the necessary introductory matters are cleared away.

It is unlikely that a profound transformation of this kind will occur simultaneously in the half dozen major industrial states. It is sufficient for the next stage to become identifiable if one country takes the lead in putting through the change and others, feeling the tug, move at their own pace and in their indigenous ways to follow suit. It is also probable that the pioneering state will install the major institutions and networks for the new arrangements piecemeal, and that a number of years will elapse before the new order is substantially in place and functioning effectively. As occurred in the era of Western modernizations, other nations will appropriate for their own purposes those arrangements of the pioneer that they find useful in their own situations.

It is easy to demonstrate statization trends in industrial societies, and the great acceleration in state expansion since the introduction of the Welfare State. It may be asserted without too much controversy, given the nature of our times, that governments will have to take over jurisdiction of more functions than they already have. But it is something else again to conclude that the climax of this process will be a comprehensive statization amounting to something close to a social revolution engineered from above. This is a prognosis—and a few words have to be said now about forecasting, with a sharp distinction drawn between the several kinds.

One genre consists of forecasting specific events: that two countries will go to war within the next six months, that today's headline of severe losses on the stock exchange is the starting point of a major economic depression, etc. These types of forecasts, where they are not frivolous, are tied to an intimate knowledge of the individuals, institutions, and countries involved, and the conclusion rests on a half-intuitive computerization of probabilities. Concrete forecasts are necessarily conditional, and the more concrete they are, the more conditional they have to be. For certain purposes they are indispensable as working data; analysts make wide use of them in drawing up recommendation papers, or they are a reference point to check unfolding events, or a hypothesis against which to monitor the activities of a hostile government. The percentage of error is large, however, either because some anticipated conditions became altered or the intersect of social vectors had been wrongly plotted to begin with.

The second type is demographic and related projections on prices, productivity, output, and population growth that sociologists, economists, and insurance firm technicians habitually employ in their calculations. They provide the basic blocks of analysis. Since the forecasting takes place within a closed system, the findings are reasonably accurate provided no "outside factors" interfere with the extrapolations. The investigator has to be aware of these limitations. When "exogenous variables," inevitably affecting other variables, disturb the smooth-flowing stream, as they often do, the projection can go awry, sometimes totally.

A rogue mutant of standard demographic forecasting is the school of futurology whose practitioners make use of the graphs for pop prognostications and slapdash theorizing. Alvin Toffler is an eminent representative of the clan. He is able to describe a coming civilization in all its concrete and vivid manifestations ranging from sexual mores to workplace attitudes because he is free of the restraints that inhibit the serious theorist. Exercises of this kind, although without claims on the social sciences, may have importance in the genre of prophetic writing in the tradition of Jules Verne.

The third type is the social forecasting attempted by Daniel Bell in *The Coming of Post-Industrial Society* and by others associated with the Academy of the Arts and Sciences Commission on the Year 2000. Here the investigators review the mass of relevant data, try to identify the main social trends, and having grasped to their satisfaction the dynamic of the process, to draw the ongoing changes to their logical limits. What the end product turns out to be depends on the method and the acuteness of the analyst. It is not my purpose to supply a rounded critique of Bell's analysis, the major contribution in this enterprise; I call attention to his work primarily to illustrate a point. It helps me flesh out my argument when I indicate why the components that make up Bell's postindustrial society lack organic unity. Here are the described characteristics of his new society due to emerge in the next thirty to fifty years: (1) the change from a goods-producing to a service economy; (2) the preeminence of the professional and technical class; (3) the centrality of theoretical knowledge (theory over empiricism) as the source of innovation and policy formulation; (4) with technological forecasting now possible, a reduced indeterminacy about society's economic future and an increased ability to plan and direct technological change, as well as to establish more advanced intellectual controls.

Two deficiencies in the enumeration are immediately apparent. The first is the absence of a political motor. This is no small matter. After all, the topic of the discussion is a dynamic of change—and the political dynamo is not listed. It is as if impersonal technological forces will break through of their own accord to shape the contours of the coming society. The absence is the more noticeable since Bell in his writings insists on the supremacy or independence of the political sector. Yet he is unable to say anything meaningful about politics or the state in his postindustrial order, leaving himself open to the accusation (that he levels at others) of technological determinism. Without some concept of the political integrant, of the role of the political establishment, the new society is left unborn for want of a midwife.

The second deficiency is in the purported preeminence of the technical class which, as he has developed the proposition, refers mainly to scientists and technologists. What does preeminence mean here? They are not to be the new governing authority, for we have been told already that the political order—whatever it is to be and whoever is going to run it—will be in charge of society's control system. Moreover the scientific intelligentsia is neither a new class nor a new mandarin caste bound by its own special interests. Nevertheless this scientific intelligentsia will stand at the hub of the social structure, for, it is hinted, like trader and capitalist elements under feudalism it will have infiltrated and will permeate the new order. Permeate it with what? "The community of science is a unique institution in human civilization. It has no ideology . . . but it has an ethos." Just as the Protestant Ethic was the ethos of capitalism and the Socialist Idea the ethos of Soviet society, so "the ethos of science is the emerging ethos of post-industrial society"; and social systems are ultimately defined by their ethos. In this case the ethos is one of professionalism, embodying formal training, certification by one's peers, dedication to one's intellectual discipline, inculcation of social responsibility, an ethic of service in place of an ethic of self-interest.

This leaves a big gap. Bell has not demonstrated that this secular priesthood, subclass, meritocracy—call it what you will—is actually the carrier of a new ethos. Furthermore how is this intelligentsia going to impose this ethos on society when it lacks political authority? In one sense scientists and engineers, particularly those whose work has military application, enjoy preeminence today. That does not mean that their elevated professional and social status can be equated with political power. In the veiled half-contest that developed in the Robert Oppenheimer case between a section of the scientific community and the Pentagon and White House bureaucracies, the scientists were brutally instructed that as scientists they carried no political credentials, that they were expected to be on tap, not on top. True, numbers of them occupy influential positions in government commissions or the inner reaches of the Pentagon—not as carriers of a distinct mission, however, but as specialists supplying input no different from their fellow bureaucrats who happen to be lawyers, accountants, or business administrators. How is the present generation of socially conformist science bureaucrats to be transmogrified to an apostolic scientific intelligentsia exuding and sanctifying an ethic of service?

One leaves Bell's big, ambitious, disorderly, in places brilliant, work with the feeling of having eaten a too-rich meal that lacked some needed ingredient. Several of the enumerated features offer glimpses of the coming society; but with Bell's map in hand, we know no more of its structure and operation, as "ideal type" or otherwise, than a blind man can understand the shape of an elephant by grasping its trunk. The reason the analytical construct is excessively abstract is because Bell has initiated his analysis by following the same paths taken by the demographers and social statisticians and then sought to conceptualize the extrapolated data. To get to the essentials of the changeovers in the coming society he should have delved into those contradictions that are responsible for ripping apart the social fabric of our present order. He should have studied those ailments that cannot be righted under ongoing political arrangements. He should have investigated those structural faults producing dislocations along planes of fracture that carry the danger of collapse—with the possibility of basic overhauls barred by corporative interests and embedded assumptions. Such a procedure is not necessarily foolproof; it will not necessarily result in the production of a manual on who will superintend the setting-up of the new works and on what principles. But such a procedure induces the analyst to keep his eye on essentials. By understanding what the questions are we can more easily grasp what the answers might be. We cannot start with technology and occupation and market trends and say, as Bell does, that we will leave open the politics of the matter to a later time. That is like staging *Hamlet* without the prince.

2

There is no need to pause very long before the recent electoral demonstrations that put conservative spokesmen in office in several countries including our own. Seesawing electoral returns have to be analyzed—where they can be rationally explained at all—in the way a psychiatrist tries to disentangle a patient's vagaries. Students of elections note that it is more usual for people to vote their hostility to the incumbents, their desire to punish officeholders dragging long trails of unredeemed promises, than to vote positive approval of the opposing party's program. Party proposals are generally murky, ambiguously designed and expressed, and their leading candidate may alter them two or three times in the course of a campaign, as well. It is no simple matter for people confused by demagogic rhetoric to conceptualize their grievances and wishes, or to have them honored in the hurly-burly of politics run by managers and handlers in the spirit of advertising campaigns. The tumult and contrived struggles of the campaign itself act as the great popular catharsis without necessarily determining the tenor of legislation to come. What the press generally interprets as a popular swing to the right or to the left may record nothing more extraordinary than customary oscillations of the electoral pendulum.

As for the factual record of the Thatcher government in England and the Reagan government in the U.S., diminishing statism is not one of either administration's accomplishments. Despite their bloodcurdling rhetoric of less government, both have been pressing for ever-greater militarization, both are amassing huge budgetary deficits, both are exerting themselves to make government martinets less, not more, accountable to the citizenry. Statistics providing the data of the actual decisions of both these administrations, when they are completed, may show little more than some shift in national income in favor of the rich. President Reagan's program to reduce the budget from over 21 to about 19 percent of GNP has already come a cropper. The average for his four budget-years will be well over 24 percent, far higher than the average during his predecessor's years.

Of greater symptomatic significance than ambiguous or contradictory messages issuing from the political pressure cookers is the widespread conviction among scholars that profound social changes are in the offing. The sense that we are at the end of an era has permeated the thought of today's sociologists, psychologists, and social scientists of varying persuasions, so that the theme spills over repeatedly into popular literature. When we consider that Plato held that a change in the mode of music forebode a change in the constitution of the political and social order, we are entitled to consider the visceral responses of intellectuals as premonitory signs of coming events. True, this seductive idea has two drawbacks. First, it is unprovable. The sociologist's vision may have profound symptomatic significance to one person and represent the vagary of an overheated imagination to another. Second, these types of apocalyptic forecasts are compromised by their having been made by artists and journalists during years that are now recognized as capitalism's heyday.

Nevertheless, that that is the perception of numbers of thoughtful scholars is not without its importance, particularly since to it is joined a more commonly held proposition. There is a disjunction, we are told, and a widening one, between social structure and culture. Official morality rests on a functional rationality requiring efficiency. Culture is increasingly hedonistic, and the huckstering crafts rooted in the social structure, with an assignment to incite consumer passions and to market goods, augment the hedonism. They deepen the hunger for possessions associated with leisure. The result is structure at war with function. The thought is commonplace that the antagonistic claims on the individual's loyalties have left capitalism with no recognizable ethic. What is debatable is whether capitalism can adapt itself to this disjunction as over its turbulent history it has accommodated its sovereignty to so many other conflicting impulses, or whether this disjunction will be the cause of drawing away vital energies over the critical years ahead.

The character of present political directorates poses for some an insuperable difficulty to accepting the reality of the profound changeovers to come. People look at these politicians in the industrial countries, those in opposition as well as those in office, and find it unrealistic to expect structural transformations to be initiated by proven dependables of the existing order, be they conservative or moderately reformist. They argue at another point that no deep-going contest over property rights and interests can ensue between multinational corporations and governments because the two sets of bureaucracies look alike and think alike. In short, if there are any Bismarcks, Cavours, or Toshimichi Okubos (architect of the Meiji Restoration) lurking in the shadows, no one is aware of their existence. Were we to accept the current crop of political practitioners as setting the boundaries for vision and élan vital, the possibility of structural transformations through elitist initiatives is farfetched. But do these coteries constitute a fixed norm? If the analysis of the gathering crisis is valid, the character of political types in office and in opposition will change. When stimuli are brutally drastic, even people in politics respond drastically. The time period in which such changes will take place is uncertain, in the range of a half to three-quarters of a century, with the change finding definition over a number of years. The shadowiness of the time frame is understandable; we are tracing a sociological trend, not attempting to cast a horoscope.

The scenario I will summarize, which I believe has relevance to the American actuality, is based on the Hundred Days of Franklin Roosevelt's initial term of office. This is not to be taken that the activities and legislation of the Hundred Days will be reenacted or that I am suggesting that the New Deal constituted a social revolution. But the scenario has validity to the extent that it illumines an existential vista as a point of reference for the changeover transition. Item number one was the crisis. It was the common perception when the new president took office that the machinery of the economy in the cities and in the countryside, in the factories and in the banks, was grinding to a halt. The crisis had penetrated the bones and brains of most people, including those in government. The result was a mass populist mood and a massive leftward shift in government. A Hyde Park patrician brought up in the school of Progressive Era elitism became the pilot of the most ambitious reform journey of the century. A professional social worker of conventional liberal persuasion became the organizer of the biggest government-financed make-work program in this or any country's history.

A traditionally interest-ridden conservative Congress was caught up in the reform whirlwind. Some legislators even wanted to go further and faster than the buoyant, self-confident figure in the White House. The antagonistic ones were overawed. They did not dare, in the reform floodtide, to pit themselves against a president riding the wave of overwhelming popularity. (Some serious students, not all, are convinced that had Roosevelt been of a mind, in the first Hundred Days he could have put through several structural reforms, that the country would have welcomed them, and that the momentary power balances would have permitted their enactment.)

The instrumentality by which the momentous changes were instituted was a revivified bureaucracy and executive organization. When word got out that the government intended to put real effort into fighting the depression, thousands of young men and women descended on Washington to participate in the great adventure—economists, lawyers, planners, journalists, social workers, professionals of every type and variety, not to mention plain office workers, secretaries, technicians—all determined to get close to the scene of action. Some came because jobs were hard or impossible to find elsewhere and Washington was hiring. Others, particularly as one went up the scale of skill and status, were fired by the ideal of enlisting in the crusade of remaking America into a more humane and participatory society.

They came from many walks of life. There were graduates of New York City slums and city colleges. There was Alger Hiss, a Harvard Law School product who had been a law clerk to Justice Holmes and thought at one time of going to Spain to fight for the Loyalists. There were Adlai Stevenson and George Ball of Forest Park's and Chicago's upper crust. There was Henry Wallace and the progressive agrarians. There was Rexford Tugwell and other experimental-minded academics. In totality they made up a decidedly liberal, in spots a left-liberal, bureaucracy the like of which had not been seen in Washington before. Liberal placemen crowded into every cranny, bureau, and department, given a sense of purpose and direction by Roosevelt's Brain Trust who reenacted and magnified the innovations of President Jackson's Kitchen Cabinet. Such were the agencies carrying through reforms in the five years of New Deal ascendancy—with the willing or grudging acquiescence of Congress. The United States, the most Tory-minded power in the industrial world in the 1920s, became for a while the most welfare-oriented.

In the crisis that will be the starting point of the Great Transformation, the feeling will be more profound that things cannot continue along the old paths. The particular blockages, disruptions, and breakdowns will not be those of 1933; they will be the culminations of present and subsequent evasions and failures. The crisis will be an aggravated one because the disorganization will have gone deeper. The demand for more sweeping reforms will well up from below because the crisis will come after Welfare State and Keynesian remedies have been found wanting and half-hearted laissez-faire revivalist attempts have been discredited. The need for more ambitious government interventions will appear inescapable.

The classes, subclasses, categories, ethnic groups, etc., that became fervent partisans of the New Deal—the Roosevelt coalition—spread across the political spectrum. The business class split; some, located in light and service industries, joined the coalition, especially in the first few years. The elder Joseph P. Kennedy, a capitalist adventurer unattached to major corporations, for example, remembered for his later role as an isolationist and backer of Sen. Joseph McCarthy, lent his voice up to the war years to rounding up support for Roosevelt in the business community, even upholding the so-called packing of the Supreme Court. Department store executives and manufacturers of light consumer goods were heavy campaign contributors. But this segment of business was a distinct minority. The foremost business leaders and organizations, most figures of the big corporations, and all but a handful of influential spokesmen, united against Roosevelt and vilified him as a traitor to his class. The press lords in 1936 overwhelmingly called for his repudiation. The atmosphere in the big-business offices, from boardrooms to ordinary company cafeterias patronized by low-echelon white-collar employees, was saturated with anti-Rooseveltianism. The managers, identified earlier as social and political conformists, found the Welfare State (until their lawyers and public relations advisers eventually quieted their fears) altogether too radical for their biases and predilections. Some of the sizable contributions to the Democrats were made not because the donors understood that reforms could no longer be avoided; these go-getters were simply taking out reinsurance (they made even larger contributions to the Republicans).

As we would expect the labor battalions, in contrast, went overwhelmingly to the Roosevelt camp. The modern working-class movement actually took shape in the Roosevelt foundry. Unions had been weak in this country up to this time, virtually unrepresented in the mass-production industries. The isolated unionized enclaves of the skilled and favored were decimated during the depression years. It was only with the rise of the CIO that employees of heavy industries were enrolled in the union fold, and the modern labor movement came into being. The climate enabling unions to expand threefold and the legal procedures directing the new militancy into orderly and bureaucratized channels was the work of government administrators and legislators.

It would be a vast oversimplification were we to counterpose leftward-oriented union leaders to rightward-oriented business leaders. The emergent labor movement, with the pronounced features of a latter-day social-democracy, was a more ambiguous social integer. On matters pertaining to social security, workshop conditions, and liberal regulations it was an indefatiguable lobbyist, consistent and persistent, for their betterment and extension—the Welfare State advocate par excellence. On more general national and international issues it was no less conformist-minded and status quo-minded than the average Rotarian businessman. George Meany, past AFL-CIO head, was an exemplar of conservatism on social questions outside his professional interests. He and most other union chieftains would out-Herod Herod in their anti-Communist pronouncements and their fervor for the free-enterprise system.

Lenin, who in pursuit of his own aims was a sharp observer of the labor scene, came to the conviction from which he never waivered, that the working class, left to its own devices, was incapable of developing an independent world outlook, that its natural bent was to trade unionism. This could only be changed when and if radical intellectuals propelled it into the Marxian stream. Workers could not "fulfill their world-historical mission of emancipating mankind if [they] concern themselves exclusively with their narrow trade interests. . . ." Actually trade unionism as a specific corporative outlook need not and does not limit itself to workshop interests and wage improvements. It encompasses in all advanced industrial countries the political dimension. Its crucial characteristic is not trade parochialism, but its stubborn rejection of "a world-historical mission to emancipate mankind," its insistence instead on concentrating on "improving labor's petty-bourgeois conditions." Hence labor's thinking, all the more pronouncedly in this country, is corporatist, not revolutionary; ameliorative, not apocalyptic; philistine, not heroic; quarreling over the distribution of the product, not over the social order under which the product is produced.

The trade union officialdom is content to take its appointed place in the liberal coalition; it lacks regal pretensions of its own. When John L. Lewis, the mine union and CIO leader—unique among union officials for his political ambitions—demanded that he be included as a vice-presidential candidate on the Roosevelt ticket and that a few laborites be placed in the cabinet, he was viewed as an insufferable climber and an ingrate by the Roosevelt entourage. What is more relevent, he was deserted by the entire non-Communist labor officialdom.

As a class American workers have no vision of a new society and no will to sovereign power. Eugene V. Debs, the fiery Socialist apostle of another day, said that he aspired to rise with the working class, not out of the working class; but his was very much a minority view. Eli Chinoy, in *Automobile Workers and the American Dream*, recorded more accurately the altogether contrary ambition of alert young workers. They aspired to get out of the working class at the first available opportunity by opening their own backyard garage or neighborhood whiskey bar. In the circumstances it is not surprising that union officials' command of their members' loyalties is a limited one. As far as one can pinpoint the leading groups, it was not the labor directors but the agglomeration of professionals, lawyers, economists, administrators, assorted political personalities, certain businessman wheeler-dealers—the middle-class intelligentsia one might call it—who were the shapers and executants of the New Deal reform program.

One can surmise that a similarly broad coalition will usher in the Great Transformation. Its specific segments will have different characteristics and the force relationships within the coalition will vary, for both social structure and social makeup have altered substantially and will alter still further in the intervening years. Because of crisscrossing subclasses and their special, not always readily reconcilable interests, coalitions of diverse groups have been the favored instrumentalities for ushering in changes throughout American history. A new coalition is the indicated agency for mediating fundamental structural reforms because no one class has emerged or can emerge as an acceptable national vanguard. Most corporate executives will seek to obstruct the passage of new enabling legislation more tenaciously and aggressively than during the introduction of the Welfare State because this time their property prerogatives will be called into greater question. Until the new state is consolidated they can be expected to be part of the opposition.

The labor movement, after preliminary soul-searching, will commit its resources and energies to the coalition for the new order because labor potentates are habituated to coming to terms with power. Whatever misgivings they may originally harbor about authoritarian dangers will be overcome by their enthusiasm for promised welfarist dispensations and the posts made available for their loyalists. Although labor's presence in the coalition is more or less indispensable, it will not be its leader any more than it was the leader of the Roosevelt coalition. This is ruled out by middle-class prejudice against union officials as well as the latter's constricted horizons.

The professionals, probably augmented with professionalized spokesmen of the new assertive minority claimants for attention, will step to the fore as both the effective bureaucracy and advance supporting cast of a new working order. This reinforced intelligentsia will shield the new regime in a manifold protective layer. At the overturn it will be a battle-ready formation reinforced over many years with specialists receptive to statist resolutions of intractable problems. A section of the bureaucracy will have already formed a subspecies whose members' careers are intertwined with state activities and who are committed to a program of state intervention. This type of popular coalition, moreover, will lend itself to the decision-wielding presidency at the center taking on Bonapartist hues in conjunction with a supportive or revamped Congress. There was an element of Bonapartism in the Roosevelt regime, indeed in the modern imperial presidency per se. The propensity for it will be greater this time because the need to balance off conflicting, enraged groups will be more pressing. The New Hundred Days will be a time in which audacity, not prudence, will be in demand.

3

Very well, we have a quasi-revolutionary regime installed at the helm. What comes next? Let us keep in mind that the regime is facing a deep crisis. That is why it came into being. It has to bring under control a raging inflation. It has to stop the uncoordinated movements of capital and plants of the multinationals and banks in and out of the country. It has to put to work millions of increasingly clamorous unemployed. It has to restore confidence in the ability of the community to manage its affairs. And the regime has to do these many things expeditiously so that serious social eruptions are avoided, the nation's morale and self-confidence are restored, and a resolute effort is underway to rectify the structural and conceptual defects that were the causes for the breakdown.

What are the leaders going to do? One of the first things they will have to do is to position the government so that it can make operative decisions. To that end they will adopt measures and take on personnel for the creation, as mentioned, of a central planning authority. For planning to rise above the rank of conventional regulation, or of the indicative variety of planning—which even in its day of glory was two parts public relations to one part state aid, and is not talked about very much any longer—the political directorate has to be in a position to operate the economic levers. Its technicians have to have authority not only to draw up blueprints but to have them acted upon.

Far more is known about indirect methods for controlling an economy than was known half a century ago. Superior technologies of knowledge storage and control are now available to would-be controllers, if the will is there to use them. Are they sufficient for an executive planning authority to carry through on its prescribed duties? Can the fiefdoms and empires be left intact under the rule of their private patriciates commanding armies of managers, treasurers, retainers? Hardly. Certain sensitive parts of the economy will have to be placed unambiguously under the administration of public servants. How extensive the nationalized sector will be, and precisely what sections will have to be included, and which ones can continue to operate under private ownership, is something that will have to be determined by practical considerations.

At issue is not the productive efficiency of specific industrial behemoths but their massed power, not their profit-taking proclivities but their narrowly corporate viewpoints. Why did De Gaulle in the 1960s, why does the Canadian government today, want to transfer some of their essential industries to the hands of their nationals? Because they did not and do not want to surrender decision-making power over their economy to outsiders. The same consideration applies within the national entity. If the state, as the surrogate for the community, is to gain decision-making powers over the economy, it has to subdue the provincial corporate sovereigns as the monarchs delegating authority to Richelieu and Mazarin subdued in their time the earls and counts running their own principalities. If planning is to be a central feature of economic organization and not a political confidence game, the state has to be in a position to monitor and supervise the activities—and there is a hundred years of experience to prove that that cannot be done by regulatory commissions. What is tolerable when the economy is advancing, people's lots are improving, and society is stable and secure, becomes intolerable when society is in crisis. Then the nation can no longer permit parochial interests to set national priorities.

In talking about planning, we are up against one of the triumphant mythologies of our time: (1) that central planning is grievously inefficient, unworkable in fact; and (2) that it spawns a sprawling, wasteful bureaucracy which inevitably results in the imposition of dictatorship, as a matter of fact, is synonymous with dictatorship. That corporation spokesmen have been able to put across these theorems as self-evident truths of political science and economic organization is a tribute to their artistry in molding public opinion. It is all the more remarkable since corporations are the foremost practitioners of centrally directed planning in our society. Planning is not just another clever idea which sprang without warning from the minds of kinky econometricians. It has a long parentage in the evolution of industrial enterprises. With the arrival of the large, multiproduct corporation that puts to use high technology and large capital accumulations, its production schedules could no longer be dependent on the ebb and flow of short-term market responses. A host of highly paid specialists in numerous disciplines spent months upon months projecting, blueprinting, reconciling the different elements of a four- or five-year plan because requisite investments are enormous and any mistake in design, concept, or calculation can be disastrous to the fortunes of the company. In the monumental study of the United States Tariff Commission previously referred to, this description of planning is offered, and offered as a testimonial to the multinationals to boot:

> The coordination of MNC operations requires planning and system-ization of control of a high order. In the largest and most sophisti-cated MNCs, planning and subsequent monitoring of plan fulfill-ment may have reached a scope and level of detail that, ironically, resemble more than superficially the national planning procedures of Communist countries. There are general goals set by top manage-ment, against which far-flung affiliates generate detailed operational plans for a year's, five years', or ten years' activity. . . . Without these devices, the large, complex MNC would disintegrate into chaos, thus forfeiting the advantages of managerial efficiency that may be its principal contribution to world economic welfare.

If the big corporations are already planning, why is it nec-essary for the state to set up its own superplan? Why will the state be a better planner than the private corporation? The indi-vidual plans of the private empires added together are not a substitute for a national plan. The drawback of the individual corporation plan is not inefficiency but narrow purpose. First, the flow of corporations' funds is designed to concentrate resources under their own control. This results in social imbalance between an affluent private sector and a starved public sector. Within the private sector there is a corresponding imbalance between the opulent big-business economy and the straitened periphery economy. Second, the various plans do not converge: they cut across each other. The individual plan, no matter how well conceived and flawlessly executed, is meant by the draftsmen and managers to further the sales, market positions, and profits of their empire, not to advance the interests of other empires. It is no part of their responsibilities to look after the needs of the general population at home, much less the populations of all the countries in which their plants are located abroad. What happens when the projects deriving from these several plans collide? What happens is that the strongest hosts garner the benefits of planning while enveloping the less favored and the generality of the populace in the higher disorganization. Hence planning of, by, and for private industrial empires is like democracy in ancient Athens, a prize for the citizen but of no application to the metic and slave.

Alongside the received wisdom that disasters unimaginable are sure to result from central planning is the dogma propounded with equal certitude that nationalization is inherently inefficient, a shopworn idea derived from obsolete Marxian texts. Nationalized companies, we are told, wherever tried, have proven an endless drain on the public treasury without offering any advantages to their own workers. Governments have no need of these cumbersome, antiquated expedients. They can instead move the economy in desired directions by utilizing sophisticated fiscal and monetary techniques perfected in recent times.

No extensive refutation of these tendentious rationalizations is called for, since I analyzed the realities of nationalizations in Western Europe in earlier chapters. The pundits have been pushing their self-fulfilling prophecies too selectively and indiscriminately for even routine journalistic purposes, dwelling on companies that lose money and skipping over the money-makers. But even if all were losers the experiment would be irrelevant for determining their efficiency or inefficiency. Nationalized firms were set up in England, France, and elsewhere on the continent as subservient auxiliaries to buttress and enhance the private sectors. As for alleged late-model sophisticated techniques, their utility has been overblown where these techniques are not entirely of the witchcraft class. They can provide an umbrella for a summer squall. They are useless in a storm.

More important than the sustained denigration of nationalizations in turning Western public opinion against a planned economy has been the Russian experience. For many, Soviet planning has demonstrated once and for all that a state-run economy is a producer of shoddy, high-priced goods, a destroyer of innovation and initiative, a generator of a monstrous bureaucracy. The defects of the Soviet economy are well known and well publicized in the West. They are the defects that stem from overcentralization and overbureaucratization, two parasitical offspring permitted to luxuriate in a society with a long history of authoritarianism, police repression, obtuse bureaucratism, illiteracy, and preindustrial slothful habits and customs. Stalinist planners thought that every detail had to be determined at the central control tower. Since it was impossible for Gosplan (the Soviet State Planning Commission) functionaries to see all, know all, and direct all, their decisions rested on questionable assumptions which all too often were far removed from the realities.

The system necessarily led to an information overload. Functionaries found themselves drowning amid an unceasing flow of paper which they could not even riffle through much less attempt to digest and evaluate. Subordinate officials and enterprise managers, thrust into a false environment and faced with impossible demands from the center, put into effect their own informal understandings with suppliers and buyers, or with unofficial expediters and fixers. Clandestine networks sprang up; informal sets of controls were devised; favors were traded. Beneath the unilateral pyramidal planning system there operate numbers of unacknowledged subordinate systems. The objectives of the national plan are often distorted or positively subverted, with subordinate officials' making decisions or engaging in activities to advance their personal or clique interests, as well as to protect their own security and careers. That Soviet planning is an abomination is understood inside and outside the bureaucracy. It is an operational model that guarantees making numerous and repeated mistakes, and that miscalculations, when made, will be big ones. Many Soviet specialists are convinced that the existing methods, whatever effectiveness they had in earlier periods, are played out, that a revision is not just desirable but unavoidable. Thus far attempts at serious reforms have been resisted by the ruling power because these carry unacceptable risks.

In 1965, in the midst of a reform wave in the satellite countries, the Soviet leadership announced a series of changes encompassing use of profits criteria, greater managerial authority in market transactions, new financial incentives tied to enterprise profitability, price reforms, etc. It was a policy looking toward decentralizing a top-heavy edifice, of controlling production by efficiency pricing. Before reforms could take effect to demonstrate their usefulness or nonusefulness, the political chieftains drew back in alarm. Very quickly they digested the fact that the technical changes carried dangerous political implications: administrative decentralization and market orientation, though rudimentary, could lead to the rise of industrial satraps, in other words, to the creation of dual centers of authority. Better to put up with an economic muddle than to accept the risk of undermining the dictatorial regime. Thus some of the glaring defects of Soviet planning and production are not necessary emanations of central planning. They are the creation of a tainted government that is presiding over an inept, corrupt bureaucracy that does not dare permit the rank and file a voice in managing the economy.

The quality of national planning and the efficiency of production in state enterprises are related intimately to the general cultural configuration of a society. The imagery may not be exact in every detail and in every instance, but by and large the character of planning and production is explicable in terms of the cultural and political attainments of a people. East Germany does far better than the Soviet Union even though operating a similarly heavy-handed Stalinist-type planning organization. Consequently the logic of the situation reads that when national planning is undertaken by advanced nations, many or most Soviet economic derelictions and blunders will be avoided.

4

An important professional literature on planning has grown up in the West since the Soviet Union popularized the concept. In the realm of theory Oscar Lange, who was professor of economics at the University of Chicago and later an official in the Gomulka government in Communist Poland, developed the proposition that socialist market economy was not only feasible

but that the market would operate more effectively under socialism than under capitalism because its functioning would no
longer be distorted by oligopolistic price-fixers. The proposition
gained a following, and Soviet economists picked it up during
the short reform springtime. They argued that because capitalism preceded socialism was no reason why the market method
of regulation cannot be employed in a socialist economy as well
to improve efficiency, that the market as a mechanism is sys-
tem-free. Their temerity, however, was short-lived, and it was
left to the Yugoslavs and then the Hungarians to demonstrate
that other systems besides capitalism can be associated with the
market.

In the Yugoslav planned economy, all enterprises of five or
more employees have to be turned over to one or another government authority. Private holdings predominate in agriculture, although about one-seventh of the arable land is owned by state
farms or collectives, and the future goal is the replacement of
private farming by self-managed, socially owned, large-scale enterprises. Urban public enterprises employing thirty or more are
run by their workers through elected council representatives,
and in their daily operation by a management committee and a
hired manager. Central control is imposed not through a compulsory plan but by state interventions, in which taxes, subsidies,
regulations, and control over new investments are employed as
instruments to guide production along desired lines. The enterprise must cover its costs and is free to establish its own markets,
to diversify production, and to apportion its profits between
wages and reinvestments.

The effectiveness of the Yugoslav system, the substantiality
of employee rule under full-time professional management, the
vitality of enterprise self-rule under the guidance of government-
directed banks and of Communist party suzerains are matters of
divergent appreciations. That Yugoslavia is not about to become
a pathfinder in world economic achievement is scarcely surprising in view of the country's longstanding economic retardation.
That the economy leaves much to be desired is evident from the
considerable unemployment, the sporadic price inflations, and
the emigration of job-seekers to Western Europe in expansionary
years. But it is an achievement of no mean order that the economy is working and growing, that the difficult experiment is a
success to the extent of binding together a country consisting of

half a dozen historically antagonistic nationalities who in the past made Yugoslavia a cockpit of Balkan conflicts.

Both theory and practice suggest that authentic national planning need not entail Soviet-style takeovers of all economic activities from large-scale factories to individually owned repair shops, from retail outlets to family farms. What is decisive is that decision-making can be engrossed by the state, and the ability of the state to plan and to carry through cannot be invalidated by the massed power of economic overloads. To achieve that, it will be sufficient that some important sections of the economy are allocated to social ownership.

Moreover those industries and facilities brought under social ownership will not necessarily function under the central state authority. Many enterprises will be owned and controlled by municipal and district authorities. In all cases, national, regional, municipal, and all sorts of communal representatives, consumer committees, or special-interest spokesmen should be able to participate in drawing up specific parts of the plan, offering proposals, making criticisms. Labor unions, while necessarily of a different character than those operating in capitalist enterprises, can continue as autonomous bodies looking after the workshop interests of their members. Consequently the final national plan worked up by professionals at central planning will not be in the form of a decree issued from on high to a servile mass below. It will be the product of the proposals and wishes of great numbers. It will also, without a doubt, given the superior economic experience and capability of advanced industrial peoples, be vastly more realistic in scheduling inputs, drawing up production schedules, and ensuring internal consistency than Soviet performance at its ultimate best. As should be clear by now, my aim is not to make a plea for this or that central-planning schema, but to argue that one or another model of this systemic type will recommend itself to decision-makers at the moment of truth.

If there is a plurality of state owners advancing sectional and group interests; if a conglomeration of committees and communal organizations press their own corporative demands; if the central authorities feel compelled to compromise on some projects in order to gain local approval for other projects; if the operative technique for crafting the plan is the tradeoff; if the cooperation of subordinate divisions can only be enlisted by log-rolling—then the question of efficacy inevitably arises. How does this type of planning eliminate the anarchy and waste of capitalist economics? The answer will have to be that in the final analysis decisions are the prerogative of the central authority, that if, after discussions, negotiations, attempts at winning cooperation with concessions or revisions, no agreement can be reached, then the central representatives will be able to say "This is the way it is going to be done."

Whether the market can or will be the important instrument of control in future planning that Lange believed it could be is uncertain. Let us first be clear about prevailing usages on both sides of the curtain. The market is not the universal controller under capitalism, and it is used in a limited way under the Soviet command system. Under capitalism, key industrial units organize production not by market but by bureaucratic dictates, notwithstanding the fact that the industrial directorates are en-meshed in a quasi-market system. All free-enterprise systems avowedly set, or permit to have set, prices administratively for airlines, railroads, telephone service, electric power usage, and unavowedly for the multitudinous products of oligopolistic in-dustries. On the other side of the divide the Soviets have a re-stricted market to recruit and assign workers, and use prices to sell consumer goods for money.

With industrial integration and accounting as refined as they are nowadays, the ascendant state can utilize the market rather than rely on brute command if it chooses to do so. Planners can direct production by purchasing final products; they can mold consumer buying habits by ordering the quantities and types of consumer goods that they think are in consonance with overall priorities, and resell them to consumers. They can conduct op-erations under one set of prices for controlling production and another set of prices for distributing to consumers. The question is: If the government guides the market to this extent, will the market emit those kinds of signals that are important for deci-sion-making? A thermometer may provide an accurate reading of a patient's temperature, but if the patient persists in swallowing hot or cold liquids while the thermometer is in place, the infor-mation recorded will be of little use to the attending physician. To what extent a market—that talks the language of costs, but waves away as externalities matters such as unemployment, health hazards, pollution, junk goods—can be used effectively by planners is something that only future practice will establish.

A different type of objection has been raised by socialist writers to reliance on the market mechanism. They point out that the market does not only emit cost signals; in its profoundest manifestation it concentrates the minds of all those enmeshed in it on material enrichment. It is the compulsive thrust of bourgeois culture upon which other attainments and fulfillments are dependent, the talisman that opens the doors to private and public success. It represents the apotheosis of the individualist creed dedicated to private aggrandizement. In its halcyon days individualism was the spur to feats of accomplishment and creativity. In our latter day, loosened from the work ethic that gave it discipline and purpose, individualism threatens like a blind Samson to tear down the pillars of the Temple. The problem with the market, therefore, is that once these egotistic furies are unleashed there is the danger that they may overwhelm new cooperative arrangements and ready the ground for the return of the competitive culture that has but recently been displaced.

This leads me to what Daniel Bell referred to as the ethos of his postindustrial society. The technician is to be at the center of it, and an ethic of service is to come ahead of an ethic of self-interest, while the ethos of science becomes the ethos of the entire society: "Capitalism was not just a system for the production of commodities . . . but a justification of the primacy of the individual and his self-interest. . . . The political ethos of an emerging post-industrial society is communal, insofar as social goals and priorities are defined by and national policy is directed to the realization of those goals."

Set aside Bell's idealized technocrat as the carrier of communal virtues and this is an accurate pointer to a necessary cultural transition. Bourgeois society presupposes, accentuates, extolls, the individualist traits. Bourgeois culture has built up, brick by brick, an acquisitive morality appropriate to the competitive struggle for wealth. Without this the system could not work. In the same way planning and the integrated state cannot function unless the nation is animated by a morality based on some form of communal commitment. Institutions cannot be lastingly refashioned unless there are corresponding transvaluations of morals. If a new morality of cooperation does not gain favor, indispensable habits will not be developed. Or if a new morality is decreed by fiat, as in the Soviet case, which cuts across the behavior of the favored, it will be cynically taken for official cant. In either case, lacking necessary "legitimacy," the postindustrial commonwealth will not last through its first serious crisis if indeed it is set up at all.

What will happen to the multinational corporations? Will the rise of planning states spell their dissolution by official fiat the way Standard Oil was broken up into its component sections by order of the U.S. Supreme Court? Would this not signify, were it to occur, a retrogression in world economic organization? Socially irresponsible and economically disorganizing though their activities are, multinational corporations are bearers of a supranational organization of production, distribution, and accounting. They carry the prodigies of capitalist-technological creativity a step further on the ascending pathway of industrial progress. They need not face dissolution under the regimes of ascendant states. One can foresee arrangements in which transmogrified multinationals are fitted into the emergent collectivities. Even now a number of multinationals, like nationally owned British Petroleum, or Renault in France, function comfortably across national boundaries. Agreements will very likely be negotiated by the new states for the continued operation of many of them. The governing authorities will have to set more stringent requirements for the corporations to observe at home and abroad. Notwithstanding this, efforts will probably be made to sustain the traditions of international cross investments and division of labor.

In a profound way today's multinational corporation is an expression of the heightened interdependence of nations in the postwar era. However distortedly, the MNC is filling the vacuum created by the default of the great nation-states in building transnational sovereignties. Given power realities and trends, it can be anticipated that several industrial colossi will remain the dominant state powers in the new order. We can envisage the formation of transnational blocs around several central states which will become the effective clearinghouses to coordinate economic tasks and regularize international exchanges.

I saved for last considerations of democracy and whether and to what extent the ascendant state's role in the economy endangers the great heritage of the commercial and industrial eras embodied in individual liberty and parliamentary representation. Practices have always lagged behind professions. There has been a yawning gap between promise and fulfillment. The counterposition of one to the other has formed the subject matter of a bulky literature of criticism and protest. But one need only compare the lot of the masses in capitalist democracies with the lot of similarly placed people in Soviet Russia and its satellites, or in the fascist countries during the interwar years, or in the military despotisms in Latin America, to realize that the loss of these rights, or many of them, would represent a profound retrogression in human affairs. It would in effect signify that in order to straighten out economic malformation, humanity had to sacrifice its political adulthood.

If the new nation builders succeed in scattering ownership of socialized property among different government subdivisions, invite popular participation in planning, and permit important parts of the economy to continue in private hands, the danger may prove to be solely an academic one. The politicians, managers, and technical experts directing economic enterprises and affairs in municipalities, regions, or the national enclave may keep watch over each other, thus providing a system of checks and balances. If, in another variant, because of related tasks, common outlooks, and professional biases these sets of bureaucrats form a caste overriding centrifugal forces and smoothing over sectional and parochial divergences, the evolution of the new society would be authoritarian and the dispersion of potential power blocs proven to have been in vain.

But need that variant gain the ascendancy? There are weighty influences militating against an authoritarian settlement. Let us recall that what is under consideration is a structual change engineered from above. This means that the new statist ministers will have to arrive at a compromise with existing business classes. The compromise that suggests itself is to compensate owners for their stocks and bonds, and to offer to integrate displaced corporation managers, fiscal officers, and technicians into the planning and supervisory apparatus of the new collectivism. Many owners of equities will simply become rentiers. Others will use the funds made available to them to buy up businesses in the private sector. It is true that business people have not been prominent in the defense of civil liberties or democratic rights in the past, and that their natural inclinations would be to underwrite authoritarian schemes. However, now they find themselves in an entirely changed personal and social situation. Whatever their previous proclivities, they now constitute a distinct social layer called upon to defend its circumscribed position.

More important is the character of the coalition that brings the new state into being. As indicated, many of the effectives making up this coalition are historically conditioned to battle for populist causes. They now have to guard libertarian rights jealously, for their group existences in the new state depend on their abilities to rent offices, issue newspapers, maintain independent unions, reinforce private organizations to watch over their special interests. Giving substance to their ambitions and claims is the embedded democratic tradition. Attempts to breach it can be expected to be met with resistance. Whatever political insulation the pioneer industrialists needed to shield themselves from the masses during their brutal "takeoff" periods, or that the Stalinist oligarchs had to provide to prevent formation of an opposition made up of all those despoiled in the Soviet primary accumulation, a repressive political apparatus is functionally unnecessary—as an imperative of economics, at any rate—for the popular acceptance of a state-conducted commonwealth.

Clearly there is no point in trying to identify specific developments or concrete alliances and contests. We cannot know. We can only try to discern through the veils obscuring our vision general tendencies and major alternatives. We can only surmise from our estimation of social players, balances, and traditions that the element of voluntarism, which plays an important part in turning points of history, will be present in the formative days of the Great Transformation. Democracy and liberty will be uplifted or encumbered congruent with the alertness and courage or apathy and indifference of key social players. Similarly it cannot be established ahead of time whether the economic features of the coming society will resemble most closely those ascribed by theorists to "state capitalism" or to "state socialism." History sometimes betrays hopes by fulfilling them in its own fashion. Conceptions of a new order, when converted from vision to actuality, undergo sweeping revisions. Institutions resemble theories only peripherally in the way the post-Constantine Christian church of the fourth century was related to the Sermon on the Mount and the Apostolic teachings. If the transformation is from above and involves a rearranging of elites, it will be a combination of both.

Notes and References

Foreword

Ali A. Mazrudi, "Marxist Theories, Socialist Policies, and African Realities," *Problems of Communism*, September-October 1980, p. 49; René König, "August Comte," *International Encyclopedia of Social Sciences* (New York: Macmillan, 1968), vol. 3; Richard Bendix, "What Is Modernization?" in Wilard Beling and George Totten, eds., *Developing Nations: Quest for a Model* (Princeton, N.J.: Van Nostrand, 1970); *Critique of Political Economy*, in Marx-Engels, *Selected Works* (New York: International Publishers, n.d.), 1: 357; id., *Selected Correspondence* (International Publishers, 1942), pp. 353–55; Karl Marx, *Capital* (New York: Modern Library, 1936), 1: 13. In his *Critique of Political Economy* Marx declares, "In broad outlines, Asiatic, ancient, feudal, and modern bourgeois modes of production can be designated as progressive epochs in the economic development of society." In his preface to *Capital* he states, "The country that is more developed industrially only shows to the less developed the image of its own future." But in comments on Russia in later years he disclaims any attempt to create "a general historico-philosophical theory" of social evolution; he insists that his analysis in *Capital* was meant to be valid for Western Europe alone. Marx did not always tie together the loose threads. Leon Trotsky, *History of Russian Revolution* (New York: Simon and Schuster, 1937), 1:4–5; Thorstein Veblen, *Imperial Germany and the Industrial Revolution* (New York: Viking, 1954, reprint of 1915 ed.), p. 19; Bendix, quoted in Theda Skocpol, *States and Social Revolutions* (New York: Cambridge University Press, 1979), p. 19; W.W. Rostow, *The Stages of Economic Growth* (Cambridge: Cambridge University Press, 1960), pp. 4–16, 145-59; Immanuel Wallerstein, "The Rise and Future Demise of the World Capitalist System," *Comparative Studies in Society and History*, September 1974; Skocpol, *States and Social Revolutions*, pp. 19–24; Engels, *Selected Works* 2:179; Barrington Moore, Jr., *Social Origins of Dictatorship and Democracy* (Boston: Beacon Press, 1966), p. 433; Otto Pflanze, *Bismarck and the Development of Germany* (Princeton: Princeton University Press, 1963), Chap. 21, pp. 157–77; Theodore S. Hamerow, *The Social Foundations of German Unification* (Princeton: Princeton University Press, 1972), pp. 100–16; A. J. Whyte, *The Political Life and Letters of Cavour* (London: Oxford University Press, 1930); Dennis

Mack Smith, *Victor Emanuel, Cavour, and the Risorgimento* (London: Oxford University Press, 1971); id., *Cavour and Garibaldi 1860* (Cambridge: Cambridge University Press, 1954); Robert L. Heilbroner, *The Limits of American Capitalism* (New York: Harper, 1966), pp. 114–20; id., "Boom and Crash," *New Yorker*, Aug. 28, 1978; Joan Robinson, "The Second Crisis of Economic Theory," *American Economic Review*, May 1972; Theda Skocpol, "Political Response to Capitalist Crisis," *Politics and Society* 10, no. 2 (1980); *Encyclopedia of the Social Sciences*, 1932 ed., s.v. "state" (14: 328–32); *International Encyclopedia of the Social Sciences*, 1968 ed. s.v. "state" 15: 143–56; Shlomo Avineri, *Hegel's Theory of the Modern State* (Cambridge: Cambridge University Press, 1972), pp. 176–84; *Daedalus*, Fall 1979 (special issue on the state).

Chapter 1. Crackup of Britain's Welfare State—I

SECTION 1

William H. Beveridge, *Power and Influence* (London: Hodder and Stoughton, 1953), pp. 319–20; Maurice Bruce, *The Coming of the Welfare State* (London: B. T. Botsford, 1961), p. ix; Karl Polanyi, *The Great Transformation* (Boston: Beacon Press, 1957), p. 166; William H. Dawson, *Bismarck and State Socialism* (London: Swan Sonnenschein, 1890, reprinted by Scholarly Press, n.d.), pp. 109–27; Kathleen Woodroofe, "The Making of the Welfare State in England," *Journal of Social History* 1, no. 4 (Summer 1968). Aneurin Bevan, *In Place of Fear* (New York: Simon and Schuster, 1952), p. 10; A. A. Rogow (with assistance of Peter Shore), *The Labour Government and British Industry 1945–1951* (Oxford: Blackwell, 1955), pp. 13, 102, 157; David Coates, *The Labour Party and the Struggle for Socialism* (Cambridge: Cambridge University Press, 1975), pp. 13, 44; *Let Us Face the Future*, Labour party statement 1945; Robert A. Brady, *Crisis in Britain* (London: Cambridge University Press, 1950), pp. 41, 509; *The Economist*, and Hogg, quoted in Rogow-Shore, *Labour Government*, pp. 155–57; Keynes, quoted in Allen Hutt, *The Postwar History of the British Working Class* (London: Gollancz, 1937), p. 239; Hugh Clegg, *Labour in Nationalized Industry*, Fabian Research Series 141; Michael Barratt Brown, "Nationalization in Britain," in Ralph Miliband and John Saville, eds., *Socialist Register 1964* (London: Merlin Press, 1964), pp. 242–55. Brady, *Crisis in Britain*, pp. 58–59, 659; Coates, *Labour and Socialism*, p. 49; J. W. Grove, *Government and Industry in Britain* (London: Longmans, 1962), p. 250; Rogow-Shore, *Labour Government*, pp. 61–63, 71; Sterling D. Spero, *Labor Relations in British Nationalized Industry* (New York: New York University Press, 1955), p. 22; Acton Society Trust, *The Men on the Boards: A Study of the Composition of the Boards of Nationalized Industry*, no. 4, pp. 6–9, 12, quoted in Rogow-Shore, *Labour Government*, Eric Hobsbawm, "Fabianism and the Fabians, 1884–1914," unpublished dissertation, Cambridge, 1951; Beatrice Webb, *Our Partnership* (Cambridge: Cambridge University Press, 1975); O. R. McGregor, "Civil Servants and Civil Service: 1850–1950," *Political Quarterly*, quoted in Rogow-Shore,

Labour Government, p. 14; Arnold J. Toynbee, in *Harvard Business Review*, quoted in John Kenneth Galbraith, *The New Industrial State* (Boston: Houghton Mifflin, 1967), p. 98.

SECTION 2
Philip Snowden, *Socialism and Syndicalism* (London: Collins, 1913), p. 241; Robert A. Dahl, "Workers Control of Industry and the British Labor Party," *American Political Science Review*, October 1947, pp. 875–900; *What Socialism Is*, Fabian Tract No. 13 (London, 1890); Gerry Hunnius et al., *Reader on Workers' Control* (New York: Random House, Vintage Books, 1973), pp. 344–56, 469–75; Ken Coates in Perry Anderson and Robin Blackburn, eds., *Towards Socialism* (Ithaca, N.Y.: Cornell University Press, 1966), pp. 291–316; André Gorz, in ibid., pp. 317–53; E. H. Carr, *The Bolshevik Revolution 1917–1923* (New York: Macmillan, 1952), 2: 63–74, 94–106; id., *Socialism in One Country 1924–1926* (New York: Macmillan, 1958), 1:114; Deborah D. Milenkovitch, "The Case of Yugoslavia," *American Economic Review*, February 1977, pp. 55–60; F. B. Singleton and Anthony Topham, *Workers' Control in Yugoslavia*, Fabian Research Series 233 (1963); Andrew Shonfield, *Modern Capitalism: The Changing Balance of Public and Private Power* (New York: Oxford University Press, 1965), pp. 89, 91, 106; J. E. Meade, *Efficiency, Equality and the Ownership of Property* (London: Allen and Unwin, 1964), p. 69; Leo Panitch, *Social Democracy and Industrial Militancy* (Cambridge: Cambridge University Press, 1976), pp. 13, 19, 29; *New York Times*, May 24, 1978, p. D1; *Labour Believes in Britain*, Labour party statement, 1949; Rogow-Shore, *Labour Government*, pp. 25–27, 140, 142–44, 151; H. H. Wilson, "Techniques of Pressure—Anti-Nationalization Propaganda in Britain," *Public Opinion Quarterly*, Summer 1951, pp. 225–42; Albert H. Hanson, *Parliament and Public Ownership* (London: Cassell, 1961), Chap. 6; *Economic Survey for 1947*, Cmnd. 7046 (London: Her Majesty's Stationery Office, 1947), pp. 5–9 and passim; Robin Marris, *Machinery of Economic Policy*, Fabian Series 168 (1954); Douglas Jay, in *The Road to Recovery*, Fabian Lectures, Autumn 1947, pp. 15–16; Herbert Morrison, *Government and Parliament* (London: Oxford University Press, 1964), pp. 299–310; *Keep Left*, New Statesman Pamphlet, April 1947, p. 21; *Statistical Material*, Cmnd. 6707, quoted in Bevan, *In Place of Fear*, pp. 206–7; Andrew Glyn and Robert Stucliffe, *British Capitalism, Workers and the Profit Squeeze* (Harmondsworth, England: Penguin, 1972), p. 35; *Challenge to Britain*, Labour party statement, 1953, p. 6; Richard M. Titmuss, *Income Distribution and Social Change* (London: Allen and Unwin, 1962), pp. 187–99; also Titmuss in Anderson and Blackburn, *Towards Socialism*, p. 360; R. J. Lampman, *Review of Economic Statistics*, November 1959, pp. 379–92.

SECTION 3
Brady, *Crisis in Britain*, pp. 246, 659; G. D. H. Cole, *Socialist Economics* (London: Gollancz, 1950), p. 53; Richard Crossman, ed., *New Fabian Essays* (London: Turnstile Press, 1952), pp. 5–6, 26–27; Michael

Foot, *Aneurin Bevan* (New York: Atheneum, 1974), 2:25–29, 349, 375–76, 574, 584; *Clem Attlee Interview*, Granada Historical Records 1967 (London: Panther Books, 1967), p.43; Robert E. Dowse, *Left in the Center* (London: Longmans, 1966), p.115; Nairn, in Anderson and Blackburn, *Towards Socialism*, pp. 159–217; Stuart Hall et al, "May Day Manifesto," in Carl Oglesby, ed., *New Left Reader* (New York: Grove Press, 1969), pp. 111–143; Ralph Miliband and John Saville, eds., *Socialist Register 1966* (London: Merlin Press, 1966), p. 23.

SECTION 4

Michael Barratt Brown, *After Imperialism* (New York: Humanities Press, 1970), pp. 69, 85–86, 228; C. H. Feinstein, *Aspects of British and Foreign Investment 1870–1913* (Cambridge: Cambridge University Press, 1960); *Statistical Tables of National Income, Expenditure, and Output 1855–1965* (Cambridge: Cambridge University Press, 1976); Clayton, quoted in Herbert Feis, *From Trust to Terror* (New York: W. W. Norton, 1970), p. 230; Boothby, quoted in Howard K. Smith, *The State of Europe* (New York: Knopf, 1949), p.88; Dean Acheson, *Present at the Creation* (New York: W. W. Norton, 1969), p. 122; Seymour E. Harris, ed., *Foreign Economic Elements in the Pax Britannica* (Cambridge, Mass.: Harvard University Press, 1958), Table 4; *British Economy: Key Statistics, 1900–1964* (London and Cambridge: Economic Service, 1965), Tables F and G; Richard N. Gardner, *Sterling Dollar Diplomacy* (Oxford: Clarendon Press, 1956), p. 230–32; *Economic Survey for 1952*, Cmnd. 8509 (London: HMSO, 1952); Brown, *After Imperialism*, p. 334, Table 21; M. M. Postan, *An Economic History of Western Europe 1945–1964* (London: Methuen, 1967), pp. 12, 17, 75; Coates, *Labour and Socialism*, p. 112; *Surveys of Germany, France, United Kingdom* (Paris: OECD, 1963); *United Nations Statistical Yearbook, 1963* (New York, 1964); Angus Maddison, *Economic Growth in the West* (New York: Twentieth Century Fund, 1964), pp. 28, 30, 37; Edward F. Denison, *Why Growth Rates Differ* (Washington, D.C.: Brookings Institution, 1967), pp. 17, 219; Postan, *Economic History*, pp. 68, 115, 135, 195–96; Brown, *After Imperialism*, pp. 254, 263–65, 278–79, Tables 14 and 15A; Geoffrey Denton et al., *Economic Planning and Policies in Britain, France and Germany* (London: Allen and Unwin, 1968), p. 51; Marvin Frankel, "Obsolescence and Technical Change in a Mature Economy," *American Economic Review*, June 1955; United Nations, *Economic Survey of Europe 1962* (New York, 1963); U.N. Economic Commission for Europe, *Economic Survey of Europe in 1961*, Part 2 (Geneva, 1964); Richard Eveley and I. M. D. Little, *Concentration in British Industry* (Cambridge: Cambridge University Press, 1960); Wilfred Beckerman, *The Labour Government's Economic Record 1964–1970* (London: Duckworth, 1972), p. 207; Joseph La Palombara and Stephen Blank, *Multinational Corporations and National Elites: A Study in Tensions* (New York: The Conference Board, 1976), p. 7; *Economic Growth 1960–1970* (Paris: OECD, 1966), p. 31.

SECTION 5
Peregrine Worsthorne, "The Trade Unions: New Lads on Top," in R. E. Tyrrell, Jr., ed., *The Future That Doesn't Work: Social Democracy's Failure in Britain* (New York: Doubleday, 1977), pp. 5, 20; Michael Shanks, *The Stagnant Society* (Harmondsworth, England: Penguin, 1961); Wilfred Beckerman et al., *The British Economy in 1975* (Cambridge: Cambridge University Press, 1965), p. 26; Shirley W. Lerner and Judith Marquand, "Workshop Bargaining, Wage Drift and Productivity in the British Engineering Industry," *Manchester School of Economic and Social Studies* 30 (January 1962); A. I. Marsh and E. E. Coker, "Shop Steward Organization in the Engineering Industry," *British Journal of Industrial Relations*, June 1963, pp. 177, 189; *Report of the Royal Commission on Trade Unions and Employers' Associations 1965–1968* (hereafter cited as Donovan Report), Cmnd. 3623 (London: HMSO, 1969); Hugh Clegg, in Allan Flanders, ed., *Collective Bargaining* (Harmondsworth, England: Penguin, 1969), pp. 352–68; Political and Economic Planning, "Trade Unions in a Changing Society," *Planning*, 1963, pp. 185–87; Beckerman, *Labour Government's Economic Record*, p. 320; International Labour Office, *Year Book of Labour Statistics 1975* (Geneva: ILO, 1975), Chaps. 2 and 9; European Management Forum, Report on the Competitiveness of European Industry, Geneva, December 1979, in ILO, *International Social and Labour Bulletin*, March 1980, no. 1, pp. 3–5; Tibor Barna, *Investment and Growth Policies in British Industrial Firms* (London: Cambridge University Press, 1962), Chap. 2 and passim; H. J. Habakkuk, *American and British Technology in the Nineteenth Century* (London: Cambridge University Press, 1962), pp. 111–14 and Chap. 6; E. J. Hobsbawm, *Industry and Empire* (Harmondsworth, England: Penguin, 1968); *The Economist*, April 22, 1978, p. 27; Richard Caves and Lawrence Krause, eds., *Britain's Economic Performance* (Washington, D.C.: Brookings Institution, 1980), distributed by Basil Blackwell; Charles Carter, ed., *Industrial Policy and Innovation* (London: Heinemann, for National Institute of Economic and Social Research, 1981); *New York Times*, Dec. 14, 1981, p. D1.

Chapter 2. Crackup of Britain's Welfare State—II

SECTION 1
Edward F. Denison, *Why Growth Rates Differ* (Washington, D.C.: Brookings Institution, 1967), pp. 294–95, 341; Charles P. Kindleberger, *Power and Money* (New York: Basic Books, 1970), pp. 88–89; Geoffrey Denton et al., *Economic Planning and Policies in Britain, France, and Germany* (London: Allen and Unwin, 1968), p. 51; Henry C. Wallich, *Mainsprings of the German Revival* (New Haven: Yale University Press, 1955), p. 279, 363; Howard D. Willey, "Growth of British and German Manufacturing 1951–1962," unpublished dissertation, Columbia University, 1966, pp. 145, 169; M. M. Postan, *An Economic History of Western Europe 1945–1964* (London: Methuen, 1967), p. 348; Wilfred

Beckerman, *International Comparisons of Real Incomes* (Paris: OECD, 1966), pp. 19, 36, 42, 51; Andrew Shonfield, *Modern Capitalism: The Changing Balance of Public and Private Power* (New York: Oxford University Press, 1965), p. 8; *Basic Statistics: International Comparisons* (Paris: OECD Economic Surveys, 1977); Allan Flanders, "Wage Movements and Wage Policy in Postwar Britain," *Annals of the American Academy of Political and Social Sciences* 310 (March 1957): 89, Table 1; Leo Panitch, *Social Democracy and Industrial Militancy* (Cambridge: Cambridge University Press, 1976), pp. 48–54; Shonfield, *Modern Capitalism*, pp. 99–101, 103; Samuel Brittan, *The Treasury Under the Tories 1951–1964* (Harmondsworth, England: Penguin, 1964), p. 162; Denton et al., *Economic Planning and Policies*, p. 109 (quote); Macmillan, quoted in Anthony Sampson, *Macmillan: A Study in Ambiguity* (London: Allen Lane, 1967), p. 160; Harold Macmillan, *Pointing the Way 1959–1961* (New York: Harper, 1972), p. 223; Samuel Brittan, *Steering the Economy: The Role of the Treasury* (London: Secker and Warberg, 1969), Chap. 6; Harold Macmillan, *At the End of the Day 1961–1963* (New York: Harper, 1973), pp. 35–36; Shonfield, *Modern Capitalism*, pp. 102, 109; Panitch, *Social Democracy*, pp. 47–57; *Incomes Policy: The Next Step*, Cmnd. 1626 (London: HMSO, 1962); Wilfred Beckerman, *The Labour Government's Economic Record 1964–1970* (London: Duckworth, 1972), Introduction and pp. 59, 300–1; George Polanyi, *Planning in Britain: The Experience of the 1960's* (London: Institute of Economic Affairs, 1967), p. 58.

SECTION 2

Paul Foot, *The Politics of Harold Wilson* (Harmondsworth, England: Penguin, 1968), pp. 135, 139, 148; Harold Wilson, *The New Britain* (Harmondsworth, England: Penguin, 1964), pp. 3–8, 23; Marcia Williams, *Inside Number 10* (London: Weidenfeld and Nicolson, 1972), p. 360; *Year Book of Labour Statistics 1976* (Geneva: ILO, 1977), p. 448; Jacques Leruez, *Economic Planning and Politics in Britain* (New York: Barnes and Noble, 1975), pp. 172–181, 303, n. 42, 43; Brown, quoted in ibid., p. 179; Brittan, quoted in ibid., p. 178; Harold Wilson, *The Labour Government: A Personal Record* (London: Weidenfeld and Nicolson, 1971), pp. 32–37; Andrew Shonfield, *International Economic Relations: The Western System in the 1960s and 1970s* (Beverly Hills and London: Sage Publications, 1976), pp. 66–70; Christopher Tugendhat, *The Multinationals* (Harmondsworth, England: Penguin, 1973), pp. 13, 164–68; Political and Economic Planning (PEP), "Inquest on Planning in Britain," *Planning* No. 499, 1966; John Brunner, *The National Plan* (London: Institute of Economic Affairs, Eaton Paper 4, 1969).

SECTION 3

Incomes in Postwar Europe (Geneva: United Nations, 1967), pp. 2–4; George Brown, *In My Way* (London: Gollancz, 1971), pp. 95–96; Panitch, *Social Democracy*, pp. 87–89; Wilson, *Labour Government*, pp. 131–32; Brittan, *Steering the Economy*, pp. 329–39, 354; Hall et al., "May Day Manifesto," *1968 Economic Review* (London: Trades Union

Congress, 1968), pp. 136–43; *Productivity, Prices and Incomes Policy in 1968 and 1969*, Cmnd. 3590 (London: HMSO, 1969); Beckerman, *Labour Government's Economic Record*, pp. 61–64; Shinwell, quoted in Panitch, *Social Democracy*, p. 155; *Financial Times* (London), May 9, 13, 1968; Donovan Report, Cmnd. 3623; *In Place of Strife*, Cmnd. 3888 (London: HMSO, 1969); Peter Jenkins, *The Battle of Downing Street* (London: C. Knight, 1970), pp. 78–84, 151–55, Chap. 8; "TUC Proposals on Industrial Relations, Report of a Meeting between the Prime Minister, First Secretary of State and the General Council," cited in Panitch, *Social Democracy*, p. 192; Beckerman, *Labour Government's Economic Record*, pp. 279, 321; Michael Kidron, *Western Capitalism Since the War* (Harmondsworth, England: Penguin, 1970), pp. 85, 100; Raymond Vernon, *Storm Over the Multinationals* (Cambridge, Mass.: Harvard University Press, 1977), p. 74; Louis Turner, *Invisible Empires* (London: Hamish Hamilton, 1970), p. 180; *Economist*, Feb. 5, 1983, pp. 59–62; Dudley Jackson et al., *Do Trade Unions Cause Inflation?* (Cambridge: Cambridge University Press, 1972), pp. 81, 83–84; David Butler and Michael Pinto-Duschinsky, *The British General Election of 1970* (London: Macmillan, 1971), p. 346; "Report to the Special Trade Union Congress," March 18, 1971, Annex, *1971 TUC Report*, British TUC documents, pp. 341–77; Panitch, *Social Democracy*, Tables 1–4, pp. 264–65; *Year Book of Labour Statistics 1975* (Geneva: ILO, 1976), p. 804; H. A. Turner and H. Zoeteweij, *Prices, Wages and Incomes Policies in Industrialized Market Economies* (Geneva: ILO, 1966), pp. 135, 144; Bob Rowthorne, "The Trap of an Incomes Policy," *New Left Review*, November-December 1956, p. 6; Arnold R. Weber and Daniel J. B. Mitchell, "Further Reflections on Wage Controls," and George P. Schultz and Kenneth W. Dam, "Reply," *Industrial and Labor Relations Review*, January 1978; Derek Robinson, "Labour Market Policies," in Beckerman, *Labour Government's Economic Record*, pp. 314–15.

Section 4
George Hutchinson, *Edward Heath* (London: Longman, 1970), pp. 145, 165, 168; *A Programme for Controlling Inflation: The First Stage*, Cmnd. 5125 (London: HMSO, 1972); *The Programme for Controlling Inflation: The Second Stage*, Cmnd. 5205 (London: HMSO, 1972); *The Counter-Inflation Programme: The Operation of Stage Two*, Cmnd. 5267 (London: HMSO, 1973); *The Price and Pay Code for Stage Three: A Consultative Document*, Cmnd. 5444 (London: HMSO, 1973); Leruez, *Economic Planning*, pp. 270, 309 n. 24, 249–51; *Financial Times* (London), Nov. 16, 1973, Jan. 3, Feb. 9, 1974; Shonfield, *Modern Capitalism*, pp. 117–19; Tibor Barna, *Investment and Growth Policies in British Industrial Firms* (London: Cambridge University Press, 1962), p. 61; Beckerman, *Labour Government's Economic Record*, pp. 183-85; Wilson, *Labour Government*, p. 561; Edmund Dell, *Political Responsibility and Industry* (London: Allen and Unwin, 1973), pp. 74–84; Brittan, *Steering the Economy*, p. 206; *The Economist*, June 17, 1978, pp. 94, 121; *New York Times*, June 14, 1980, p. A14; T. Ward, "The New Cambridge School," *British Review of Economic Issues*, no. 7 (November

1980); Ajit Singh, "UK Industry and the World Economy: A Case of De-Industrialization?" *Cambridge Journal of Economics,* June 1977; Daniel Bell, "A Report on England," *Public Interest* 51 (Spring 1978): 48; Wynn Godley et al., "Costs to Britain of Belonging to EEC," (British) *Economic Policy Review of Cambridge,* March 1978; J. M. Keynes, *The General Theory of Employment, Interest and Money* (New York: Harcourt, Brace, 1936), p. 383; *The Economist,* Jan. 31, 1981, p. 48; ibid., June 27, 1981, p. 17; ibid., May 14, 1983, p. 12.

Chapter 3. French Planning Revisited

SECTION 1
Stanley Hoffmann et al., *In Search of France* (Cambridge, Mass.: Harvard University Press, 1963), pp. 3–11, 219, 254, 267; *Year Book of Labour Statistics 1947–1948* (Geneva: ILO, 1948), p. 14, 1949–1950, p. 18; John E. Sawyer, "The Entrepreneur and the Social Order: France and the United States," in William Miller, ed., *Men in Business* (New York: Harper Torchbooks, Harper and Row, 1962), pp. 7–22; Georges Lefranc, *Histoire du front populaire* (Paris: Payot, 1965), pp. 131, 141, 146; Dorothy M. Pickles, *The French Political Scene* (London: Nelson, 1939), p. 130; Shepard B. Clough et al., *Economic History of Europe: Twentieth Century* (New York: Walker, 1968), pp. 255–63; Andrew Shonfield, *Modern Capitalism: The Changing Balance of Public and Private Power* (New York: Oxford University Press, 1965), pp. 85n–86n; Charles De Gaulle, *War Memoirs,* Vol. 3, *Salvation 1944–1946* (London: Weidenfeld and Nicolson, 1960), pp. 101–5; Ralph Miliband, *The State in Capitalist Society* (New York: Basic Books, 1969), pp. 114–15; Angus Maddison, *Economic Growth in the West* (New York: Twentieth Century Fund, 1964), pp. 105, 107; John Sheahan, *Promotion and Control of Industry in Postwar France* (Cambridge, Mass.: Harvard University Press, 1963), p. 31; Warren C. Baum, *The French Economy and the State* (Princeton, N.J.: Princeton University Press, 1958), pp. 174–80; Charles P. Kindleberger, in Hoffmann et al., *In Search of France,* pp. 152, 154; Stephen S. Cohen, *Modern Capitalist Planning: The French Model* (Berkeley: University of California Press, 1977), pp. 25–26; *Economic Survey of Europe in 1954* (Geneva: United Nations, 1955), pp. 172-73, 181; *Economic Survey of Europe in 1974* (Geneva: United Nations, 1975), 2:248.

SECTION 2
Economic Survey, 1954, pp. 176–77, 189–90; Hoffmann et al., *In Search of France,* pp. 371–72, 163 (long quotation); Cohen, *Modern Capitalist Planning,* p. 92; Baum, *French Economy,* p. 43ff; John Sheahan, "Problems and Possibilities of Industrial Price Controls: Postwar French Experience," *American Economic Review,* June 1961, pp. 345–48; Alexander Werth, *France 1940–1955* (Boston: Beacon Press, 1966), pp. 246–49, 300, 353; Cohen, *Modern Capitalist Planning,* pp. 38, 93–95; Kuznets, quoted in Sheahan, *Promotion and Control,* pp. 13–14; Charles Rist, "The French Financial Dilemma," *Foreign Affairs,* April

1947, pp. 452–53; European Cooperation Administration, *France: Data Book 1951*, p.5; Harriman, quoted in Cohen, *Modern Capitalist Planning*, p. 124; Val R. Lorwin, *The French Labor Movement* (Cambridge, Mass.: Harvard University Press, 1954), p. 133; *Business Week*, Oct. 21, 1950, p. 124; ibid., June 19, 1978, p. 42; *Labor Costs in European Industry*, new series, no. 52 (Geneva: ILO, 1959), pp. 89, 91; Shonfield, *Modern Capitalism*, pp. 92, 171, 292; Hoffmann et al., *In Search of France*, pp. 43, 70; M. M. Postan, *An Economic History of Western Europe 1945–1964* (London: Methuen, 1967), pp. 351–52; Peter Coffey, *The Social Economy of France* (London: Macmillan, 1973), pp. 110, 115; Sheahan, *Promotion and Control*, pp. 116–17, 190, 200, 206; Thomas Marschak, "Capital Budgeting and Pricing in the French Nationalized Industries," *Journal of Business*, April 1960, pp. 133–56; Charles P. Kindleberger, in Hoffmann et al., *In Search of France*, p. 154; André G. Delion, *L'Etat et les entreprises publiques* (Paris: Sirey, 1958), pp. 168–69; Giscard, quoted in Cohen, *Modern Capitalist Planning*, p. 270, see also p. 196; *Economic Survey 1954*, p. 174; Werth, *France 1940–1955*, p.404; *Economic Surveys, Basic Statistics* (Paris: OECD, 1977, 1978); *France Enters the 70s* (Geneva: Business International, S.A., 1970), Research Report 70–2, p. 40; *The Economist*, March 11, 1978, pp. 66–67; ibid., March 18, 1978, p. 72; ibid., Sept. 9, 1978, p. 94; "Survey of France," ibid., Jan. 27, 1979, p. 26.

SECTION 3
Merry Bromberger and Serge Bromberger, *Jean Monnet and the United States of Europe* (New York: Coward-McCann, 1969), pp. 10–19, 223–25; Shonfield, *Modern Capitalism*, pp. 3, 5; Shepard B. Clough, "Economic Planning in a Capitalist Society: France from Monnet to Hirsch," *Political Science Quarterly* 71, (December 1956); Werth, *France 1940–1955*, p. 498; Walter B. Blass, "Economic Planning, European Style," *Harvard Business Review*, September-October 1963; Cohen, *Modern Capitalist Planning*, p. 29; Sheahan, *Promotion and Control*, pp. 172, 181; David Granick, *The European Executive* (Garden City, N.Y.: Doubleday Anchor, 1964), p. 150; Pierre Bauchet, *Economic Planning: The French Experience* (London: Heinemann, 1964), pp. 59–60; Cohen, *Modern Capitalist Planning*, pp. 88–194 passim; Phillippe Bauchard, "La Mystique du Plan," quoted in ibid., p. 197; *Les Motifs d'Execution du Plan*, quoted in ibid., p. 164.

SECTION 4
Bauchet, *Economic Planning*, pp. 47, 127; Shonfield, *Modern Capitalism*, pp. 128, 130, 138, 143; Sheahan, *Promotion and Control*, p. 179; Block-Lainé, quoted in Cohen, *Modern Capitalist Planning*, p. 198; Shonfield, *Modern Capitalism*, pp. 98, 109–10, 131, 159; G. D. N. Worswick and P. H. Ady, eds., *The British Economy in the Nineteen-Fifties* (London: Oxford University Press, 1962), p. 337; Werth, *France 1940–1955*, p. 564; Sheahan, "Problems and Possibilities"; Cohen, *Modern Capitalist Planning*, pp. 170, 231, 276; Bureau de Recherche et d'Action Economique study, quoted in ibid., p. 65; Jacques Leruez, *Economic Planning*

and *Politics in Britain* (New York: Barnes and Noble, 1975), pp. 134–35, 147, 153; Sheahan, *Promotion and Control*, p. 30; Bernard Nossiter, *Britain—A Future That Works* (Boston: Houghton Mifflin, 1978), p. 31.

SECTION 5
Cohen, *Modern Capitalist Planning*, p. 277; Commissariat Général du Plan, "Rapport général sur le Premier Plan de Modernisation et d'Equipment: Rapport d'Execution du VI Plan," quoted in Cohen, *Modern Capitalist Planning*, p. 25; *The Economist*, March 18, 1978, p. 71; ibid., July 1, 1978, p. 11; ibid., March 3, 1979, p. 45; ibid., March 31, 1979, p. 53; ibid., Jan. 21, 1980, p. 78; Quarterly Economic Review of France, Fourth Quarter 1979 (London: The Economist Intelligence Unit, 1979), on the Eighth Plan; *Business Week*, June 30, 1980, p. 49; U.S. Department of Labor, Bureau of Labor Statistics, May 22, 1980, release on international comparisons of productivity and labor costs; *Economic Surveys: France*, February 1979, International Comparisons (Paris: OECD, 1979); James O. Goldsborough, "Giscard's New Revolution: Capitalism," *Fortune*, April 9, 1979.

Chapter 4. American Goliath

SECTION 1
Randolph S. Churchill, ed., *Sinews of Peace: Postwar Speeches of Winston S. Churchill* (Boston: Houghton Mifflin, 1949), p. 120; U.S. Bureau of the Budget, *The United States at War* (Washington, D.C.: U.S. Government Printing Office, 1946), p. 112; Robert E. Sherwood, *Roosevelt and Hopkins* (New York: Harper, 1948), p. 474; James W. Fesler et al., *Industrial Mobilization for War* (Washington, D.C.: Civilian Production Administration, 1947), pp. 207–26; *Historical Statistics, Colonial Times to 1957* (Washington, D.C.: U.S. Bureau of the Census, 1958), p. 139; Joel Seidman, *American Labor from Defense to Reconversion* (Chicago: University of Chicago Press, 1953), pp. 270–71; H. M. Douty, "A Review of Basic American Labor Conditions," in E. Colston Warne, ed., *Labor in Postwar America* (New York: Remsen Press, 1949), pp. 109–36; Charles P. Kindleberger, "U.S. Economic Foreign Policy 1776–1976," *Foreign Affairs*, January 1977, pp. 406, 409; *Statistical Abstract 1976* (Washington, D.C.: U.S. Government Printing Office, 1977), pp. 760, 839, 861, 977; *Historical Statistics, From Colonial Times to 1970* (Washington, D.C.: U.S. Government Printing Office, 1971), Pt. 1, p. 199; Angus Maddison, *Economic Growth in the West*, (New York: Twentieth Century Fund, 1964), p. 166; Andrew Shonfield, *International Economic Relations: The Western System in the 1960s and 1970s* (Beverly Hills: Sage Publications, 1976), p. 66.

SECTION 2
Kindleberger, "U.S. Economic Foreign Policy," p. 413; Shonfield, *International Economic Relations*, pp. 9, 34; *Business Week*, June 30, 1980, pp. 59, 65, 82; Seymour Melman, *The Permanent War Economy*

(New York: Simon and Schuster, 1974), p. 97; phone interview with Melman, Dec. 18, 1978; John Kenneth Galbraith, "Economics of Arms Race—and After," *Bulletin of the Atomic Scientists*, June-July 1981, pp. 13–16; Robert M. Dunn, Jr., *Economic Growth Among Industrialized Countries: Why the United States Lags* (Washington, D.C.: National Planning Association, 1980), Chaps. 1–4; Michael Harper, "The Role of Capital Formation in the Recent Slowdown in Productivity Growth," Working Paper #27, U.S. Bureau of Labor Statistics, Office of Productivity, January 1979.

SECTION 3

Jack Behrman, *National Interests and the Multinational Enterprise* (Englewood Cliffs, N.J.: Prentice-Hall, 1970), pp. 10–11, 104–13; id., *Some Patterns in the Rise of the Multinational Enterprise*, Research Paper No. 18 (Chapel Hill, N.C.: University of North Carolina Business School, 1969), pp. 45–48; Howard V. Perlmutter, "Super-Giant Firms in the Future," *Wharton Quarterly* 3 (Winter 1968); *Fortune*, May 8, 1978, p. 239; ibid., May 7, 1979, p. 268; ibid., May 2, 1983, p. 227; *Business Week*, March 12, 1979, p. 41; ibid., March 19, 1979, p. 104; *Handbook of Economic Statistics* (Arlington, Va.: Central Intelligence Agency, 1976), pp. 1, 31; *Yearbook of National Accounts Statistics 1976* (New York: United Nations, 1977), vol 2; Raymond Vernon, *Storm over the Multinationals* (Cambridge, Mass.: Harvard University Press, 1977), p. 12; id., "The Multinationals: No Strings Attached," *Foreign Policy* 33 (Winter 1978–1979): 122, 129; id., *Sovereignty at Bay: The Multinational Spread of U.S. Enterprises* (New York: Basic Books, 1971), pp. 7, 11, 214–15; id., "Multinational Enterprise and National Sovereignty," *Harvard Business Review*, March-April 1967; *The Multinational Corporation and the World Economy*, U.S. Senate Committee on Finance, Subcommittee on International Trade staff study, 93rd Cong., 1st sess., February 1973; Richard J. Barnet and Ronald E. Müller, *Global Reach: The Power of the Multinational Corporations* (New York: Simon and Schuster, 1974), p. 109; "500 Largest U.S. Industrial Corporations," *Fortune*, May 8, 1978, pp. 238–39; *Fortune*, May 7, 1979, pp. 268–69; Karl Kaysen, in Edward S. Mason, ed., *The Corporation in Modern Society* (Cambridge, Mass.: Harvard University Press, 1959), pp. 89–99; Dr. Mueller, quoted in Ferdinand Lundberg, *The Rich and the Super-Rich* (New York: Lyle Stuart, 1968), p. 742; U.S. Senate Committee on the Judiciary, Subcommittee on Antitrust and Monopoly, Hearings, 91st Cong., 2d sess., November 1969–February 1970, p. 4544; John M. Blair, *Economic Concentration* (New York: Harcourt Brace, 1972), pp. 69–70; *Statistical Abstract 1977*, pp. 566, 793, 797; Karl Kaysen and Donald F. Turner, *Antitrust Policy: An Economic and Legal Analysis* (Cambridge, Mass.: Harvard University Press, 1959), pp. 27ff.; Robert T. Averitt, *The Dual Economy* (New York: W. W. Norton, 1968), pp. 21, 43–44; Robert Dorfman, *The Price System* (Englewood Cliffs, N.J.: Prentice-Hall, 1964), p. 102; John Kenneth Galbraith, *The New Industrial State* (Boston: Houghton Mifflin, 1967), pp. 186, 200–1; id., *American Capitalism: The Concept of Countervailing Power* (Boston: Houghton Mifflin, rev. ed.,

1956), pp. 41, 119, 123; Averitt, *Dual Economy,* p. 69; Werner Sombart, *Der Bourgeois: Zur Geistesgeschichte des modernen Wirtschaftsmenschen* (Munich: Duncker & Humblot, 1913), p. 74; Thorstein Veblen, *Absentee Ownership and Business Enterprise in Recent Times* (New York: Huebsch, 1923), pp. 305–6; E. H. Chamberlin, *The Theory of Monopolistic Competition* (Cambridge, Mass.: Harvard University Press, 1932), pp. 119ff.; Max Horkheimer and Theodor W. Adorno, *Dialectic of Enlightenment* (New York: Herder and Herder, 1972), pp. 161–67; Edward D. Hollander et al., *The Future of Small Business* (New York: Praeger, 1967) (This study by Robert Nathan Associates was done under contract with the U.S. Small Business Administration); Harmon Ziegler, *The Politics of Small Business* (Washington, D.C.: Public Affairs Press, 1961), pp. 2–3; *Statistical Abstract 1976,* pp. 516, 525; Milton Friedman, *Capitalism and Freedom* (Chicago: University of Chicago Press, 1962), p. 133; Earl F. Cheit, ed., *The Business Establishment* (New York: Wiley, 1964), p. 163.

SECTION
    Alfred D. Chandler, Jr., *Strategy and Structure* (Cambridge, Mass.: MIT Press, 1962), Chap. 1, pp. 78–80, 84–85, 103–9; Alfred D. Chandler, Jr., and Stephen Salsbury, *Pierre S. Du Pont and the Making of the Modern Corporation* (New York: Harper, 1971), Chap. 9; Alfred P. Sloan, *My Sixty Years with General Motors* (Garden City, N.Y.: Doubleday, 1964), Chap. 7; Ralph L. Nelson, *Merger Movements in American Industry 1895–1956* (Princeton, N.J.: Princeton University Press, 1959), pp. 33–34; Fortune Editors, *The Conglomerate Commotion* (New York: Viking, 1970); "The Merger Movement Rides High," *Fortune,* February 1969; "Why Leasco Failed to Net Chemical," *Business Week,* April 26, 1969; *Statistical Abstract 1981,* p. 537; Statistics of 1900, quoted in Gabriel Kolko, *The Triumph of Conservatism* (Chicago: Quadrangle, 1967), pp. 22–23; *Newsweek,* July 27, 1981, p. 52.

Chapter 5. Multinational Corporations

SECTION 1
    James W. Vaupel and Joan P. Curhan, *The Making of Multinational Enterprise* (Boston: Harvard School of Business, 1969), Chap. 3; European press, quoted in Raymond Vernon, *Sovereignty at Bay: The Multinational Spread of U.S. Enterprises* (New York: Basic Books, 1971), p. 81; Alfred D. Chandler, Jr., *The Visible Hand: The Managerial Revolution in American Business* (Cambridge, Mass.: Harvard University Press, 1977), p. 16; Christopher Tugendhat, *The Multinationals* (New York: Random House, 1972), pp. 12–16; Commerce Department figures, quoted in Stephen H. Hymer, *The International Operations of National Firms: A Study of Direct Foreign Investment* (Cambridge, Mass.: MIT Press, 1976), p. 5; Mira Wilkins, *The Maturing of the Multinational Enterprise: American Business Abroad from 1914 to 1970* (Cambridge, Mass.: Harvard University Press, 1974), pp. 55, 61, 155–56, 182–83, 329; Ludwell Denny,

America Conquers Britain (New York: Knopf, 1930), pp. 140–42; Histori-cal Statistics to 1957 (Washington, D.C.: U.S. Bureau of the Census, 1958), p. 564; Leon Trotsky, Europe vs. America: Two Speeches, July 1924 and February 1926 (Colombo, Ceylon: Lanka Samasamaja, 1961), pp. 23, 28; Foreign Aid by the United States Government 1940–1951 (Washington, D.C.: U.S. Department of Commerce, 1952), pp. 65–66; Jo-seph La Palombara and Stephen Blank, Multinational Corporations and National Elites: A Study in Tensions (New York: Conference Board, 1976), pp. 6–7; Rainer Hellman, The Challenge to U.S. Dominance of the International Corporation (New York: Dunellen, 1970), p. 306; Multina-tional Corporations in World Development (New York: United Nations, 1973), pp. 138–39; Andrew Shonfield, International Economic Relations: The Western System in the 1960s and 1970s (Beverly Hills: Sage Publica-tions, 1976), p. 70; Statistical Abstract 1981 (Washington, D.C.: U.S. Bu-reau of the Census, 1982), p. 833; Jean-Jacques Servan-Schreiber, The American Challenge (New York: Atheneum, 1969); Hugh Stephenson, The Coming Clash (New York: Saturday Review Press, 1973), p. 45; Mul-tinational Corporations, a compendium of papers of the U.S. Senate Committee on Finance, Subcommittee on International Trade, 93rd Cong., 1st sess., February 1973, p. 69; Vernon, Sovereignty at Bay, pp. 121, 155; Richard Eells, Global Corporations: The Emerging System of World Economic Power (New York: Interbook, 1972), pp. 28–29; Wilkins, Maturing, pp. 402–5; John H. Dunning, The Role of American Investment in the British Economy (London: PEP Broadsheet 507, February 1969), p. 178; John Fayerweather, Foreign Investment in Canada (White Plains, N.Y.: International Arts and Sciences Press, 1973), p. 6; Donald T. Brash, American Investment in Australian Industry (Cambridge, Mass.: Harvard University Press, 1966), p. 33; Charles P. Kindleberger, The International Corporation (Cambridge, Mass.: MIT Press, 1970), pp. 294–95; Raymond Vernon, Storm over the Multinationals (Cambridge, Mass.: Harvard Uni-versity Press, 1977), pp. 51, 74, 108–9; Louis Turner, Invisible Empires (London: Hamish Hamilton, 1970), pp. 180–82; Jack Behrman, National Interests and the Multinational Enterprise (Englewood Cliffs, N.J.: Pren-tice-Hall, 1970), pp. 151, 159–65; Shonfield, International Economic Re-lations, p. 71; id., Modern Capitalism, pp. 370–74; Charles P. Kindle-berger, in Courtney Brown, World Business: Promise and Problems (New York: Macmillan, 1970), p. 101; Jeremy Main, "The First International Bankers," Fortune, December 1967, p. 143; New York Times, Jan. 7, 1979, p. 57; ibid., Jan. 25, 1979, p. D3; Multinational Enterprises (Geneva: ILO), p. 6; The Economist, Sept. 13, 1975, p. 56; ibid., April 3, 1976, pp. 111–12.

SECTION 2
   The Multinational Corporation: Studies in U.S. Foreign Investment (Washington, D.C.: U.S. Department of Commerce, 1972), 1:13; Shon-field, International Economic Relations, p. 72; Wilkins, Maturing, pp. 330, 353–54; Rolfe and Damm, quoted in Raymond Vernon, ed., The Economic and Political Consequences of Multinational Enterprise (Bos-ton: Harvard Graduate School of Business Administration, 1972), pp.

126–27; id., *Storm Over the Multinationals*, p. 70; Joseph La Palombara and Stephen Blank, *Multinational Corporations in Comparative Perspective* (New York: Conference Board, 1977), pp. viii–ix; A. K. Cairncross, *Home and Foreign Investment 1870–1913* (Cambridge: Cambridge University Press, 1953), pp. 183, 185, 223–24; A. R. Hall, ed., *The Export of Capital from Britain 1860–1914* (London: Methuen, 1968), p. vii; C. Fred Bergsten, "Coming Investment Wars?" *Foreign Affairs*, October 1974, p. 138; *International Economic Report of the President, 1973*, p. 66; ILO, *International Labour Review* 117, no. 3 (1978): 273–79; Sidney E. Rolfe and Walter Damm, eds., *The Multinational Corporation in the World Economy* (New York: Praeger, 1970); Charles P. Kindleberger, *The World in Depression 1929–1939* (Berkeley: University of California Press, 1973), p. 38; id., in Brown, *World Business*, pp. 103–4; Hymer, *International Operations*, p. 13, 23, 66; Robert B. Stobaugh, Jr., "Where in the World Shall We Put That Plant?" reprinted in A. Kapoor and Phillip D. Grub, eds., *The Multinational Enterprise in Transition* (Princeton, N.J.: Darwin Press, 1972), pp. 292–304; Tugendhat, *The Multinationals*, pp. 151–52; Vernon, *Sovereignty at Bay*, pp. 72–73, 156; Harvard Multinational Project, in Vernon, *Storm Over the Multinationals*, pp. 22–23, 35; U.S. Tariff Commission, *Implications of Multinational Firms for World Trade and Investment and for U.S. Trade and Labor*, presented to the U.S. Senate Committee on Finance, Subcommittee on International Trade (Washington, D.C.: U.S. Government Printing Office, 1973), pp. 3, 116–17; H. D. Willey, "Direct Investment Controls," in Charles P. Kindleberger, ed., *The International Corporation* (Cambridge, Mass.: MIT Press, 1970); Report to the President, reprinted in Vernon, *Economic Political Consequences*, p. 69; id., "Sovereignty at Bay," *Foreign Affairs*, October 1968; Theodore H. Moran, "Foreign Expansion as an 'Institutional Necessity' for U.S. Corporate Capitalism," *World Politics*, April 1973; Shonfield, *International Economic Relations*, p. 72; Jack Behrman, *Some Patterns in the Rise of the Multinational Enterprise*, Research Paper No. 18 (Chapel Hill, N.C.: University of North Carolina Business School, 1969), pp. 24–25; Judd Polk et al., *U.S. Production Abroad and the Balance of Payments* (New York: National Industrial Conference Board, 1966), pp. 105, 132–36.

Section 3
    Shonfield, *International Economic Relations*, pp. 66–67, 69–70; U.S. Tariff Commission, *Implications*, pp. 4, 322–23; Vernon, *Sovereignty at Bay*, p. 16; Tugendhat, *The Multinationals*, pp. 108, 131, 134; Marie T. Bradshaw, "U.S. Exports to Foreign Affiliates of U.S. Firms," *Survey of Current Business* 49 (May 1969): 37; *Multinational Corporations*, U.S. Senate Committee on Finance, Subcommittee on International Trade, p. 45; Benoit, in Brown, *World Business*, p. 21; *Multinational Enterprises* (Geneva: ILO, 1973), p. 26; Joseph S. Nye, Jr., "Multinational Corporations in World Politics," *Foreign Affairs*, October 1974, p. 153; Vernon, *Storm Over the Multinationals*, pp. 119, 121–23; Sidney Robbins and Robert B. Stobaugh, *Money in the Multinational Enterprise* (New York: Basic Books, 1973), p. 41; Jack Behrman, *National Interests and the Mul-*

tinational Enterprise (Englewood Cliffs, N.J.: Prentice-Hall, 1970), pp. 80–81; *Multinational Corporations in the Dollar Devaluation Crisis: Report on a Questionnaire*, U.S. Senate Committee on Foreign Relations, Subcommittee on Multinational Corporations, 94th Cong., 1st sess., 1975; Obie G. Whichard, "U.S. Direct Investment Abroad in 1978," *Survey of Current Business*, August 1979.

SECTION 4
Jane D'Arista, "U.S. Banks Abroad," in *Financial Institutions and the National Economy*, compendium of papers, 94th Cong., 2nd sess., June 1976, 2:812; *Foreign Government Restraints on U.S. Banking Operations Abroad*, U.S. Congress, Joint Economic Committee, 90th Cong. 1st sess., 1967, Paper No. 10, pp. 30, 114; Raymond Vernon, "International Investment and International Trade in the Product Life Cycle," *Quarterly Journal of Economics* 80 (May 1966): 190–207; Kindleberger, *International Corporation*, p. 9; *New York Times*, Jan. 27, 1974, p. 56; Budzeika, quoted in Richard J. Barnet and Ronald E. Müller, *Global Reach: The Power of the Multinational Corporations* (New York: Simon and Schuster, 1974), pp. 271–72; Robert T. Averitt, *The Dual Economy* (New York: W. W. Norton, 1968), pp. 122–23; Robert Stobaugh et al., *U.S. Multinational Enterprises and the U.S. Economy*, Harvard Business School Report for the Department of Commerce, January 1972; Lawrence Krause, "Private International Finance," in Robert O. Keohane and Joseph S. Nye, Jr., eds., *Transnational Relations and World Politics* (Cambridge, Mass.: Harvard University Press, 1973), pp. 177, 180; H. David Willey, in Kindleberger, *International Corporation*, p. 100; Wilkins, *Maturing*, pp. 329, 335–36, 343; Behrman, *National Interests*, p. 92; Shonfield, *International Economic Relations*, pp. 66–68; Lamfalussy, cited in ibid., pp. 66–67; "Controlling the Euromarkets," *The Economist*, June 2, 1979, p. 83; *New York Times*, June 12, 1979, p. D1; ibid., Nov. 12, 1979, p. D1; ibid., June 10, 1981, p. 1; ibid., June 15, 1981, p. D1; Morgan Guaranty Trust Company, *World Financial Markets*, December 1977, p. 12; ibid., December 1978, pp. 11, 13; Bank for International Settlements, 48th Annual Report (Basle, June 12, 1978), pp. 101–2, 107; *The Euro-Dollar and Its Public Policy Implications*, U. S. Congress, Joint Economic Committee, 91st Cong., 2nd sess., 1970; U.S. Tariff Commission, *Implications*, pp. 478, 537–39, 548; Meigs, quoted in Barnet and Müller, *Global Reach*, p. 28; *Wall Street Journal*, Aug. 20, 1971.

SECTION 5
Charles P. Kindleberger, "U.S. Foreign Economic Policy, 1776–1976," *Foreign Affairs*, January 1977, p. 417; Stephen Hymer and Robert Rowthorne, "Multinational Corporations and International Oligopoly: The Non-American Challenge," in Kindleberger, *International Corporation*, pp. 80–81, 91; Stephen H. Hymer, "The Multinational Corporation and Uneven Development," statement read before Subcommittee on Foreign Economic Policy of the Joint Economic Committee, 91st Cong., 2nd sess., pp. 906–10; Bergsten, "Coming Investment Wars?" p. 148; Hellmann, *Challenge to U.S. Dominance*, pp. 172, 181–82; Rolfe and

Damm, eds., *The Multinational Corporation in the World Economy*, special studies, pp. 40, 55; *New York Times*, March 29, 1979, p. D11; ibid., March 12, 1979, p. D1; ibid, March 17, 1979, p. 25; ibid., May 16, 1979, p. D1; *Survey of Current Business*, December 1978, pp. 39, 58; *Statistical Abstract 1978*, pp. 865–66; ibid., *1979*, pp. 850, 852; *The Economist*, March 31, 1979, banking survey, after p. 46; ibid., Aug. 30, 1980, p. 54; *Financial Institutions and the Nation's Economy*, U.S. Congress, House Committee on Banking, Subcommittee on Financial Institutions Supervision, 94th Cong., 1st sess., 1975 (Andrew Brimmer); *Business Week*, March 12, 1979, p. 76; U.S. Tariff Commission, *Implications*, p. 159; Earl H. Fry, *Financial Invasion of the U.S.A.* (New York: McGraw-Hill, 1980), pp. 91, 94, 141, 163, 174; ibid., pp. 39, 46–51, 128–29; *New York Times*, May 28, 1976, p. C4; ibid., Sept. 16, 1976, p. 63; ibid., June 15, 1977, p. D1; ibid., Oct. 26, 1978, p. D15; ibid., Oct. 12, 1980, p. F1; *Business Week*, Feb. 6, 1978, p. 106; Obie G. Whichard, "U.S. Direct Investment Abroad in 1980," *Survey of Current Business* 61, no. 8 (August 1981); Ned G. Howenstine, "Growth of U.S. Multinational Companies 1966–1977," *Survey of Current Business* 62, no. 4 (April 1982); Benjamin C. Cohen, "Europe's Money, America's Problem," *Foreign Policy* 35 (Summer 1979); Raymond Vernon, in Kindleberger, *International Corporation*, p. 386; Vernon, *Storm Over the Multinationals*, p. 73.

Chapter 6. Politics and Economics

SECTION 1

Rolfe, in Charles P. Kindleberger, *The International Corporation* (Cambridge, Mass.: MIT Press, 1970), p. 87; Peter F. Drucker, "Multinationals and Developing Countries: Myths and Realities," *Foreign Affairs*, October 1974, p. 133; John Fayerweather, "The Internationalization of Business," *Annals of the Academy of Political and Social Science* 403 (September 1972): 1–11; A. W. Clausen, "The Internationalized Corporation: An Executive's View," *Annals of the Academy of Political and Social Science* 403 (September 1972): 12–21; Christopher Tugendhat, *The Multinationals* (New York: Random House, 1972), p. 221; Courtney Brown, *World Business: Promise and Problems* (New York: Macmillan, 1970), pp. 12, 14; George Ball, in Brown, *World Business*, pp. 330–38; George Ball, "The Promise of the Multinational Corporation," *Fortune*, June 1, 1967; Charles P. Kindleberger, *American Business Abroad* (New Haven, Conn.: Yale University Press, 1967), p. 207; Stanley Hoffmann, *Gulliver's Troubles* (New York: McGraw-Hill, 1968), pp. 18, 22, 40–42; E. H. Carr, *Nationalism and After* (London: Macmillan, 1945), pp. 31, 47, 51, 64, 66; George W. Ball, "Citizenship and the MNC." *Social Research* 41 (Winter 1974); Stephen Hymer, *The International Operations of National Firms: A Study of Direct Foreign Investment* (Cambridge, Mass.: MIT Press, 1976), pp. 28–31; Simmonds, in Brown, *World Business*, pp. 45, 48; Raymond Vernon, *Sovereignty at Bay: The Multinational Spread of U.S. Enterprises* (New York: Basic Books, 1971), p. 146;

Howard V. Perlmutter, "The Tortuous Evolution of the Multinational Corporation," in A. Kapoor and Phillip D. Grub, eds., *The Multinational Enterprise in Transition* (Princeton, N.J.: Darwin Press, 1972), p. 64; John Thackray, "Not So Multinational, After All," *Interplay*, November 1968, pp. 23–25; *Business Week* and corporation chairman, quoted in Christopher Tugendhat, *The Multinationals* (New York: Random House, 1972), pp. 195–96; Hugh Stephenson, *The Coming Clash* (New York: Saturday Review Press, 1973), p. 10; Ronald Müller, in Charles K. Wilber, ed., *The Political Economy of Development and Underdevelopment* (New York: Random House, 1973); John C. Shearer, in Solomon Barkin et al., eds., *International Labor* (New York: Harper, 1967), p. 123.

SECTION 2
Jack Behrman, "Multinational Corporation, Transnational Interests, and National Sovereignty," *Columbia Journal of World Business*, March-April 1969, pp. 15–22; Francis X. Sutton et al., *The American Business Creed* (Cambridge, Mass.: Harvard University Press, 1956), p. 186; Earl F. Cheit, ed., *The Business Establishment* (New York: Wiley, 1964), p. 23 (Mason quote), p. 180 (Clark Kerr quote); Abdul A. Said and Luiz R. Simmons, *The New Sovereigns: Multinational Corporations as World Powers* (Englewood Cliffs, N.J.: Prentice-Hall, 1975), pp. 108–119; Raymond Vernon, *Storm Over the Multinationals* (Cambridge, Mass.: Harvard University Press, 1977), pp. 52–53, 144; David F. Noble, *America by Design: Science, Technology, and the Rise of Corporate Capitalism* (New York: Knopf, 1977), Chap. 9; John P. Gannemann, ed., *The Nation-State and Transnational Corporations in Conflict* (New York: Praeger, 1975), p. 72; William H. Whyte, *The Organization Man* (Garden City, N.Y.: Doubleday Anchor, 1956), pp. 69, 150, 152; "The Crown Princes of Business," *Fortune*, October 1953, p. 152; William Miller, ed., *Men in Business* (New York: Harper, 1962), pp. 291, 301–3; Chester I. Barnard, *The Functions of the Executive* (Cambridge, Mass.: Harvard University Press, 1968), pp. 121, 225; James Burnham, *The Managerial Revolution* (Bloomington: Indiana University Press, 1960); Robert K. Merton et al., eds., *Reader in Bureaucracy* (Glencoe, Ill.: The Free Press, 1952), pp. 118–21 (Bendix), 364–68 (Merton); Diane Rothbard Margolis, *The Managers* (New York: Morrow, 1979), pp. 24–25, 43.

SECTION 3
The U.S. Economy in 1980, Bulletin No. 1673 (Washington, D.C.: U.S. Bureau of Labor Statistics, 1970); Victor Fuchs, *The Service Economy* (New York: Columbia University Press, 1968), pp. 16–17; *Statistical Abstract 1978* (Washington, D.C.: U.S. Bureau of the Census, 1979), pp. 407, 414–16; *Historical Statistics, Colonial Times to 1957* (Washington, D.C.: U.S. Bureau of the Census, 1958), p. 73; Maurice Lengelle, *The Growing Importance of the Service Sector in Member Countries* (Paris: OECD, 1966); Gur Oter, *The Service Industries in a Developing Economy* (New York: Praeger, 1967); Robert Paul Wolff, ed., *1984 Revisited* (New York: Knopf, 1973), pp. 165–67; Robert L. Heilbroner, "Economic Problems of a 'Post-industrial' Society," *Dissent*, Spring 1973; *Statistical*

Abstract 1978, pp. 256–58, 287–94; ibid., *1982*, pp. 276, 421, 832–33; Rainer Hellman, *The Challenge to U.S. Dominance of the International Corporation* (New York: Dunellen, 1970), p. 32; U.S. Tariff Commission, *Implications of Multinational Firms for World Trade and Investment and for U.S. Trade and Labor*, presented to the U.S. Senate Committee on Finance, Subcommittee on International Trade (Washington, D.C.: U.S. Government Printing Office, 1973), pp. 890–901; Daniel Bell, *The Coming of Post-Industrial Society: A Venture in Social Forecasting* (New York: Basic Books, 1973), p. 159; *R & D Efforts in Member Countries* (Paris: OECD, 1967, 1968); G. C. Hufbauer and J. R. Nunns, "Tax Payments and Tax Expenditures on International Investment and Employment," *Columbia Journal of World Business*, Summer 1975, p. 13; *Multinational Corporations and United States Foreign Policy*, U.S. Senate Committee on Foreign Relations, Subcommittee on Multinational Corporations, 93rd Cong., 1st sess., 3:3–7; Peggy Musgrave, "Tax Preferences," in U.S. Congress Joint Economic Committee, *The Economics of Federal Subsidy Programs* (Washington, D.C.: U.S. Government Printing Office, 1972), 2:177, 214; *A Foreign Economic Policy for the 1970s*, U.S. Congress Joint Economic Committee, Subcommittee on Foreign Policy, 91st Cong., 1st sess., 1:11; Peter Drucker, *The Age of Discontinuity* (New York: Harper, 1960), p. 63; James O'Connor, *The Fiscal Crisis of the State* (New York: St. Martin's Press, 1973), p 97.

SECTION 4

AFL-CIO, "An American Trade Union View of International Trade and Investment," in *Multinational Corporations*, a compendium of papers of the U.S. Senate Committee on Finance, Subcommittee on International Trade, 93rd Cong., 1st sess., February 1973, pp. 75–76; Elizabeth Jager and Markley Roberts, "The Export of Jobs and Technology by U.S. MNCs' " January 1977 (available from the AFL-CIO); statement by Markley Roberts before Joint House Committees on Science and Technology, June 24, 1980 (available from the AFL-CIO); *American Federationist*, December 1977, pp. 7–9; ibid., May 1978, pp. 16–20; ibid., August 1977, pp. 9–12; Stanley H. Ruttenberg and Assoc., *Needed: A Constructive Foreign Policy* (AFL-CIO, October 1971), pp. 62–63; American Enterprise Institute for Public Policy Research, *The Burke-Hartke Foreign Trade and Investment Proposal*, Legislative Analyisis No. 4, U.S. Senate, 93rd Cong., 1st sess., Feb. 22, 1973; *The Multinational Corporation and the National Interest* (Robert Gilpin), U.S. Senate Committee on Labor and Public Welfare, 93rd Cong., 1st sess., 1973; *Direct Investment Abroad and the Multinationals: Effects on the U.S. Economy* (Peggy B. Musgrave), U.S. Senate Committee on Foreign Relations, Subcommittee on Multinational Corporations, 94th Cong., 1st sess., 1975; National Association of Manufacturers, "International Activities of U.S. Multinational Corporations," in *Multinational Corporations*, U.S. Senate Committee on Finance, pp. 559–63; National Foreign Trade Council, "The Impact of U.S. Foreign Direct Investment and U.S. Employment and Trade," in ibid., p. 666; *The Multinational Corporation, Studies on U.S. Foreign Investment* (Washington, D.C.: U.S. Department of Commerce, Bureau of International Commerce, January-February 1972), 1:14–16; *Special Survey of U.S. Multinational Companies* (Washington, D.C.: U.S. Department of Commerce, Bureau of Economic Analysis, 1972); U.S. Tariff Commission, *Report to the President on Economic Factors Affecting the Use of Items 807 and 806.30 of the Tariff Schedules of the United States*, Publication 339 (Washington, D.C., September 1970), pp. 232–33; Robert B. Stobaugh, *Nine Investments Abroad and Their Impact at Home* (Cambridge, Mass.: Harvard Business School, 1976), p. 34; Jack Behrman, Symposium on "Labor's International Role," *Foreign Policy* 26 (Spring 1977): 225–27; U.S. Tariff Commission, *Implications*, pp. 645–72; foreign employment of American MNC affiliates built up from Vernon's 1966 estimates, in *Sovereignty at Bay*, p. 156; Fred C. Bergsten et al., *American Multinationals and American Interests* (Washington, D.C.: Brookings Institution, 1978), p. 4; Robert Gilpin, *U.S. Power and the Multinational Corporation* (New York: Basic Books, 1975), pp. 203–4; Samuelson, quoted in ibid., pp. 205–6.

Chapter 7. Unfinished Business

SECTION 1
   The Economist, March 4, 1978, p. 92; ibid., April 1, 1978, pp. 17–18; ibid., Dec. 10, 1978, p. 40; quote, in ibid., Feb. 24, 1979, p. 69; Wolfgang Friedmann, ed., *Public and Private Enterprise in Mixed Economies* (New York: Columbia University Press, 1974), pp. 4–8, 44–48, 200–1, 364, 377–81; Ralph Miliband, *The State in Capitalist Society* (New York: Basic Books, 1969), pp. 8–9; James O'Connor, *The Fiscal Crisis of the State* (New York: St. Martin's Press, 1973), pp. 181–89; Andrew Shonfield, *Modern Capitalism: The Changing Balance of Public and Private Power* (New York: Oxford University Press, 1965), pp. 178–79, 191; R. Kelf-Cohen, *Twenty Years of Nationalization: The British Experience* (New York: St. Martin's Press, 1969), p. 49; Warren G. Baum, *The French Economy and the State* (Princeton, N.J.: Princeton University Press, 1958), pp. 32–39; John Sheahan, *Promotion and Control of Industry in Postwar France* (Cambridge, Mass.: Harvard University Press, 1963), pp. 190, 193; documents from France: The Nationalizations 82/35, Press Service of the French Embassy, New York, N.Y.; Neil W. Chamberlain, *The Place of Business in America's Future* (New York: Basic Books, 1973), pp. 301–3; Joseph Schumpeter, "The Crisis of the Tax State," *International Economic Papers*, No. 4 (New York: Macmillan, 1954); Howard Smith, "The Budget as an Instrument of Legislative Control and Executive Management," *Public Administration Review*, Summer 1964; Shonfield, *Modern Capitalism*, pp. 341, 372; Seymour Melman, *The Permanent War Economy* (New York: Simon and Schuster, 1974), p. 80; Raymond Vernon, *Sovereignty at Bay: The Multinational Spread of U.S. Enterprises* (New York: Basic Books, 1971), p. 90; *Statistical Abstract 1978* (Washington, D.C.: U.S. Bureau of the Census, 1979), pp. 261, 624–25; *National Patterns of R & D Resources 1953–1978* (Washington, D.C.: U.S. National Science Foundation,

1978); *Reviews of National Science Policy: United States* (Paris: OECD); OECD national statistics, in *The Economist*, Dec. 30, 1978, p. 40; *New York Times*, July 30, 1978, "Week in Review," p. 3; interview with Walter Heller, in *Think*, IBM publication for employees, March-April 1976; Paul A. Baran and Paul M. Sweezy, *Monopoly Capital* (New York: Monthly Review Press, 1966), pp. 146, 152–53; Raymond W. Goldsmith, *The National Wealth of the United States in the Postwar Period* (Princeton, N.J.: Princeton University Press, 1962), pp. 98–99; *Economic Report of the President 1977*, January 1978, p. 270; Alan T. Peacock and Jack Wiseman, *The Growth of Public Expenditures in the United Kingdom* (Princeton, N.J.: Princeton University Press, 1961), p. 13; Henry C. Wallich, "Public versus Private: Could Galbraith Be Wrong?" *Harpers*, October 1961.

SECTION 2
    World Military and Arms Transfers 1967–1976 (Washington, D.C.: U.S. Arms Control and Disarmament Agnecy, 1977), pp. 1–11; McNamara, quoted in Richard J. Barnet, *Intervention and Revolution* (New York: World, 1968), p. 4; David Wood, quoted in Zbigniew Brzezinski, *Between Two Ages* (New York: Viking, 1970), p. 7; Ronald Steel, *Pax Americana* (New York: Viking, 1970), pp. 290, 300, 303; Michael J. Crozier, Samuel P. Huntington, and Joji Watanuki, *The Crisis of Democracy* (New York: New York University Press, 1975); footnote on neoconservatives, see Christopher Jencks in *New York Times Book Review*, July 1, 1979, p. 1; George Katona, *The Mass Consumption Society* (New York: McGraw-Hill, 1964), pp. 142–53; Barbara Ward, *The Rich Nations and the Poor Nations* (New York: W. W. Norton, 1962), p. 15; Vance Packard, *The Hidden Persuaders* (New York: David McKay 1957); Peter Steinfels' *The Neoconservatives* (New York: Simon and Schuster, 1979), pp. 50–55, 179; Eugene V. Rostow, *Planning for Freedom* (New Haven, Conn.: Yale University Press, 1959), p. 43; Edward S. Mason, "Interests, Ideologies, and the Problem of Stability and Growth," *American Economic Review* 53 (March 1963); Colm, quoted in Schonfield, *Modern Capitalism*, pp. 351–52; Arthur M. Schlesinger, Jr., *The Coming of the New Deal* (Boston: Houghton Mifflin, 1958), pp. 153, 179, 445; Eric F. Goldman, *Rendevous with Destiny* (New York: Random House, Vintage Books, 1958), p. 272; Arthur Miller and Ralph Ferrara, "Public and Private Enterprise in the United States," in Friedmann, ed., *Public and Private Enterprise*, pp. 291ff., 353; I. F. Stone, "In the Bowels of the Behemoth," *New York Review of Books*, March 11, 1971.

SECTION 3
    Crozier et al., *Crisis of Democracy*, p. 22; Walter Dean Burnham, letter to the editor, *New York Times*, May 23, 1979, p. A26; Thomas R. Malthus, *An Essay on the Principles of Population* (New York: Dutton Everyman's Library, 1914), pp. 69–70; David Ricardo, *Works and Correspondence* (New York: Cambridge University Press, 1951), 1:290; John Stuart Mill, *Principles of Political Economy* (New York: Colonial Press, 1900), pp. 153, 173; Frederick Engels, *On Britain* (Moscow: Foreign Language Publishing House, 1953), 319–22; Karl Marx, *Capital* (Chi-

cago: Kerr, 1912), 1:675–77, 693–96; ibid., (Moscow: Foreign Language Publishing House, 1959), 3:655–57, 751–52; *Communist Manifesto*, in Karl Marx, *Selected Works* (New York: International Publishers, 1933), 1:208, 210; Gifford Pinchot, *Breaking New Ground* (New York: Harcourt, Brace, 1947), pp. 190, 252; Samuel P. Hays, *Conservation and the Gospel of Efficiency: The Progressive Conservation Movement 1890–1920* (New York: Atheneum, 1969), Preface and pp. 1–10; David Riesman, "Some Observations on Changes in Leisure Attitudes," reprinted in id., *Individualism Reconsidered* (Garden City, N.Y.: Doubleday Anchor Books, 1955); id., "Leisure and Work in Post-Industrial Society," in Eric Larrabee and Rolf Meyersohn, eds., *Mass Leisure* (Glencoe, Ill.: The Free Press, 1958); Robert Perrucci and Marc Pilisuk, comps., *The Triple Revolution: Social Problems in Depth* (Boston: Little, Brown, 1968); Herman Kahn and Anthony Wiener, *The Year 2000* (New York: Macmillan, 1968), p. 213; D. H. Meadows et al., *The Limits to Growth* (New York: Universe Books, 1972); Jay Forrester, *World Dynamics* (Cambridge, Mass.: Wright-Allen Press, 1971); Karl Kaysen, "The Computer That Printed Out W*O*L*F," *Foreign Affairs* 50 (July 1972); Theodore Roszak, *The Making of a Counter Culture* (Garden City, N.Y.: Doubleday, 1969), p. 35.

SECTION 4
Robert L. Heilbroner, *American Business in Decline* (New York: W. W. Norton, 1976), pp. 103–7; id., *An Inquiry into the Human Prospect* (New York: W. W. Norton, 1974), pp. 44, 50, 54; Louis J. Halle, "Does War Have a Future?" *Foreign Affairs* 52 (October 1973): 23; report for the Energy Department, quoted in the *New York Times*, June 9, 1979, p. 12; space scientists' study, reported in the *New York Times*, Aug. 22, 1981, p. 1; Charles F. Cooper, "What Might Man-induced Climate Change Mean?" *Foreign Affairs* 56 (April 1978); footnote, *New York Times*, July 8, 1979, p. A7; ibid., July 6, 1979, p. A1; ibid., July 7, 1979, p. 22; ibid. April 1, 1981; ibid., Sept. 24, 1982; Kindleberger, quoted in ibid., Nov. 25, 1982; Lyle P. Schertz, "World Food: Prices and the Poor," *Foreign Affairs* 52 (April 1974); Jean Mayer, "Coping with Famine," *Foreign Affairs* 53 (October 1974); Emma Rothschild, "Food Politics," *Foreign Affairs* 54 (January 1976); Paul Ehrlich and Anne Ehrlich, *The End of Affluence* (New York: Ballantine Books, 1974), pp. 104–10; id., *Population, Resources, Environment* (San Francisco: Freeman, 1972), Chap. 6; A. L. Hammond, in *Harper's*, January 1973, pp. 30–34; Jeremy Rifkin, *Entropy* (New York: Viking Press, 1980); Julian Simon, *The Ultimate Resource* (Princeton, N.J.: Princeton University Press, 1981).

Chapter 8. The State in Ascendance

SECTION 1
Alvin Toffler, *Future Shock* (New York: Bantam Books, 1971); id., *The Third Wave* (New York: Bantam Books, 1981); Daniel Bell, *The Coming of Post-Industrial Society: A Venture in Social Forecasting* (New York: Basic Books, 1973), pp. 3–8, 14, 26, 38, 373–77, 380, 391–

92, 400, 409; Zbigniew Brzezinski, *Between Two Ages* (New York: Viking, 1970), p. xv; Robert Nisbet, "Has Futurology a Future?" *Encounter*, November 1971; Otis Duncan, "Social Forecasting: The State of the Art," *Public Interest*, Fall 1969; Talcott Parsons, "Professions," *International Encyclopedia of the Social Sciences*, vol. 12; Don K. Price, *The Scientific Estate* (Cambridge, Mass.: Harvard University Press, 1967), Chap. 7; Max Weber, "Science as a Vocation," in H. H. Gerth and C. Wright Mills, eds., *From Max Weber: Essays in Sociology* (New York: Oxford University Press, 1958), pp. 129–47; *In the Matter of J. Robert Oppenheimer*, Transcript of Hearing before Personnel Security Board, U.S. Atomic Energy Commission, 1954; Philip M. Stern, *The Oppenheimer Case: Security on Trial* (New York: Harper, 1969), Chap. 15.

SECTION 2

The Economist, Feb. 9, 1980, pp. 13, 19–20; ibid., March 15, 1980, pp. 66–67, 86–87; *New York Times*, March 31, 1980, p. D1; Kenneth Boulding, *The Meaning of the Twentieth Century: The Great Transition* (New York: Harper, 1964), pp. 156–79; Daniel Bell, *The Cultural Contradictions of Capitalism* (New York: Basic Books, 1976), pp. 69, 75; Angus Campbell et al., *The American Voter* (New York: Wiley, 1960), p. 320; Angus Campbell et al., *Election and the Political Order* (New York: Wiley, 1966), pp. 289–91; Walter Karp, *Indispensible Enemies: The Politics of Misrule in America* (Baltimore: Penguin, 1973), p. 73; Robert Putnam, *The Beliefs of Politicians* (New Haven, Conn.: Yale University Press, 1973), pp. 54, 62–69, 105; Arthur Miller, "Political Issues and Trust in Government 1964–1970," *American Political Science Review* 68 (September 1974); Plato, quoted in Irving Kristol and Paul Weaver, *The Americans 1976* (Lexington, Mass.: D. C. Heath, 1976), 2:xviii; Carl E. Schorske, *Fin-de-Siècle Vienna: Politics and Culture* (New York: Knopf, 1980), Chaps. 5–7; Edmund Wilson, *Memoirs of Hecate County* (New York: Noonday Press, 1959), sections 5–6; Arthur M. Schlesinger, Jr., *The Coming of the New Deal* (Boston: Houghton Mifflin, 1959), p. 266; William Leuchtenberg, "The New Deal and the Analogue of War," in John Braeman et al., eds., *Change and Continuity in Twentieth Century America* (Columbus: Ohio State University Press, 1964); Andrew Hacker, "The Elected and the Anointed: Two American Elites," *American Political Science Review* 56, no. 3 (September 1961); Nicos Poulantzas, *Political Power and Social Classes* (London: NLB, trans. 1973), p. 272; Ferdinand Lundberg, *America's 60 Families* (New York: Vanguard, 1937), pp. 480–85; Arthur M. Schlesinger, Jr., *Robert Kennedy and His Times* (New York: Ballantine, 1979), pp. 24–26; Eli Chinoy, *Automobile Workers and the American Dream* (Boston: Beacon Press, 1965); V. I. Lenin, *What Is To Be Done?* (New York: International, 1929), pp. 40–42; id., "Agrarian Draft Thesis," *Collected Works* (Moscow: Progress, 1958), 31:159–61.

SECTION 3

Charles E. Lindblom, *Politics and Markets: The World's Political-Economic Systems* (New York: Basic Books, 1977), pp. 111–13, 154–55, 171–72; Neil W. Chamberlain, *Private and Public Planning* (New York:

McGraw-Hill, 1965), Chap. 1; U.S. Tariff Commission, *Implications of Multinational Firms for World Trade and Investment and for U.S. Trade and Labor*, presented to the U.S. Senate Committee on Finance, Subcommittee on International Trade (Washington, D.C.: U.S. Government Printing Office, 1973), p. 159; Alfred G. Meyer, *The Soviet Political System* (New York: Random House, 1965), p. 112; David Granick, *The Red Executive* (Garden City, N.Y.: Doubleday Anchor Books, 1961), Chap. 1; id., *Enterprise Guidance in Eastern Europe* (Princeton, N.J.: Princeton University Press, 1975); Phillippe J. Bernard, *Planning in the Soviet Union* (London: Pergamon Press, 1966), Chaps. 2–6; Moshe Lewin, *Political Undercurrents in Soviet Economic Debates* (Princeton, N.J.: Princeton University Press, 1974), p. 127 forward; Stephen F. Cohen et al., eds., *The Soviet Union Since Stalin* (Bloomington: Indiana University Press, 1980), pp. 11–31; U.S. Congress Joint Economic Committee, *Soviet Economy in a Time of Change* (Washington, D.C.: U.S. Government Printing Office, Oct. 10, 1979), p. 794.

Section 4

Lindblom, *Politics and Markets*, pp. 300–7, 325–26; Benjamin Lippincott, Oscar Lange, and Fred M. Taylor, eds., *On the Economic Theory of Socialism* (New York: A. M. Kelley, 1970); Oscar Lange, "Marxism Economics and Modern Economic Theory," *Review of Economic Studies*, Cambridge, England, June 1935; id., *Essays on Economic Planning* (Bombay: Asia Publishing House, 1967); Henry M. Pachter, "Three Models of Society," *Dissent*, Spring 1954; Alec Nove, *Political Economy and Soviet Socialism* (London: Allen and Unwin, 1979), pp. 112–32; Fred Hirsch, *Social Limits to Growth* (Cambridge, Mass.: Harvard University Press, 1976), p. 118; Joseph A. Schumpeter, *Capitalism, Socialism and Democracy* (New York: Harper Colophon Books, 1976), pp. 61, 415–19; Ljobo Sirc, *The Yugoslav Economy Under Self-Management* (New York: St. Martin's Press, 1979); Ellen T. Comisso, *Workers' Control Under Plan and Market: Implications of Yugoslav Self-Management* (New Haven, Conn.: Yale University Press, 1979); Gary K. Bertsch and Josip Obradovic, "Participation and Influence in Yugoslav Self-Management," *Industrial Relations*, no. 3 (Fall 1979); Egon Neuberger and Estelle James, "The Yugoslav Self-Managed Enterprise," in Morris Bornstein, ed., *Plan and Market* (New Haven, Conn.: Yale University Press, 1973); see for debate with Galbraith on markets, consumers, etc., Robert M. Solow, "The New Industrial State: A Discussion," *Public Interest* 9 (Fall 1967); Robert L. Heilbroner, "What Is Socialism," *Dissent*, Summer 1978; Bell, *Post-Industrial Society*, pp. 380, 386, 481; Robert A. Rothman, "A Dissenting View on the Scientific Ethos," *British Journal of Sociology* 23, no. 1 (March 1972); Emile Durkheim, *Professional Ethics and Civic Morals* (New York: The Free Press, 1958), pp. 51–64; R. H. Tawney, *The Acquisitive Society* (New York: Harcourt Brace, Harvest Books, n.d.), pp. 13–15, Chaps. 6 and 7; Andrew Martin, "The Politics of Economic Development in Advanced Industrial Societies," unpublished manuscript, August 1976.

Index

223